— Praise for *Thaddeus Stevens*

"At last, Thaddeus Stevens, one of the nineteenth century's greatest proponents of racial justice, gets the biography he deserves. Drawing on a career of scholarly engagement with the Civil War era, Bruce Levine expertly relates how Stevens navigated the currents of the Second American Revolution, how he helped to bring about the destruction of slavery and was a leader in the effort during Reconstruction to make the United States a biracial democracy. We need Stevens's passion for equality today."

—Eric Foner, Pulitzer Prize–winning author of
The Fiery Trial: Abraham Lincoln and American Slavery

"He was called everything from Robin Hood to Robespierre to evil genius to fanatic and worse. He was a 'radical' in a time when that was not always derogatory. This book reveals in many dimensions a Thaddeus Stevens, who with vicious wit and shrewd political skill, was a primary founder of the second American republic. Through deep understanding of all the contexts of the Civil War era and vivid writing, Bruce Levine gives us the best biography of this towering figure yet written, and a timely story about the power of racial equality."

—David W. Blight, Pulitzer Prize–winning author of
Frederick Douglass: Prophet of Freedom

"Bruce Levine . . . restores [Stevens] fully to his place in the American pantheon."

—*The Wall Street Journal*

"Often reviled and generally misunderstood, Thaddeus Stevens has been relegated to a dark corner of the American historical stage. The distinguished historian Bruce Levine not only brings Stevens back into the light but also reveals his significance to the revolutionary dynamic of the Civil War and Reconstruction. Levine's is a riveting read and a thought-provoking biography, more timely than ever."

—Steven Hahn, Pulitzer Prize–winning author of
The Political Worlds of Slavery and Freedom

"Spirited."

—*The Civil War Monitor*

"Vital."

—*The Guardian*

"Levine deftly weaves political, social, and intellectual history into eleven brief chapters . . . helping us to understand 19th-century America as Americans of the time knew it, instead of as Lost Cause advocates . . . reimagined it in the years after the Civil War."

—*The National Review*

"Levine's book, written in crisp and no-nonsense language . . . succeeds in recovering a richer, more complicated Stevens. . . . Appreciated here in full, his career gives the lie to the oft-repeated idea, common in politics and certain kinds of history, that radical ideals and practical achievements are inevitably and always at odds. . . . Levine's study of the neglected, much maligned Stevens offers an opportunity to reflect on what this country might have been—and the merest glimmer of hope for what it might still be."

—*The Baffler*

"Levine writes in lucid prose with a great depth of understanding. . . . It's impossible to read this book without seeing a reflection of our own combustible times."

—*BookPage*

"This is the fullest, most nuanced, and best written explication of the political career and principles ever written about one of the key figures of nineteenth-century America. It is a major contribution to antebellum, Civil War, and Reconstruction studies and to American political biography. Anyone interested in how the war evolved and why its aftermath was both so promising and so disappointing needs to read this book."

—Stephen V. Ash, author of *A Massacre in Memphis:*
The Race Riot that Shook the Nation
One Year after the Civil War

"W.E.B. Du Bois called the pioneering antislavery politician Thaddeus Stevens a 'seer of democracy.' In this superb biography, Bruce Levine has conjured Stevens's bold vision of equality, revealing that Stevens was a profound thinker who saw the essential connection between civil rights and economic rights. Levine deftly traces Stevens's dramatic political journey, with attention to setbacks and missteps as well as to the progress Stevens achieved for America. This is a timely tale of an inspirational leader."

—Elizabeth R. Varon, author of
Armies of Deliverance: A New History of the Civil War

"In this taut, authoritative, and much-needed modern biography of Thaddeus Stevens, the benchmark racial egalitarian of the Civil War era, Bruce Levine elegantly captures the steely moral fiber and unwavering political radicalism of an unsettling colleague and formidable foe. This is very fine history. Additionally, Stevens, implacable in the pursuit of racial justice, provides a relevant, stirring, and essential model for our own times."

—Richard Carwardine, author of *Lincoln's Sense of Humor*

"At long last, the principled yet astute Thaddeus Stevens is the subject of a sympathetic modern biography. Bruce Levine's adept book gives us a compelling portrait of the Radical Republican extraordinaire, especially when he was at the apex of his political career during the Civil War and Reconstruction."

—Manisha Sinha, author of
The Slave's Cause: A History of Abolition

"This succinct and compelling biography . . . casts Stevens as a congressional leader of the drive to abolish slavery and implant civil and political equality in the Constitution, though Congress failed in the end to adopt his plan to attack economic inequality by land reform in the reconstructed South."

—James M. McPherson, Pulitzer Prize–winning author of
Battle Cry of Freedom: The Civil War Era

ALSO BY BRUCE LEVINE

The Fall of the House of Dixie: The Civil War and
the Social Revolution That Transformed the South

Confederate Emancipation: Southern Plans to
Free and Arm Slaves during the Civil War

Half Slave and Half Free: The Roots of Civil War

The Spirit of 1848: German Immigrants,
Labor Conflict, and the Coming of the Civil War

THADDEUS STEVENS

Civil War Revolutionary,
Fighter for Racial Justice

— BRUCE LEVINE —

SIMON & SCHUSTER PAPERBACKS
New York   London   Toronto   Sydney   New Delhi

To longtime and long-suffering pals
Josh Brown, Scott Ware, and Elliott Gorn

Simon & Schuster Paperbacks
An Imprint of Simon & Schuster, Inc.
1230 Avenue of the Americas
New York, NY 10020

First Simon & Schuster trade paperback edition March 2022

SIMON & SCHUSTER PAPERBACKS and colophon are registered trademarks
of Simon & Schuster, Inc.

For information about special discounts for bulk purchases,
please contact Simon & Schuster Special Sales at 1-866-506-1949
or business@simonandschuster.com.

The Simon & Schuster Speakers Bureau can bring authors to your
live event. For more information or to book an event contact
the Simon & Schuster Speakers Bureau at 1-866-248-3049
or visit our website at www.simonspeakers.com.

Interior design by Paul Dippolito

Manufactured in the United States of America

1   3   5   7   9   10   8   6   4   2

Library of Congress Cataloging-in-Publication Data is available.

ISBN 978-1-4767-9337-5
ISBN 978-1-4767-9338-2 (pbk)
ISBN 978-1-4767-9339-9 (ebook)

Contents

Bringing "the Spirit of John Brown" into Government

I n the summer of 1863, the third year of the Civil War, Confederate general Robert E. Lee launched a raid into Pennsylvania that culminated in the epic battle of Gettysburg. During that raid, one of Lee's division commanders, General Jubal A. Early, looted and demolished the Caledonia Iron Works, located outside of town. The ironworks' owner and the attack's personal target was Republican congressman Thaddeus Stevens. Jubal Early regretted only that he hadn't encountered Stevens on the premises. If he had, the general swore, he would have moved then and there to hang him, "divide his bones and send them to the several States as curiosities." Early had destroyed the ironworks to make an example of the man who, he said, had inflicted more harm on the Confederacy than any other in the U.S. Congress. Frederick Douglass, the former slave and abolitionist leader, agreed with Jubal Early about almost nothing. But he did second the general's appraisal of Stevens's importance. "There was in him," Douglass said, "the power of conviction, the power of will, the power of knowledge, and the power of conscious ability," qualities that "at last made him more potent in Congress and in the country than even the president and cabinet combined."[1]

As chairman of the House of Representatives' Ways and Means

Committee, Stevens ensured that the Union war machine received the funding it needed. Perhaps even more important, he fought eloquently and doggedly in Congress for the strong antislavery and antiracist war policies to which other Republicans would come around only later. Stevens was "always in advance of public opinion," one associate recalled, and "constantly antagonized it with a valor and boldness unequalled. Usually political leaders ascertain the current and drift of public sentiment and accommodate themselves to it." But Stevens "created public opinion and moulded public sentiment." Although he did, in fact, on occasion hesitate in the face of public disapproval, he far more often defied such opposition in order to champion causes close to his heart, especially the destruction of slavery and the fight against racial discrimination in general.[2]

Over the course of the Civil War, President Abraham Lincoln grew impressively into the role of leader of the Second American Revolution, moving to confiscate and then emancipate Confederate slaves and to bring black men into Union armies. But at each stage of Lincoln's evolution, he found Thaddeus Stevens marching ahead of him, pushing for further advances. Stevens also demanded a constitutional amendment outlawing slavery throughout the United States a year before Lincoln endorsed the idea. In arguing for these and other measures, Stevens helped to educate and reshape public opinion in the North, thereby permitting or inducing other political figures to move eventually in the same direction.

Stevens's pioneering role did not end with the Confederacy's defeat and Lincoln's death. In the first years of postwar Reconstruction, he demanded equal civil rights for African Americans. Before long he was fighting as well to grant them political rights, the rights to vote and hold office, doing that before most of his Republican colleagues endorsed the constitutional amendments that enshrined those advances, amendments that paved the legal way for the civil rights movement of the twentieth century. Reflecting on this record of determined and militant struggle for black equality, Republican congressman Ignatius L. Donnelly observed that Stevens "brought the spirit of John Brown into the work of the statesman."[3]

Stevens's opposition to slavery began early. The same was true of Abraham Lincoln. But Stevens's hostility was more passionate and deeply rooted. Although opposing bondage since boyhood, Lincoln said and did relatively little about it until the middle of the 1850s. Stevens became a full-bore abolitionist decades earlier, at a time when white people calling for slavery's destruction constituted only a widely despised handful. And he stood even then not only for the prompt abolition of slavery but for equal rights for African Americans, north and south. At a convention revising Pennsylvania's state constitution in 1837, thus, Stevens rejected the finished document because it denied black men the right to vote. In the 1840s, Abraham Lincoln opposed the war with Mexico and the seizure of Mexican land. When the United States nonetheless absorbed half of that country, a political crisis blew up over slavery's status in the newly acquired region. Lincoln embraced the famous Compromise of 1850 that ended the crisis, while Stevens repudiated it for allowing slavery to spread and for including a law that facilitated the enslavement of people accused of fleeing bondage.

Thaddeus Stevens joined the newborn Republican Party in 1855, the party that put Lincoln in the White House six years later. When slaveholders rose in armed revolt against Lincoln's election, an associate recalled, "Stevens was the one man who never faltered, who never hesitated, who never temporized, but who was ready to meet aggressive treason with the most aggressive assaults." And while "he and Lincoln worked substantially on the same lines, earnestly striving to attain the same ends," it was Stevens who pointed the way forward. "While Lincoln ever halted until assured that the considerate judgment of the nation would sustain him," Stevens "was the pioneer who was ever in advance of the government." A northern newspaper that often opposed Stevens's initiatives had to agree in retrospect. "He comprehended the magnitude of the crisis," it acknowledged, "while the majority about him saw but dimly its proportions." Stevens, it conceded, "realized the necessity of bold, strong measures, while others clung to hopes of pacification and compromise. He was one of the few who are not afraid to grasp first principles and lay hold of great truths, or to push them to their remotest logical result."[4]

As Thaddeus Stevens understood, uprooting slavery meant overthrowing the economic system in half the United States, a labor system that underpinned the wealth and political power of the South's elite and that nourished much of the South's social and cultural life. Emancipation would therefore constitute a social and political revolution of tremendous dimensions and consequences. Surveying the postwar landscape, a Tennessee editor observed that "the events of the last five years have produced an entire revolution in the entire Southern country. The old arrangement of things is broken up." "Society has been completely changed by the war," agreed ex–Confederate general Richard Taylor. Even the stormy French Revolution of the previous century, he thought, "did not produce a greater change in the 'Ancien Regime' than has this in our social life." Georges Clemenceau, then a Parisian journalist based in the United States, marveled at "one of the most radical revolutions known in history." Watching the Civil War from afar, Karl Marx observed approvingly at the end of 1864 that "never has such a gigantic revolution occurred with such rapidity."[5]

Thaddeus Stevens was among the first to recognize and embrace the Civil War's profound significance and to demand that the Union act accordingly. "We must treat this as a radical revolution," he urged his party. And to complete and secure the gains of that revolution, Stevens called for confiscating the large slaveholders' estates and dividing them among the former slaves. "He considered himself as a sort of legal Robin Hood," a friend would recall, "authorized to take from the rich and give to the poor." Many likened him to leaders of the French Revolution. The hostile *New York Herald* sourly observed in 1868 that "we are passing through a similar revolution to that of the French," one in which Stevens displayed "the boldness of Danton, the bitterness and hatred of Marat, and the unscrupulousness of Robespierre."[6]

These politics naturally made Thaddeus Stevens one of the earliest and most implacable foes of Abraham Lincoln's successor in the White House, Andrew Johnson. A former slaveholder from Tennessee, Johnson had nonetheless opposed secession in 1861, remaining in the Union as a "War Democrat" and becoming Lincoln's running mate in 1864. But when Lincoln's murder catapulted him into the presidency, Johnson began helping the southern elite to regain political power and to force the freedpeople down into a new form of racial subordination. Stevens fought the accidental president from start to finish, pressed the House to impeach him, and came close to ejecting Johnson from office.

Thaddeus Stevens owed his high visibility and effectiveness not only to the substance of his views but also to a number of personal qualities and skills. He displayed an iron will and great courage, moral as well as physical, repeatedly refusing to bend before opposition, cower before threats, or grovel or pander for voter support. "He did not play the courtier," as one congressman observed, and "he did not flatter the people; he never was a beggar for their votes."[7] He also became a shrewd and skillful parliamentarian, using the rules of procedure to outmaneuver congressional opponents.

Those who clashed with Stevens discovered that he had a quick wit and sharp tongue and was happy to give free rein to both. On one occasion, while speaking in the House of Representatives, he agreed to yield the floor so that an adversary could make "a few feeble remarks." He declared of a pro-slavery Pennsylvania congressman that "there are some reptiles so flat that the common foot of man cannot crush them." Walking down a narrow lane one day, he found himself confronting a political antagonist. "I never get out of the way for a skunk," the other man sneered. "I always do," Stevens replied, and promptly stood aside. Stevens displayed this penchant for colorfully pointed language early in his career. When still a member of the Pennsylvania legislature, he referred to a hostile opponent who had entered the chamber as "the thing which has crawled into this House and adheres to one of the seats by its own slime." No wonder that a fellow member of the U.S. House of Representatives confessed years later that he would no sooner tangle verbally with Stevens than he would "get into difficulty with a porcupine."[8]

Thaddeus Stevens's views, words, and actions provoked both deep admiration and bitter denunciation. Within the Union, opponents of the Republican Party hated Stevens almost as much as did Jubal Early. Republicans who were more conservative than Stevens deplored his influence. "On the subject of Reconstruction," declared the *New York Times*, "Mr. Stevens must be considered the Evil Genius of the Republican Party."[9]

That dark view of Stevens grew more widespread later when politicians and intellectuals turned against the radicalism that had saved the Union and abolished slavery. From the late nineteenth century through the middle of the twentieth, professional historians generally looked balefully at Stevens and the policies that he championed. Professor William A. Dunning of Columbia University, who influenced generations of historians, damned Stevens as "truculent, vindictive, and cynical." To James G. Randall, once considered the dean of Lincoln scholars, Stevens seemed filled with "vindictive ugliness," "unfairness, intolerance, and hatefulness."[10]

Historical literature directed at a wider public likewise scorned Stevens. A popular 1929 biography of Andrew Johnson denounced

Stevens as a "horrible old man . . . craftily preparing to strangle the bleeding, broken body of the South," a man who thought it would be "a beautiful thing" to see "the white men, especially the white women of the South, writhing under negro domination." Two years later, James Truslow Adams's bestselling *The Epic of America* called Stevens "the most despicable, malevolent and morally deformed character who has ever risen to power in America." John F. Kennedy's Pulitzer Prize–winning *Profiles in Courage* (1955) sang the praises of Andrew Johnson while breathing hostility to Thaddeus Stevens, "the crippled, fanatical personification of the extremes of the Radical Republican movement." Hollywood began early to foster public hostility to Stevens's memory. D. W. Griffith's widely seen film *The Birth of a Nation* (1915) celebrated the Ku Klux Klan and featured a villainous congressman named Stoneman who was obviously modeled on Stevens. Almost thirty years later, an MGM movie about Andrew Johnson repeated that message, with Lionel Barrymore portraying Stevens as the vindictive persecutor of a helpless defeated South.[11]

It took the civil rights movement of the mid-twentieth century to make many writers and filmmakers reconsider both Reconstruction and Thaddeus Stevens. Fawn M. Brodie's 1959 psycho-biography of Stevens expressed appreciation for his efforts on behalf of African Americans. But even she attributed to the man "an arbitrary righteousness mingled with cynicism" and a neurotic perfectionism. "For it is in the nature of the crusader," Brodie wrote, "—the radical, the Jacobin, the revolutionary, the true believer: call him what you will—that he is never sated. . . . This is because his crusade is likely to be a substitute for deeper needs, and there is no success but finds him empty and lonely still." In Tony Kushner and Steven Spielberg's film *Lincoln* (2012), which celebrates the passage of the Thirteenth Amendment, Tommy Lee Jones's portrayal of Thaddeus Stevens brought the latter unprecedented modern notice. But it presented its audience with an obstinate, doctrinaire Stevens, too radical for his time and therefore as much of an obstacle to emancipation as a force behind its achievement.[12]

Two twentieth-century scholars portrayed Stevens in sharply conflicting but nonetheless instructive ways. Hans Trefousse dubbed him a "nineteenth-century egalitarian." But that label is not very precise. In Stevens's era, self-styled egalitarians came in many shapes and sizes—including laissez-faire libertarians, women's suffragists, land reformers, trade unionists, utopian community builders, socialists, and anarchists—depending upon how they defined equality. Richard N. Current objected to calling Stevens any kind of egalitarian, arguing that what motivated Stevens was not the achievement of human equality but merely his own "frustrated personal ambitions" and a "desire to keep his party in power and make it a vehicle for industrialists like himself," adding that in pursuit of those aims Stevens "did his part in bringing about the Age of Big Business."[13]

These two historians seized upon aspects of Stevens's outlook without grasping its essence. The egalitarianism that Stevens espoused drew inspiration from and sought to promote the system of "free labor" capitalism then developing in the United States's northern states. But the attempt to counterpose Stevens's devotion to that economic system to his fervent hostility to human slavery was misguided. With Stevens, they were only different facets of a single outlook.

Human lives contain many dimensions. That was as true of Thaddeus Stevens as of anyone else. Before throwing himself into politics, he became an able and prominent attorney. As his law practice prospered, he invested in real estate and iron production. Family was important to him. He attributed much of his success in life to his mother, who doted on him as a child, and he visited and remained devoted to her throughout her life. In 1848, a widow of mixed-race ancestry, Lydia Hamilton Smith, came to work for Stevens as a housekeeper, and the two developed a close friendship and working relationship. Hoping to tarnish Stevens's image, enemies accused him of taking Mrs. Smith as a lover, and Spielberg's *Lincoln* treats that claim as true, although no firm evidence substantiates it.

Thaddeus Stevens: Civil War Revolutionary, Fighter for Racial Justice focuses on his role as a public figure, on his fight against chattel slavery and racial discrimination, on the key part he played in the Union war effort and in the postwar struggle to bring racial democracy to the South and the nation at large. It will also ask how such a key figure came into being. One of Stevens's longtime associates, Alexander Hood, later mused that "when a man of peculiar qualifications is required to push the world onward . . . , Providence always furnishes an instrument adapted to the work." "Sometimes," Hood continued, "the chosen one seems to come forth like Minerva from the hand of Jove, fully developed and equipped at all points for the work." Sometimes, but by no means always. "At other times, it would appear that a long course of vigorous training is required to fit the destined leader for his work." The latter, Hood suggested, was the case with Thaddeus Stevens. The man known to the Civil War era took shape over the course of prior decades that exposed him to a multitude of influences and confronted him with a host of challenges. Those influences and challenges and what he made of them shaped the person that Stevens would eventually become. Only understanding that process makes his evolution comprehensible.[14]

As Alexander Hood understood, Stevens's evolution was not a simple, straightforward one. It passed through a series of stages that a number of his previous biographers have left barely examined. He began life in a poor farm family in Vermont in the aftermath of major social and political struggles that shook that place and left its mark on its values and politics. His family immersed him in the Baptist faith, and schooling exposed him to the Greek and Roman classics. In college he discovered teachers and books steeped in the Enlightenment. Some of the ideas he encountered in those years complemented one another; others did not. In adulthood, Stevens would have to sort through and test them in practice and grapple with their inconsistencies. In doing so, he trod a path that contained zigs and zags. The chapters that follow seek to explain how that path led Stevens to his crucial place in the Second American Revolution.

CHAPTER ONE

A Son of Vermont

Shortly after noon on Thursday, December 17, 1868, the U.S. House of Representatives put aside pressing business to pay tribute to one of its most influential members and surely its most colorful one. Thaddeus Stevens of Pennsylvania had died late in the previous summer, and on this day one man after another took the floor to honor his courage, integrity, eloquence, slashing wit, and especially his dedication to and achievements on behalf of human freedom. Stevens was born and raised in Vermont, and one of its congressmen read aloud a resolution from its legislature that claimed the deceased as "a son of Vermont." Another congressman from that state explained that its people had always held "that the strong love of freedom and independence for all men" that the mature Stevens displayed—"his hatred of all forms of oppression, and his efforts to elevate and benefit the masses"—that these qualities and others "were, to some extent, due to his being born in Vermont."[1]

Stevens had indeed grown up in a state proud of its recent struggle to protect its small farms and achieve a democratic form of government. His family's strong Baptist faith stressed individual rights, egalitarianism, and mutuality. Schooling exposed him to the classics of the ancient world, an Enlightenment-influenced Protestantism, and liberal capitalist principles. These and other early influences con-

tributed to the young man's evolving personality, values, and view of
the world.

Stevens's parents had moved to Vermont from Methuen, Massachusetts, in 1786, just three years after the Revolutionary War ended.
Along with some other families, Joshua Stevens and Sarah Morrill
Stevens left their homes in hopes of escaping the economic hard-
ships then afflicting Bay State farmers by resettling in a place whose
soil was both cheaper and more fertile. Traveling 150 miles north-
ward, they reached Danville, a small Vermont hill town set near a
tributary of the Connecticut River. A few years later, Joshua managed to obtain a mortgage with which to purchase a farm there, and
Sarah before long gave birth to four sons—Joshua Jr. in 1790; Thaddeus in 1792; Abner in 1794; and Alanson in 1797.[2]

Even in their new home, the Stevenses continued to struggle
against poverty. The first two sons, Joshua Jr. and Thaddeus, were
born with club feet—Joshua with two, Thaddeus with one. That left
the boys unable to perform all the heavy labor that farming required.
It also exposed them to ridicule. Someone who knew Stevens in his
youth recalled that other youngsters would "sometimes . . . laugh at
him, boy-like, and mimic his limping walk." Thaddeus, that neighbor
added, "was a sensitive little fellow, and it rankled."[3]

The Stevens family's difficulties deepened when Thaddeus's father disappeared around 1804. The cause of that disappearance is
unclear. Some suggest that Joshua Sr. simply fled his family's woes.
Some say that after abandoning his family, he died in the War of
1812. After trying for three years to manage the Danville farm without a mate or sufficient aid from her children, Sarah moved herself
and her sons to nearby Peacham to live with her brother. Thaddeus
then remained in Vermont another seven years, until 1811, when he
was nineteen.[4]

Vermont's political atmosphere in those years encouraged commitment to equality and democratic government. As Congressman Luke Poland noted in a eulogy for Stevens, that state was born in a fierce and protracted fight against what its residents viewed as "unlawful and unjust" attempts to oppress them. At stake in that fight were access to land and the right of democratic self-government. Although that struggle preceded Thaddeus's birth, Poland also noted, "the heroes and statesmen who were her leaders in those trying days were still alive" during Stevens's youth, and they continued to give "tone and temper to public sentiment and opinion for many years" afterward.[5]

Both before, during, and after the American Revolution, the region eventually known as Vermont—then commonly called the New Hampshire Grants—was claimed by both New Hampshire and New York. New Hampshire usually provided would-be settlers from New England with comparatively inexpensive land titles. But the colonial province of New York pronounced those claims invalid and during the 1760s bestowed titles of its own upon Yorker landlords and businessmen; some of those titles covered thousands of acres that overlapped with claims that Yankee farmers and speculators had previously staked.[6]

Even Yankee farmers whose deeds Yorkers did not challenge had good reason to oppose New York's claim to govern the region. The colonial province of New York contained huge manors, especially along the Hudson and Mohawk Rivers, where many hundreds of poor, landless tenants worked land owned by wealthy families who wielded great power in provincial government. That power enabled the province's elite to enforce payment of the often heavy debts of the region's hard-pressed small farmers.[7]

When Yorkers, most of them absentee owners, tried to supplant Yankee farmers in the Hampshire Grants, the Yankees resisted, often violently. They rioted when Yorker-created courts tried to enforce the small farmers' debts. They attacked, kidnapped, and even jailed officials attempting to evict them; freed neighbors arrested by such officials; destroyed the fences, crops, homes, and other property of Yorker newcomers; and forced the closing of local courts.[8]

In 1775, the Grants declared themselves a self-governing republic, eventually adopting the name of Vermont (from the French *les Verts Monts*, after the Green Mountain range that runs from north to south down the middle of the region).[9] Although the small Vermont republic remained independent until admitted to the United States as a state in 1791, Vermont troops fought alongside the other insurgent colonies against Britain early in the war. That struggle further fanned the flames of social conflict at home. In the summer of 1777, revolutionary Vermont moved to finance the war's costs by seizing property belonging to imperial Loyalists and selling it at public auction. Such land seizures, when added to acreage forfeited by Yorkers and Loyalists who fled Vermont, represented a major transfer of property from one group of people to another. While speculators took advantage of the situation, this agrarian upheaval enabled many poor settlers—those already in Vermont as well as others who arrived from elsewhere in New England after the revolution—to obtain farms at low prices.[10]

Thaddeus Stevens was thus born in a state that owed its very existence to struggle by small farmers for land. In waging that struggle, Vermont's Yankee settlers drew strength from and reinforced a code of cultural, economic, and political values deeply rooted in New England. Those included belief in democratic government based on a broad-based suffrage and a conviction that the best society was one whose members owned their own small farms and whose mutual assistance helped to prevent creation of great extremes of wealth and poverty. Individual rights were prized, but personal interest must not threaten the welfare of the community.[11]

*   *   *

As colonists in North America waged their war for home rule against the British Empire, a second conflict broke out over who would rule at home. What kind of constitutions should newly born states adopt, and what kinds of state governments should those constitutions create? Some states, like New York, adopted constitutions structured to protect the interests of the social and economic elite against the dangers of too much democracy. They created weak and unwieldy bicameral legislatures in which effective veto power lay with upper houses elected solely by citizens with considerable property. They often placed more power in the hands of state governors whose lengthier terms of office placed them further above the reach of voters.[12]

Vermonters rejected that government model in favor of a more democratic one. The constitution they adopted in 1777 created a unicameral legislature that was stronger than the governor. Its members would be elected annually, with nearly all adult males enfranchised. (The one striking exception to this inclusive approach was a religious one. Vermont's constitution guaranteed full religious freedom only to Protestants and limited membership in the legislature to them.)[13]

The generally democratic spirit that suffused Vermont politics and structured its government did something else of historic importance. Vermont's constitution was the first in North America to condemn the enslavement of human beings. Echoing and elaborating upon the Declaration of Independence, its preamble announced that "all persons are born equally free and independent, and have certain natural, inherent, and unalienable rights, amongst which are the enjoying and defending life and liberty, acquiring, possessing and protecting property, and pursuing and obtaining happiness and safety." From that premise Vermonters drew at least one conclusion absent from the U.S. Constitution, adopted a decade later. "No person born in this country, or brought from over sea," Vermont's constitution held, "ought to be holden by law, to serve any person as a servant, slave or apprentice, after arriving to the age of twenty-one years." To be sure, that passage was ambiguous and incomplete. It rejected the enslavement of adults more clearly than it actually outlawed it. And it said nothing about the enslavement of children. Still, it expressed greater hostility to slavery than did any U.S. state (or the British Empire) at that time.[14]

Of course, Vermont's population was not homogeneous politically, and being born and raised there did not guarantee growing up to be Thaddeus Stevens. Stephen A. Douglas, whose political principles the adult Stevens despised, also spent his youth in that state. But Stevens's family displayed a marked attachment to Vermont's democratic and egalitarian traditions. Joshua and Sarah apparently named their second son after Tadeusz Kościuszko, the Polish-Lithuanian soldier who had joined the American fight for independence. More tellingly, Thaddeus long remembered his family's regard for the revolution's most egalitarian document, the Declaration of Independence. From his "earliest youth," he would later recall, he was taught to read it and "to revere its sublime principles."[15]

The Stevens family's Baptist faith echoed and reinforced those principles. Sarah Morrill Stevens was very devout and saw to it, as she later recalled, that her son was "taught the scriptures" at an early age. The town of Danville's first Baptist congregation formed in the year of Thaddeus's birth, and his family duly joined it.[16]

The Baptist denomination had arisen in England within seventeenth-century Puritanism, which prized simplicity of doctrine and ritual and the active involvement of church members. Puritans were also Calvinists and held to the doctrine of predestination, believing that God decided the spiritual fate of all humans before their births and that the great mass of humanity would be damned. Only the few, the "elect," would be saved, and God would stand by them, strengthen their arms, and relieve them of any conflicting obligations to earthly powers, including kings.[17]

Baptists subscribed to much of that general Puritan outlook, in some ways further emphasizing personal choice and responsibility. Their name reflected insistence that the full church membership conveyed in the ceremony of baptism should occur not routinely at birth but only once a person reached adulthood and made a conscious decision to accept the church's doctrines and responsibilities. The same stress on individual choice led Baptist congregations to permit, even to encourage, their members to amend or challenge the sermons of their ministers.[18]

Complementing and somewhat qualifying this stress on personal choice and responsibility, Baptists prized membership in a community bound together by ties of mutual respect and mutual assistance, helping one another both spiritually and practically.[19] Thaddeus's mother personified that commitment. When spotted fever struck the county in 1805, she threw herself into the work of nursing the afflicted back to health. Her son accompanied her as she did so, and his mother's selfless conduct reinforced his sense of responsibility to the unfortunate and fostered an open-handed generosity toward them.[20]

The Baptists of Vermont were strongly egalitarian and democratic in their political inclinations. They remained acutely conscious that they had suffered persecution in England, and in both Massachusetts and Vermont they found themselves taxed to support another (the Congregational) church. In reaction, they favored separation of church and state, an expansive freedom of religion, and a democratic form of government, expecting that greater democracy would better protect their liberties. The same concerns led them to demand transparency in government and to oppose secretive fraternal associations, fearing that secrecy could cloak authoritarian and repressive plotting against their rights.[21]

*   *   *

The next stage of Stevens's early shaping took place in schools. Sarah Stevens doted upon this son and made him (as a close colleague of his later put it) "the Joseph of the family." She determined early that he must obtain a good education and prepare himself for one of the professions. Thaddeus himself recalled that this "very extraordinary woman" had "worked night and day to educate me." She taught him to read, helped kindle in him a love of reading and a hunger for reading matter, and enrolled him in the state's public ("common") schools. Finding books scarce in rural Vermont, Thaddeus tried at age fifteen to establish a library in his community. In 1807 he began attending the Peacham Academy, a tuition-based high school, to prepare himself for college.[22]

Four years later, Stevens enrolled in Dartmouth College in Hanover, New Hampshire. For reasons that are unclear, he passed all or part of his junior year at the University of Vermont, returning to Dartmouth for his senior year and graduation. Like many others with few means, he helped to finance his higher education by working as a teacher in a nearby school. He also skipped the freshman year at Dartmouth, enrolling instead as a sophomore. This was another stratagem that indigent students commonly used to reduce the cost of their education. In order to do that, Stevens would have had to perform well on the entrance examination by demonstrating an acquaintance with the Greek and Latin classics, something that the young man had probably obtained at the Peacham Academy.

To which ideas was Stevens exposed in college? One influence would have been the Dartmouth faculty, which was Federalist in political sympathy and therefore likely to prefer some restrictions on the suffrage and to support government aid to commercial and industrial development. A second influence would have been the particular books listed in the college curricula, which included works by John Locke, William Paley, Joseph Butler, Jonathan Edwards, and the Swiss theorist Jean-Jacques Burlamaqui.[23]

Neither a lazy nor a frivolous student, Stevens doubtless took his reading assignments seriously.[24] In those books he would encounter strenuous efforts to grapple with the Enlightenment's challenge to religion. That took the form not of demanding blind faith in received doctrine but of asserting that human reason was not only perfectly compatible with belief in God and acceptance of Christianity but led naturally to belief and acceptance.[25] Those books would also expose Stevens to strong views about subjects later called sociology, political science, and history. Jean-Jacques Burlamaqui argued for strong and activist government in the hands of an educated and capable elite. In *Principles of Moral and Political Philosophy*, William Paley endorsed policies that served existing social and political relations. He held that private property was necessary for productivity, prosperity, and social order and must be protected, and he criticized trade unions for fomenting social turmoil. Allowing people who owned no property to vote was dangerous, Paley also explained, because the poor were volatile and undependable; a really broad-based political democracy would lead to mob rule.

But the young Stevens would not have found in Paley's book a complacent satisfaction with all aspects of the status quo. Private property could produce abuse and exploitation, Paley conceded. And that author flirted with some egalitarian-seeming notions, criticized the idleness and self-indulgence of the rich, contemplated a graduated income tax, and urged a significant degree of religious freedom.[26]

The books that Stevens read probably had an ambiguous impact upon students' thinking. In religious, social, and political terms, the authors were basically conservative, aiming to defend Christianity and existing society by inoculating readers against religious skepticism and social and political radicalism. But, as some feared, their adaptation to the Enlightenment might also serve as a bridge out of strong religious belief. And their acknowledgment of societal inequities could encourage more extensive and more fundamental kinds of social and political questioning.[27]

On one subject, however—human slavery—Stevens's formal education would have had a straightforward effect, bolstering the aversion to bondage that was common among New Englanders and that Vermonters had written into their own constitution. In the ancient classics, he later recalled, he "found . . . one unanimous denunciation of tyranny and of slavery, and eulogy of liberty. Homer, Aeschylus the great Greek tragedian, Cicero, Hesiod, Virgil, Tacitus, and Sallust, in immortal language, all denounced slavery." As early as 1808, students at the University of Vermont were engaging in organized debates over the rights and wrongs of slavery and emancipation. Paley's *Principles of Moral and Political Philosophy* contained an extended and passionate denunciation of slavery, deeming property in human beings an abomination. "The slaves, torn away from parents, wives, children, from their friends and companions, their fields and flocks, their home and country," Paley protested, "are transported to the European settlements in America, with no other accommodation on shipboard than what is provided for brutes." Once in the Americas "the miserable exiles are . . . placed, and that for life, in subjection to a dominion and system of laws, the most merciless and tyrannical that ever were tolerated upon the face of the earth" and did so "with rigour and brutality."[28]

How could this great moral wrong be righted? Paley's basic conservatism made him quail at the thought of eliminating even so abominable a tyranny hastily. "The emancipation of slaves should be gradual," he said, "and be carried on by provisions of law, and under the protection of civil government." Paley counted on the spread of Christian enlightenment to put an end to "this odious institution." "By the mild diffusion of its [Christianity's] light and influence," he wrote, "the minds of men are insensibly prepared to perceive and correct the enormities, which folly, or wickedness, or accident, have introduced into public establishments." Wasn't that, after all, the way that "Greek and Roman slavery, and, since these, the feudal tyranny, has declined before it"?[29]

After graduating from Dartmouth in August 1814, Stevens moved to southern Pennsylvania, evidently hoping to find a teaching job where a friend had already done so.[30] He succeeded in the town of York and began teaching at the York Academy while studying law. In late August 1816, at twenty-four, he passed the bar in neighboring Maryland and then opened a law office in Gettysburg, the small county seat of Adams County. A lawyer and judge who knew him then observed "a mind which instantly and clearly comprehended" any problem at hand and a "strength of judgment" that quickly produced "a sound solution." Stevens's manner of speaking, moreover, was both "eloquent and curt" and "impressed the force of his convictions" upon his listeners. Even a longtime political opponent conceded his skill at "present[ing] the strong points of a case in a more powerful manner" than could most other lawyers. The young attorney's appearance was impressive, too. He was tall and physically imposing. Just under six feet in height, he boasted a large frame and, despite his limp, had become muscular and athletic. His face radiated dignity, intelligence, and intensity. (His hair was brown until he lost it all in his mid-thirties to alopecia, after which he never appeared in public without a wig.)[31]

As his law practice prospered, Stevens invested in local real estate and ironworks and launched a political career. Between 1822 and 1831 his neighbors elected him to the borough council, where he served for a time as its president. In 1833 voters sent him to the Pennsylvania House of Representatives and did so again in each of the next two years. He failed to win reelection in October 1836 but the following month became a delegate to the Pennsylvania constitutional convention of 1837–38. He returned to the state House in 1837. In the summer of 1842, financial reverses induced him to move to the larger town of Lancaster, which offered greater opportunities to a rising attorney and politician.

When he settled in Pennsylvania, Thaddeus Stevens's general outlook reflected what he had internalized, modified, or discarded from his family and their values, his Vermont neighbors, and his formal education. His relationship to the Calvinism of his youth was complicated. Raised by and long close to his devout mother, he claimed at the end of his life that he had "always been a firm believer in the Bible" and that only "a fool . . . disbelieves in the existence of a God." And while admitting that he had not lived piously, he also insisted that, having been "raised a Baptist," he continued to "adhere to their belief." Apparently bolstering that claim was the fact that Stevens rented church pews while living in Gettysburg as well as Lancaster.[32] And throughout his life he would invoke both God and scripture in support of his political convictions.

But the Thaddeus Stevens whom his friends and acquaintances knew differed from this image. His law student and then political associate Alexander Hood saw in him a religious skeptic whose mind rebelled against any belief that was "in conflict with his own reason." Another longtime friend and ally, Edward McPherson, agreed in an unpublished memoir that Stevens was not "a Christian in any religious sense," that he "gave the same admiration to Socrates [that] he did to Jesus." Indeed, McPherson went on, "in regard to Religion, for nearly the whole of his life he sat 'in the seat of the scornful'" and while "as a general thing he was too guarded to speak his thoughts openly," still "at times, among those whom he thought it would not too deeply offend," he expressed views on that subject that "were exceedingly course and extremely contemptuous."[33] It seems most likely, therefore, that although the adult Stevens believed in God, he had little use for organized religion.

The Baptist faith that surrounded Stevens in his youth seems nonetheless to have left its mark. McPherson noted that Stevens remained "at all times a reader of the Scriptures" and that "his knowledge of them was extensive and accurate." Hood recalled seeing Stevens vigorously defend the doctrine of predestination against a critic. In doing so, Hood said, Stevens demonstrated "such an intimate acquaintance with the theological writers of the Calvinistic school" that the critic asked if he had ever trained for the clergy. Stevens replied with a dismissive grunt and a curt affirmation that he had "read the books."[34]

As students of religion have noted, belief in predestination has commonly served to bolster the optimism and self-confidence of subscribers who presume themselves to be among the "elect." But if Stevens no longer adhered fully to Calvinist doctrine, what belief animated his defense of predestination that day? It seemed to Hood that even though Stevens was no longer genuinely religious, he remained "a *fatalist* in the strongest sense of the term." Stevens's assertion decades later that neither secession nor the Civil War was an "accidental" occurrence but were instead "predetermined and inevitable" seems to accord with Hood's claim.[35] But if it was not grounded in Calvinism, what was the nature of Stevens's fatalism? Was it a belief in some kind of cosmic fate? Or was it simply an understanding that real, often intractable earthly circumstances—including material conditions, human frailties, and large social forces—limited options and shaped the lives of individuals and nations?[36]

Stevens also retained the dark view of human nature that underlay Calvinism's belief that only a few would achieve salvation. McPherson recorded that while Stevens in later years agreed "that an honest man was not an impossibility," he continued to believe that such men "were very few indeed."[37] He would invoke that view publicly at the end of his life in a shorthand explanation of the nation's decades-long "depart[ure] from the principles of the Declaration of Independence" in tolerating slavery and racial inequality for so long. That had occurred, he summarized, because "man still is vile."[38]

Stevens's personal life exhibited an ambivalence similar to the one apparent in his spiritual life. Although when still "a young man he would occasionally take a glass of wine," he would later abstain from both tobacco and alcohol. He "was not an immoral man," Hood observed, but neither was it accurate "to say he had no vices." Stevens was an enthusiastic gambler and, perhaps, something of a sexual libertine. Later in his life he confessed to having spent "too much" of it "in idleness or frivolous amusement." The abolitionist Protestant minister Jonathan Blanchard called him "one of that sort of prophets who . . . are at once the violators of God's law, and the champions of His cause."[39]

One of Stevens's oft-noted characteristics was a pronounced and lifelong sympathy for the disadvantaged and mistreated. As another colleague later put it, "nature had given Mr. Stevens a generous heart," so "he seemed to feel that every wrong inflicted upon the human race was a blow struck at himself." Observers and chroniclers have attributed that generosity of spirit to various sources, especially his own physical handicap, and perhaps that did play a part. Stevens himself credited the indigence he had known in Vermont. "When I reflect," he said in the 1830s, "how apt hereditary wealth, hereditary influence, and, perhaps, as a consequence, hereditary pride are to close the avenues and steel the heart against the wants and the rights of the poor, I am induced to thank my Creator for having, from early life, bestowed upon me the blessing of poverty."[40]

But perceiving poverty's silver lining did not make Stevens idealize his straitened, provincial youth. It seems clear, on the contrary, that at an early age he found life in his hard-pressed rural community wanting. His first direct exposure to a world outside it apparently occurred in 1804; in that year, at age twelve, he went on a family trip to visit relatives in Boston. Although the adult Stevens rarely discussed that trip, Alexander Hood inferred that it convinced young Thaddeus that he must "become rich and live like the wealthy men did there." But Hood admittedly had trouble squaring that inference with the fact that "there never was a man who cared less for money to be spent upon himself" than Thaddeus Stevens. Other acquaintances agreed about Stevens's relative disinterest in wealth.[41]

Whether or not exposure to Boston ignited an ambition for personal gain, it probably opened young Thaddeus's eyes to a kind of life that was not only materially richer but also more stimulating, exciting, and filled with opportunities than was his own, which he would some years later refer to sardonically as "indigent obscurity." Appreciation of economic development's benefits would shape much of his adult life.[42]

CHAPTER TWO

A Young Man's Outlook

In aspiring to a more comfortable and interesting life than the one he'd been born into, Thaddeus Stevens mirrored the experience of other contemporaries. One of those was, once again, Abraham Lincoln, who as an adult looked back without nostalgia upon his own provincial youth in rural Kentucky and Indiana. Being "raised to farm work," the mature Lincoln regretted, his existence had contained "absolutely nothing to excite ambition for education." Horace Greeley, who would become the founding editor and publisher of the widely read and influential *New York Tribune*, was the son and grandson of small-scale Baptist and Methodist farmers in New Hampshire. When Horace was nine years old, debt stripped the Greeleys of their land and consigned them to hard, low-paid agricultural labor. It was a life that struck Horace as "a mindless, monotonous drudgery" in which "there was neither scope for expanding faculties, incitement to constant growth in knowledge, nor a spur to generous ambition." He, too, therefore "turned from it in dissatisfaction, if not in disgust, and sought a different sphere and vocation."[1]

With backgrounds like these, it is scarcely surprising that Lincoln, Greeley, and Stevens all came to look upon the expansion of commerce and manufacturing as essential to the nation's prosperity, cultural enrichment, and societal health. In Stevens's case, university education reinforced and helped him to articulate that opinion. At his Dartmouth graduation ceremony he delivered an oration that strongly advocated such development, arguing that it benefited not only the capitalist but all members of society. Nor was that benefit only material. It was just such "improvement," the young Stevens asserted, ". . . that has banished barbarism, despotism, and superstition from a great portion of the globe."[2]

Confidence in industrial development as an engine of human progress remained central to Stevens's outlook and politics for the rest of his life. He would aver in the 1850s that "every highly cultivated Nation has made the protection of domestic industry the special care of Government" because "nations, without manufactures, may be highly respectable, but cannot be highly refined." Kindred views gained great popularity in the country's Northeast during the first half of the nineteenth century.[3]

In his Dartmouth graduation speech, the young Stevens did not deny that, in addition to increasing wealth and facilitating enlightenment, the economic system eventually known as capitalism also fostered significant inequality. But like William Paley, he accepted such "unequal distribution of wealth" as a necessary by-product of progress. Economic development and class distinctions seemed to him inseparable, because "as men advance in refinement, distinction of ranks and orders multiply." So rejecting inequality required rejecting progress, too. Had human beings "been content to remain in a state of equality," he told his audience, they would "likewise have remained in a state of barbarism."[4]

And if capitalism fostered economic inequality, the young Thaddeus Stevens believed, it could nevertheless improve the lives of all of society's members. An expanding commerce and industry could benefit not only those at the top of the economic ladder but also those currently perched on its lower rungs. His own ascent from poverty into the professions seemed to bear out this optimistic view, and he continued to defend that doctrine in later decades.[5]

Still, Stevens did not believe that economic development and prosperity were inevitable. Nor did he assume that all deserving people would inevitably partake of whatever prosperity should occur. Those happy outcomes would transpire only on two conditions.

First, government must actively and deliberately stimulate the development of capitalism, especially its commercial and manufacturing sectors. Speaking in the Pennsylvania House of Representatives in 1834, Stevens praised federal financing, in whole or in part, of the construction and maintenance of roads, bridges, canals, ports, and railroads to facilitate commerce. He praised the Second U.S. Bank, a privately owned but federally chartered corporation charged with handling the national government's fiscal transactions and regulating the issuance of credit by private banks. To Stevens, the Bank's value lay in its ability to prevent "sudden and calamitous fluctuations of the currency," thereby smoothing the way for greater trade across the miles and aiding the government's ability to borrow. No less valuable in his eyes was a tariff to protect the domestic market for the United States' fledgling manufacturing sector against European, especially British, imports. (Henry Clay of Kentucky was the outstanding champion of all these measures. [6])

Second, government must take positive steps to *ensure* to all an equal chance to partake of prosperity's blessings. Such equal economic opportunity required a parallel guarantee of equal treatment by and before the law. That was essential because in Stevens's eyes true "human oppression" was chiefly political, not social or economic, in origin; it arose from an "inequality of rights," legal rights. So while Stevens accepted wealth inequality born of a free market, he rejected anything that to him smacked of caste. In his own words, Stevens repudiated "distinctions . . . made by your laws between the different classes of society." A corollary evil for him was hatred, contempt, or condescension toward the poor. The "aristocracy of the most odious and insolent kind," he held, was "the aristocracy of wealth and pride."[7] The capitalism that Thaddeus Stevens idealized was a humane and legally egalitarian and humane one.

Even as society enshrined legal equality, Stevens held, so must it act affirmatively to help prepare all of its members to take advantage of economic opportunities on offer. Here, too, Stevens saw a positive role for government. So in 1834 he supported in the Pennsylvania legislature a law creating a system of public ("common") schools funded by state revenues. Such a system, he expected, would further reduce the likelihood of classes hardening into castes; it could enable "the poor man's son," once schooled, to "far outstrip and bear off the laurels from the less industrious heirs of wealth."[8]

But Stevens soon faced vociferous demands for the new school law's repeal. Other Pennsylvanians, it developed, embraced a far narrower conception of government's proper role and a more limited view of citizens' responsibilities to one other. "Many of our industrious, frugal, agricultural population," recalled one colleague, "believed that every man should take care of his own family and educate his children or not, as seemed to him best. The idea of taxing one man to pay for schooling the children of another was looked upon by them as an innovation and an injustice." In Lancaster County, this view appears to have been especially common among the large "Pennsylvania Dutch" (actually, colonial-era German American immigrant) population.[9]

Those numerous and emphatic objections did soon induce the state Senate to repeal the common schools law, doing so by a margin of almost two to one, substituting a far smaller system serving only those who could be certified as paupers. This new Senate bill went to the state's House of Representatives for approval.

Stevens's constituents demanded that he approve this move to repeal and replace. He refused. Instead on April 11, 1835, he took the floor of the state House to explain that common schools for all were essential building blocks of good government, preparing the citizenry to exercise the franchise knowledgeably. Those schools were also essential in order to share widely the benefits of prosperity and to avoid humiliating the poor. Stevens urged Pennsylvania to follow the example of his native New England, where "free schools plant the seeds and the desire of knowledge in every mind, without regard to the wealth of the parent or the texture of the pupil's garments." He celebrated "the exquisite feelings" that poor parents experience "when they see their children receiving the boon of education" and because of that education overcoming the obstacles that "hereditary poverty" placed in their way. Invoking his own history even more specifically, he noted that the free common schools that New England's "generous public" supported also provided economic sustenance to "those who have but scanty means, and are pursuing a *collegiate* education" and "find it necessary to spend a portion of the year in teaching common schools" to pay for it.[10]

New England's taxpayers made all that possible, Stevens continued, because they understood the necessity of supporting institutions such as schools that might not necessarily serve them directly. He regretted that so many in his adopted state lacked that understanding, "complain[ing] of the school tax not so much on account of its amount, as because it is for the benefit of others and not themselves." Here Stevens pointed an accusing finger directly at public education's more well-to-do critics, including "the industrious, thrifty, rich farmer" and especially the farmer who had inherited his wealth, "whose fat acres have descended to him, from father to son in unbroken succession." Such people, Stevens regretted, "can scarcely feel any sympathy with, or understand the necessities of the poor."

But Stevens insisted that well-to-do voters' hostility toward common schools was "a mistake," one that revealed a shortsighted understanding of their true self-interest. They should recognize that ensuring the education of the general public redounds to "their own benefit," he explained, because "it perpetuates the government and ensures the due administration of the laws under which they live, and by which their lives and property are protected." Tight-fisted citizens who demand that every government function yield direct, personal dividends to them should instead value institutions that sustained the kind of society in which they could prosper and feel secure in their property. By all accounts, Stevens's words strongly moved other legislators. The Pennsylvania House then rejected the attempt to replace the common schools with paupers-only schools by a nearly two-thirds majority, and the state Senate agreed.[11]

It was probably Stevens's defense of the public school system that cost him reelection to the legislature in 1836. But his neighbors did vote that same year to send him as a delegate to the state constitutional convention that met in 1837. Encountering the same education controversy there, he elaborated upon his opposition to paupers-only publicly supported schools. He despised "this setting up on one side, those possessed of wealth, and branding another class as plebeians and poor." No law must shame people by branding them as paupers, not least because such public snobbery "has broken down the spirit of many of your young men, and lowered them in their own estimation." No, education "ought to be as free as the air to every human being in society." Indeed, Stevens wished to see a publicly funded education guaranteed not only to the young but to all in need of it, regardless of age.[12]

Stevens made common cause in this fight and a few others with some Pennsylvania Democrats, including the governor. In general, however, and especially in national politics, Stevens opposed the Democratic Party on nearly all questions. At the national level, that party was largely controlled by slaveholding leaders of its southern state organizations. Within the South itself, Democrats obtained mass support partly by arguing that slavery and white supremacy benefited poorer whites as much as plantation owners. In the free states, Democratic politicians regularly presented themselves to voters as champions of the white man of little or no property, promising to foil attempts both by despised free blacks to gain any kind of legal or social parity with him and by wealthy "monopolists" to infringe upon either his political rights or his economic opportunities. On the latter score, northern Democrats commonly denounced attempts to create national banks, protective tariffs, and taxation to pay for internal improvements; such things, they claimed, were nothing but schemes to benefit the northern rich at the expense of the poor and middle class, rural and urban alike.[13]

That stance offended Thaddeus Stevens. At this stage of his life, as noted, the egalitarianism of his Vermont youth had been at least qualified by confidence in the curative power of economic development. A firm believer in the North's free-labor capitalist society, Stevens in the 1830s opposed the stoking of hostilities among its social classes as unjustified and dangerous to prosperity, social order, and republican government. As a delegate to Pennsylvania's constitutional convention, he decried "attempt[s] to sever the community in twain, to render the rich and the poorer classes antagonist to each other, and thus to convert into enemies, those whose interests are mutually dependent," in the process "rob[bing] thrift and industry of their earnings and their security." To Stevens, such divisive appeals and the measures they promoted echoed rabble-rousers who subverted the republics of ancient Greece and Rome, seventeenth-century England, and eighteenth-century France. "Whenever demagogues in any country, had a design against the institutions of their country," he warned, "they began by arraying the poor against the rich, and the laborer against the capitalist." In ancient Greece "they denounced the wealthy aristocracy, and passed laws to expel the wealthy, for the purpose of dividing their property with the poor. . . ." During the French Revolution, "Robespierre and others, have preached precisely the same doctrines. . . . They inveighed against the rich, and denounced the moneyed power." In each case, he warned, such policies brought on economic ruin and the dissolution of republican government into either anarchy or despotism. The Jacksonian Democrats, he warned, now confronted the United States with a similar peril.[14]

At least as threatening as demagogues, in Stevens's view, was a public easily seduced by them. Because there are rabble-rousers in "every age," the Democrats of Andrew Jackson's era were only the current version. But "what is most calculated to make discerning men despair of the republic is the subserviency of the people," he continued, "the facility with which they abandon their own principles for those of their rulers." And among the people generally, which group was most susceptible to the demagogues' siren song? Those without property, Stevens believed, especially the urban poor. That, once again, was an answer supplied by republican theory since Aristotle and others in ancient Greece and Rome, and later codified in the writings of seventeenth-century English writers, including James Harrington and John Locke.[15] Only the ownership of property, these republican writers held, allowed a man enough leisure to obtain the education and information needed to vote intelligently, and only a degree of wealth gave him a sufficient stake in society to make him exercise the franchise judiciously and in a manner respectful of his neighbors' property rights. Society's poorest residents, who were concentrated especially in its large cities, had no such qualifications.

Stevens had likely absorbed this idea, too, from his youthful study of the classics and from his college years. That there was a tension between this view of the independent farmer as the ideal citizen and his own lifelong advocacy of manufacturing based on wage labor seems never to have occurred to him.

Stevens championed the classical view at Pennsylvania's constitutional convention, most directly when addressing the issues of voting rights and representation in the state legislature. He wished to deprive the state's largest urban centers of proportional representation there. Devotion to capitalist development did not necessarily bring with it affection for the biggest cities. Many champions of manufacturing, on the contrary, looked upon those places with a jaundiced eye. They saw there great extremes of wealth and poverty, greater than they considered necessary or healthy, and rich and powerful metropolitan merchants who derived their wealth not from useful service or production but from exploiting bottlenecks in commerce between true producers and consumers in order to rob both. Industry's proponents also knew that major port-based merchants who battened upon international trade usually opposed the tariff protections that appeared necessary to the country's infant manufacturing sector. Meanwhile, they believed, legions of propertyless individuals in big cities became willing political pawns of wealthy patrons and so politically strengthened the hands of the mercantile urban elite.

At Pennsylvania's constitutional convention, Stevens proposed that, no matter how large its population, "no city or county should ever have more than six representatives" in the lower house of the state's legislature. His views became still clearer when the convention turned to the subject of individual voting rights. The existing state constitution, passed in 1790, offered a ballot to "every freeman" aged twenty-one who had lived in the state and paid taxes there for two years. Mounting popular objections to that relatively lengthy residence requirement and to the taxpayer qualification had helped bring the current convention into existence. Endorsing those objections, Democratic delegate John Dickey insisted that "the citizen had a right to vote, whether he had property, or no property, or whether he had one dollar, or one hundred thousand dollars." Dickey "would not disqualify . . . any poor man, because he could not pay a tax."[16]

Convention delegate Phineas Jenks defended that requirement

precisely because it denied political power to "individuals who had no interest in society." Stevens also opposed eliminating the taxpaying requirement. He had no objection, he said, to enfranchising "the honest farmer, mechanic, or laborer," but he balked at giving the vote to those he viewed as vagrants and transients, to "the vile, the vagabond, the idle and dissipated," to the man who "lodged in a barn" and "washed his cravat in a mud hole." He therefore joined a sizable convention majority in voting to preserve the taxpayer qualification.[17] Although it is not clear that this requirement disfranchised a significant number of adult white males, Stevens's aversion to what seemed too-ample a democracy was apparent.

When Thaddeus Stevens graduated from college in 1814, he had branded loyalty to a political party as a mortal threat to the nation. "Party spirit is the nurse of treachery and revenge," the young man recited, "and the parent of corruption." It fomented political division among the citizenry, which "soon grows up into civil tumults, and worse. Then every tie which connects society is rent asunder." As proof, Stevens once again cited the doleful experience of Greece and Rome, as recounted in the classics he had read.[18]

But this was one of the views that experience would shortly lead Stevens to alter. In a political universe already structured by partisan alliances, anti-party axioms had little practical utility. So as he embarked upon his own political career in the late 1820s, he jettisoned that principle. He joined and soon became a leader of a new political party known as the Anti-Masons.[19] He attended that party's first two national conventions in 1830 and 1831, and when he won election to the Pennsylvania House of Representatives in 1833, he did so as the Anti-Masonic candidate.

William Seward of New York—destined like Stevens to become a leader of another fledgling party, the Republicans, decades later—

met the Pennsylvanian at the Anti-Masons' 1830 convention. When Seward discovered that Stevens was "an advocate of popular education, of American industry, and of internal improvement," he realized that they were joined together by "an earnest sympathy of political views." Such a meeting of minds was not unusual. Among the heterogeneous foes of Andrew Jackson's party, quite a few of the more pro-development forces gravitated toward the Anti-Masons.[20]

As their name suggests, Anti-Masons were defined by hostility to the Freemasons, which was at the time a secret fraternal order. That hostility seems to most modern writers bizarre and even paranoid, and more than a few historians have depicted Anti-Masonry that way. It appears less odd when viewed in the context of its era. Freemasons then, generally prosperous and often quite influential, bound themselves with solemn oaths to support one another in preference to all others in politics and in other spheres as well. As the Masonic order grew greatly in strength in the decade or so after 1815, many others reacted with alarm, viewing them as a serious danger to republican government, a cabal capable through its secret oaths of mutual support of wielding outsize control over the country. The Anti-Masonic party's second national convention thus declared that "secret and affiliated societies . . . benefit the *few*, at the expense of the *many*, by creating a *privileged class*, in the midst of a community entitled to enjoy equal rights and privileges," which made the struggle against Masonry a fight for "the liberty of the press, the liberty of speech, equal rights."[21]

Thaddeus Stevens opposed secrecy in politics, regarding it as a device for "keeping the people in total darkness, as to the affairs of the Commonwealth." Freemasons, he warned, "swear to promote one another's political preferment," and that secret alliance "corrupts the fountain of justice; stays the arm of the law; stops the regular action of government; binds the mind in darkness." At the end of 1834, Stevens brought a resolution into the Pennsylvania legislature that denounced Masonry because "it secures an undue, because unmerited[,] advantage to members of the fraternity over the honest and industrious uninitiated farmer, mechanic, and laborer, in all the business transactions of life." And in politics, he asserted, the Masons constituted "an antirepublican and an insidious and dangerous enemy to our democratic form of government," since "its whole tendency is to cherish a hatred of democracy, and a love of aristocratic and regal forms of power."[22]

Here, too, his views and actions put Stevens in sync with his state of birth, with his family, and with their coreligionists. Vermont became Anti-Masonry's chief national bastion. Caledonia County, the home of Stevens's family, became an especially strong Anti-Mason stronghold. And New England Baptists generally were wary of Freemasons. They had gained religious equality only recently and remained on guard against attempts to deprive them of it anew. They were therefore particularly sensitive to the kind of covert political maneuvering in which they believed Masons engaged. So in 1830 Thaddeus's pious Baptist mother congratulated him on his participation in the "good cause" of Anti-Masonry while cautioning that such participation would array dangerous "enemys" (*sic*) against him.[23] Anti-Masonry also proved popular in central Pennsylvania. And when in the summer of 1842 Thaddeus Stevens left Gettysburg, it was to resettle in Lancaster, where the state's Anti-Masonic movement originated.[24]

Ultimately, the very success of that party proved its undoing. The size and virulence of Anti-Masonic sentiment eventually drove the Freemasons into retreat and decline. That, in turn, reduced the urgency and appeal of the Anti-Masonic cause. By the second half of the 1830s, it was on its way toward oblivion. The principal beneficiary was the Whig Party, which shared many of the other values that Anti-Masons like Stevens and Seward cherished, notably enthusiasm for government-supported economic development. Faced with the decline of Anti-Masonry, Stevens and his followers became Whigs.[25]

Thaddeus Stevens saw nothing inherently illegitimate about wealth inequality produced by the marketplace. But physically imposed and enforced servitude—and especially outright enslavement—was manifestly wrong and deplorable in his eyes. He had absorbed that belief, he said later, from his family's devotion to the Declaration of Independence, from his study of the classics, and through "the divine inspirations of Jesus."[26] Life in southern Pennsylvania, on the border of the slave state of Maryland, forced him to confront the institution of human slavery more directly and immediately than would have been necessary back in Vermont.

Not that Stevens instantaneously became a committed abolitionist. He displayed a strong antipathy toward slavery during the 1820s without initially waging a consistent struggle against it. One likely reason was pragmatic. Although northern Pennsylvania contained many in-migrants from largely antislavery New England, the Keystone State's southern tier did not. That region was more influenced by the pro-slavery sentiments widespread in the adjacent slave state of Maryland, with whose residents south Pennsylvania did considerable business. Stevens doubtless felt pressure to adapt somewhat to the conservative political climate that this association promoted. Confidence in a progressive human destiny and the enlightening effects of economic development may also have made him expect that slavery would before too long decline even without the need for a concerted political struggle. Like some other future Republicans, Stevens seemed not yet to grasp just how politically aggressive slave masters were and would soon become on behalf of their "peculiar institution."

In the early years of his law practice, therefore, Stevens kept his antislavery views strictly separate from business. He served as attorney both for people accused of *being* fugitive slaves and for slaveholders seeking to *capture* alleged fugitives. In 1821 he helped a Maryland man assert property rights in a woman named Charity Butler and her two daughters. Two years later, Stevens offered an antislavery toast at an Independence Day dinner party. "The next President," he proposed, "may he be a freeman, who never riveted fetters on a human slave."[27] Expressing that wish, however, did not prevent Stevens from subsequently supporting the presidential bids of several slaveholders.

Such inconsistency was not uncommon, but it became more obvious and awkward as slavery-related issues pushed toward the forefront of national consciousness and national politics. Future Republicans began to reevaluate their priorities in light of those changing political circumstances at different points in their careers. In Stevens's case, the change in stance occurred sometime between the fall of 1835 and the spring of 1836, when sectional tensions were rising.

The decade of the 1830s brought a sharp increase in public attention to the issue of slavery. In late August 1831, the slave Nat Turner led the bloodiest rebellion of the nineteenth century in Pennsylvania's neighboring state of Virginia. By then some of slavery's opponents (soon known as abolitionists) had begun elaborating a more radical and militant form of antislavery doctrine and movement than had prevailed previously, demanding immediate steps to bring slavery to an end and seeking full civil equality for free blacks in the United States. In 1833, abolitionists met in Philadelphia to create the American Antislavery Society (AAS). Its founding document called slavery a sin "unequalled by any other on the face of the earth" and demanded that everyone, regardless of race, be made "secure in his own right to his own body—to the products of his own labor—to the protections of the law—to the common advantages of society."[28]

For years afterward, free black residents of the North provided abolitionism with much of its support. But the new movement also demonstrated strength among whites in New England, including among Baptists. His hometown of Peacham, Vermont, formed its own branch of the AAS. In July 1836, an abolition society formed as well in Gettysburg's Adams County, Pennsylvania.[29]

The slavery issue soon provoked a major national showdown. The Nat Turner slave revolt and the rise of abolitionism provoked a strong reaction in the South and especially in South Carolina. The Palmetto State contained unusually high concentrations of slaves and a fabulously wealthy slave-owning aristocracy in its rice- and cotton-growing districts. In 1832, that elite initiated the so-called nullification crisis. The nominal trigger was the protective tariffs that Congress imposed on manufactured imports in 1828 and 1832, tariffs that Carolinians, overwhelmingly agriculturalists, portrayed as a tax upon themselves for the benefit primarily of the industrializing Northeast. In November 1832, prominent South Carolinians announced that henceforth the tariff "shall not be lawful . . . within the limits of this state" and that any federal attempt to collect it by force might well drive their state out of the Union.[30] That announcement precipitated an unprecedented constitutional crisis.

South Carolina's John C. Calhoun explained privately that the tariff was not in fact "the real cause of the present unhappy state of things." The fundamental factor was his fellow Carolinians' fears for slavery. "The truth can no longer be disguised," Calhoun warned, "that the peculiar domestick [*sic*] institutions of the Southern States, and the consequent direction which that and her soil and climate have given to her industry, has placed them . . . in opposite relation to the majority of the Union." If the federal government were permitted to disregard southern interests in the tariff matter, it might soon turn its power directly against slavery, the state's key "domestick institution."[31] By barring enforcement of this particular federal law, Calhoun and his allies meant to warn the national government that they would permit it to enforce *no* law harmful to their interests within their state's borders.

After a period of tense confrontation between South Carolina and the federal government, the issue was resolved without violence. Congressional leaders agreed to reduce tariffs sharply over the next nine years; South Carolina agreed to repeal its nullification ordinance. But that state had by then made clear the extreme lengths to which it was ready to go in defense of slavery, including not only nullification but also outright secession. And it had forced the national legislature to surrender on the substance of tariff protection for northern industry.

To Thaddeus Stevens, as to many other northerners, especially those in iron-producing Pennsylvania, that concession was a foul betrayal. In brokering the deal, Stevens cried, Whig leader Henry Clay had "abandoned the American System," had "laid violent hands on his own child," had "sacrificed" the "dearest interests of our country" and thereby "gave strength and dignity and future hope to triumphant treason." Indeed, Stevens would later argue, concessions like that one formed "the bitter root" of all subsequent sectional conflict, because they signaled to the South that resorting to extreme tactics would succeed. Stevens judged that if Andrew Jackson, president during the nullification crisis, had chosen to put down the Carolinians more forcefully, and even to "execute the traitors, if need be," the country would "never again have heard a rebellious minority shouting 'disunion!' 'civil war!' 'bloody devastation!' "[32]

Despite their success in forcing the withdrawal of the protective tariff, however, slaveholders' grievances continued to mount during the 1830s. Central to those grievances were the activities of the abolitionists. In just its first three years of life, the American Antislavery Society distributed more than a million pieces of antislavery literature, mostly by mail and some of it sent into the South. Congress received antislavery petitions from the free states that bore hundreds of thousands of signatures; an especially popular one called for out-lawing slavery in the nation's capital.[33]

Pro-slavery forces met the growing size, energy, and determination of the abolitionist movement with an escalation of pro-slavery repression and violence. A crowd in Charleston, South Carolina, broke into its post office in July 1835, seizing and setting ablaze stacks of what it took to be abolitionist literature addressed to southerners. A few months later, President Jackson called for legislation to criminalize the mailing of such "incendiary publications" into slave states. Southern leaders demanded that their northern counterparts join them in silencing abolitionists and, indeed, in suppressing all public talk of abolition. Virginia congressmen warned northerners that they "cannot attack the system of slavery without attacking the institutions of our country, our safety, and our welfare," and that therefore "for the people of non-slaveholding States to discuss the question of slavery, at all" was "to attack the foundations of the union itself."[34]

Prominent residents of the free states strove to reassure their southern colleagues. New York City's mayor presided over a large public meeting in 1835 that, while defending citizens' right to discuss slavery, stressed that the North neither agreed with "immediate abolitionism" nor would tolerate any "violent or aggressive means for the purpose of abolishing" bondage. The Constitution, said the New Yorkers, had "recognized as lawful the condition of slavery in the southern states." To be sure, the meeting's organizers claimed, they would "hail the day, if it shall ever come," when the southern states themselves "may be able and willing to abolish it" on their own. But until such a time, "the citizens of the north have no political right to interfere with the slavery of the southern states." As for antislavery publications, the meeting condoned their being mailed only to those southern whites who had specifically requested them, and it especially condemned any attempt to place such literature in the hands of slaves. Attendees then expressed the hope that the current "excitement at the south" about abolitionism would now subside, since the only thing that might "sustain" that small radical movement would be "intemperate opposition" to it.[35]

Thaddeus Stevens was by now becoming increasingly outspoken about his antislavery sentiments. When William Seward encountered him in 1830, he discovered a man "abhorring slavery in every form" and a man "bent on breaking up the combination between a subservient party in the North and the slave power of the South," the combination that sustained Andrew Jackson's national Democratic Party.[36] In this respect, Stevens and Seward personified Anti-Masonry's stronger aversion to slavery than was typical of either the Democratic or Whig parties.

Still, Stevens did at first give ground before the anti-abolitionist reaction that arose during that decade. On September 12, 1835, he played a prominent role in a Gettysburg gathering that in some ways echoed New York City's while in other ways departing from it. Although the Gettysburg meeting "deplore[d] the existence of slavery and all the evils which attend it," it refused to condemn slave ownership as intrinsically immoral and denied "the obligation and feasibility of immediate emancipation." It also disparaged abolitionism for "tend[ing] to array the excited feelings of one portion of our citizens against another, and to occasion violence and disunion." But unlike the New Yorkers, these Pennsylvanians condoned the mailing of abolitionist literature even to those white southerners who had *not* solicited it. They also expressed the hope that the North's clear refusal to embrace abolitionism would "arrest the tendency to hasty and injurious measures at the south," including "all riotous or violent proceedings, all outrages on persons and property, and every illegal interference with the rights of citizens"—presumably referring to anti-abolitionist and anti-black riots such as Charleston's and one that had occurred in New York City itself in 1834.[37]

But violent attacks on abolitionists and African Americans continued to erupt in parts of the North, as they did in Utica, New York; Boston; and Cincinnati. And southern leaders grew ever more demanding in their drive to suppress antislavery speech and action. As petitions seeking abolition in the District of Columbia poured into the U.S. House of Representatives, southern congressmen insisted that those memorials be suppressed. In May 1836, the House agreed, adopting a "gag rule" specifying that "all petitions, memorials, resolutions, propositions, or papers relating in any way or to any extent whatever to the subject of slavery" would be tabled and "no further action shall be taken thereon." For the next four years, each session of Congress renewed that gag rule. And from 1840 to 1844, the House instituted an even more extreme policy, now refusing even to acknowledge receipt of abolitionist petitions.[38] Antislavery northerners protested in vain that this procedure effectively gutted the citizens' constitutionally guaranteed right to petition their government.

Southern state legislatures also called upon the North to follow the South in criminalizing antislavery speech and activity. The governor of Virginia sent a battery of legislative resolutions to that effect to northern state capitals, including Pennsylvania's. Insisting that "congress has no power to abolish slavery in the district of Columbia, or the territories of the United States," Virginia demanded that Pennsylvania punish any of its citizens found to be "forming associations for the abolition of slavery, [and] printing, publishing and circulating seditious or incendiary publications, designed, calculated, or having a tendency to operate on her population."[39]

Anti-abolitionist violence and the South's imperious diktats provoked a number of northerners to step up their resistance to proslavery forces and to stiffen their opposition to slavery itself. It had that effect on Stevens, who now changed his public stance fundamentally. "We are not slaves here in Pennsylvania," he growled.[40]

Stevens's change of front revealed itself publicly in his response to Virginia's demands upon the North. As chair of the Pennsylvania House of Representatives' judiciary committee, he presented its report on the Virginia resolutions to the full House in May 1836. That report refused to restrict Pennsylvanians' right to discuss slavery. "Every citizen of the non-slaveholding slates," it said, "has a right freely to think and publish his thoughts on *any* subject of national or state policy. Nor can he be compelled to confine his remarks to such subjects as affect only the state in which he resides." The members of Stevens's committee also emphasized their own disgust with slavery itself. "To witness droves of human beings," they said, "bound together with iron fetters, and lashed forward to hopeless servitude," and to see that being done by free men even as they pontificated "loudly and boastfully on the blessings of liberty"—this was "a moral anomaly," one that "fails to shock only because of its familiarity." Finally, the committee not only affirmed that "congress *does* possess the constitutional power . . . to abolish slavery and the slave trade within the District of Columbia"; it also urged Congress to exercise that power. The failure to do so before this, it added for good measure, stood as "a reproach upon our national legislature." Just how far ahead of public opinion his committee had thereby ventured became apparent when Stevens called on the Pennsylvania House to endorse the report. That body steadfastly declined to do so.[41]

Another way to evaluate Stevens's position is to compare it to Abraham Lincoln's. The Illinoisan, then a member of his own state's legislature, also addressed himself to Virginia's demands that spring. Much like Stevens, Lincoln declared "that the institution of slavery is founded on both injustice and bad policy." But while he agreed with Stevens that Congress had the legal power to abolish slavery in the District of Columbia, Lincoln advised Congress not to exercise that power unless "the people of said District" (meaning, of course, its white residents) asked it to do so. Since the District of Columbia was located in the South, sandwiched between the slave states of Maryland and Virginia, that was obviously not about to happen.[42] A dozen years later, by then a member of the U.S. House of Representatives, Lincoln contemplated introducing a bill to gradually abolish slavery in the District of Columbia. Even then, however, he expected to give the district's white male population the right to veto the initiative.[43]

During the next few years, Stevens made his support for abolition still clearer. In February 1837 he invited the Vermont-born Congregationalist minister Jonathan Blanchard, widely hated for his abolitionist views and activities, to dine with him publicly at Nagle's hotel in Gettysburg. And over dinner, Stevens donated money to Rev. Blanchard's cause. Doing all this was a public statement, for as Blanchard later noted, "no minister of my acquaintance (except some few slavery-haters like myself), would have cheerfully done the like," especially since "some 100 political friends and enemies of yourself who then boarded at Nagle's would bitterly condemn you for harboring or encouraging me."[44]

In the month that followed, Blanchard engaged in public debates about slavery and abolition in Gettysburg. At one of those events, anti-abolitionist audience members pelted him with eggs, shutting the meeting down. Stevens was then out of town, but at the third of these debates, he forcefully and successfully defended Blanchard's right to express himself freely. "What freeman," demanded a disgusted Stevens, "does not feel himself covered all over with burning blushes to find himself surrounded by *such* freemen!"[45]

Stevens did attend another anti-abolitionist gathering a few months later, a large one convened in Pennsylvania's state capital of Harrisburg. Calling itself the "Friends of the Integrity of the Union," it rejected any federal law restricting slavery in the nation's capital and seconded the slaveholders' attempt to ban all discussion of abolition. "Every attempt by the citizens of one state," it declared, even to "denounce" the "established institutions of another" was "unwarranted by the constitution, and hostile to the peace and harmony of the Union." Not content to abjure criticism of slavery, the convention went on to defend the principle of nullification, justifying in advance any state's future decision to declare null and void all federal measures "which should violate its internal security and peace, or abrogate the rights of property of its citizens." The Harrisburg meeting concluded by announcing that the "colonization" (that is, the organized emigration) to Africa of slaves freed by their owners was the only appropriate method of achieving "the ultimate abolition of slavery."[46]

Stevens managed to get himself sent to this meeting as a delegate from his home county. Once there, he behaved very differently than he had at the Gettysburg anti-abolition meeting eight months earlier. While still calling "some" unspecified things that abolitionists did "exceedingly ill judged," he nonetheless introduced a strongly antislavery resolution. The Declaration of Independence's egalitarian language, it said, compelled the government "to protect every human being in all his inalienable rights, so far as it can be done without violating the fundamental laws of the government." In the name of that duty, Stevens called upon the meeting to endorse key abolitionist principles. Instead of agreeing that the emigration of manumitted blacks was the only proper manner with which to end slavery, he called for direct federal action to cripple slavery at home. The meeting, he said, should clearly announce that the U.S. Congress "possesses the constitutional right to abolish Slavery and the Slave trade, in the District of Columbia, and the territories of the United States." It should also both affirm that "Congress possesses power to prohibit the admission of any State into the Union, which tolerates Slavery by its Constitution" and declare that it was Congress's positive "*duty* to enforce such prohibition." The federal government, said his resolution, should also outlaw the country's so-called internal slave trade—that is, should legally ban the sale of slaves "between the Several States and Territories." Stevens presumably believed that the power to do that derived from the Constitution's granting to Congress control over interstate commerce. Such a ban, Stevens held, would happily "tend to the abolition of Slavery within this nation."[47]

The Harrisburg gathering of conservative sectional conciliators rejected Stevens's inflammatory resolution. But by putting it forward, he had clarified the actually pro-slavery content of the meeting's professed devotion to the Union. And he had thrown into sharp relief his own categorical opposition to it.

In fact, Stevens had accomplished still more. There, and throughout the preceding months, he had endorsed and helped publicize an abolitionist program of action that seemed to overcome constitutional obstacles. He was experimenting with an antislavery strategy known as the de-nationalization of slavery, which modern historians most closely associate with abolitionists such as James G. Birney, Theodore Dwight Weld, and Salmon P. Chase. Underlying this strategy was the view that abolitionists legally *could* bring the slave-labor system to its knees without transgressing constitutional barriers between federal and states' rights, barriers that slavery's defenders so strongly cherished and regularly invoked. Abolitionists could continue to agitate against slavery publicly, including through the mails and in Congress, and thereby change public opinion. They could seek federal abolition of slavery in the nation's capital, in the federal territories, and in interstate commerce. They could block the admission into the Union of any additional slave states, thereby ensuring that political supremacy in Washington would slide steadily into the hands of current and prospective free states. During the following decade, those eventually known as "radical Republicans"— those most adamantly opposed to slavery's survival—would rally to this standard.[48]

A few months after disrupting the anti-abolitionist Friends of the Union gathering, Stevens again condemned slavery in harsh and sweeping terms, this time on the floor of the convention then meeting to amend Pennsylvania's state constitution. "The domestic slavery of this country," he declared, "is the most disgraceful institution that the world had ever witnessed, under any form of Government, in any age."[49] And in the spring of 1838, Stevens offered a ringing endorsement of abolitionism in a letter to the Pennsylvania Antislavery Society. That society had invited Stevens to attend the opening of a Pennsylvania Hall for the Free Discussion of Liberty, and equality of Civil Rights and the evils of Slavery, an opening scheduled to occur in Philadelphia on May 14.

Replying to that invitation, Stevens regretted his inability to attend since "I know of no spectacle, which it would give me greater pleasure to witness, than the dedication of a Temple of Liberty." To be sure, the U.S. Constitution (which, he said, "contradicts the principles of our Declaration of Independence") did give slaveholders legal rights, and so long as the Constitution "remains unchanged, it must be supported." But obeying unjust laws did not require praising or even respecting them. While "we must yield to existing laws," he said, we must not surrender "our sense of justice." He could "never acknowledge the *right* of slavery" in moral terms, Stevens explained, and he would "bow down to no Deity however worshipped by professing Christians . . . whose footstool is the crushed necks of groaning millions, and who rejoices in the resoundings of the tyrant's lash, and the cries of his tortured victims." "Your object," he told his correspondents, "*should* meet with the approbation of every freeman," and "it *will* meet with the approbation of every man, who respects the rights of others, as much as he loves his own." Stevens then expanded on that optimistic assessment of abolitionism's future. "Interest, fashion, false religion, and tyranny may triumph for a while," he wrote, "and rob man of his inalienable rights." But "the people cannot always be deceived, and they will not always be oppressed." That Stevens's optimism was premature, however—that anti-abolitionist and racist sentiment remained virulent—soon became clear. Three days after the Philadelphia abolitionists dedicated their building, a mob burned it down and then torched an African American neighborhood as thousands of whites looked on.[50]

Unlike most abolitionists, white and black—but like quite a few people who would later become radical Republicans—Thaddeus Stevens did in those days support what was called "colonization," the emigration of free blacks from the United States. In 1835, indeed, he not only attended a meeting of Gettysburg's Young Men's Colonization Society but even joined a committee charged with raising funds to further its work.[51] Many white colonizationists favored the idea as a way to usher free blacks out of the country because they could not imagine or would not tolerate legally free black people making their homes in the United States. Others sought *both* to assist those free blacks who wished to leave *and* to win equal rights for those who chose to remain. Stevens was among the latter.

Most northern states before the Civil War imposed onerous legal restrictions, burdens, and disabilities upon legally free African Americans. Laws and state constitutions either barred free black people from even entering a given state or at least required them to post high bonds to guarantee behavior acceptable to the whites while there. Other legal measures denied them equal access to public schools, forbade them to testify against whites in court, and excluded them from both juries and the electorate. Less formal but no less effective barriers kept black people out of most jobs, neighborhoods, schools, and public accommodations. The 1837 convention that amended Pennsylvania's state constitution was invited to join the ranks of such exclusionary states. One delegate suggested considering a measure to "prohibit the future emigration into the State of persons of color and fugitive slaves from other States and territories." Stevens denounced that idea as "totally at war with the principles of the Declaration of Independence, the Bill of Rights, and the spirit of our institutions."[52]

The convention did not act upon this exclusionary suggestion.

But a proposal to deny the vote to all African Americans received a warm reception. The state's existing constitution, adopted in 1790, stated only that "every freeman . . . shall enjoy the rights of an elector." In practice, different locales interpreted this wording in different ways, some (including Philadelphia, which contained by far the state's largest black population) simply defining all African Americans out of the category of "freemen." By 1837, large numbers of white Pennsylvanians were demanding that such discrimination be made more explicit, formal, and universal. Speaking in favor of that call was convention delegate John Sterigere, a Democratic Party leader from just north of Philadelphia. He moved to add the word "white" to the state constitution's definition of a legitimate voter.[53]

Black residents of Pittsburgh had until then been accustomed to voting. Now, having "heard, with surprise and alarm," of plans to disfranchise them, members of this approximately 2,500-strong community held a mass meeting to discuss the problem. That meeting appointed a committee to draw up and submit a memorial to the state's constitutional convention. On July 8, 1837, Anti-Masonic delegate Harmar Denny of Pittsburgh's Allegheny County brought that petition before the convention's delegates. The Pittsburgh memorial's overall text and tone were deeply respectful, even conservative, in content, striving to prove that black Pittsburghers were law-abiding, hardworking, taxpaying people who were "worthy of the land of William Penn" and therefore deserved "the honors and high responsibilities of freemen." But it included some stronger language, too, decrying the fact that "in many of the States, one half of the community is the absolute property of the other" and consequently "subject to the despotic will, nay to the passion, caprice, and cruelty of a master." More forcefully still, the memorial attributed current attempts to disenfranchise black Pennsylvanians to "barbarous prejudices."[54]

Some convention delegates strove to suppress the memorial.

Charles Brown, a Philadelphia Democrat, fumed that referring to "barbarous prejudices" was "not very courteous." Another Philadelphia Democrat, Charles Ingersoll, protested against "language rather harsh against citizens of other States."[55]

But Stevens insisted that the whole convention hear, consider, and print the petition from Pittsburgh's black residents. "Those who petitioned this body," he said, "whether black or white, had a right to be heard, whether on this or any other subject, relative to the business before the Convention," and a right to have their views given "respectful consideration." He brushed aside complaints that the petition was discourteous as mere racist subterfuge. "Such a memorial, coming from white men," Stevens noted pointedly, "would not be considered offensive." And claims that African Americans had "no right to petition, because they are degraded and debased," simply outraged him. If those people are degraded, he said, "they have been reduced to this degraded condition *by our acts* and . . . they have been prevented *by us* from rising in the scale of moral dignity." So now, Stevens demanded, "shall we turn upon them, and say—we have debased you—we have decreed that you shall never improve your condition—and how dare you come here with petitions to be allowed to participate in any of the privileges of freemen?"[56] Was not such hypocrisy glaringly obvious?

The urge to deny the vote to Pennsylvania's blacks sprang from at least two sources. As Stevens noted, disfranchisement's proponents most often justified their position by alleging the inferiority of blacks, their consequent unfitness for political rights, and the white citizenry's supposed aversion to sharing those rights with such inferiors. "It is an insult to the white man to propose this association, and ask him to go to the polls, and exercise the right of a freeman with negroes," John Sterigere asserted. But Sterigere and his Pennsylvania allies also hoped that denying votes to African Americans would reassure the white South that their state would have no truck with movements for black rights. This line of argument was especially popular among Democrats, though quite a few conservative Whigs also came around to it, fearing to offend the South regarding what Whig Daniel Agnew called "a question which had so much reference to the policy and action of many of our sister states."[57]

Convention delegates who resisted black disfranchisement included a sprinkling of less conservative Democrats but many more Whigs and Anti-Masons. And Anti-Masons continued to resist still longer than did most Whigs, who felt pressured by the southern wing of their national party. Stevens made himself the most visible spokesman for this resistance. He scorned those who called for disfranchising black men for the sake of appeasing southern slaveholders. "Let those who stand in fear of the South," he snarled, "truckle to their debasing tyranny." He, for one, "would rather be the degraded subject of a southern master, than to be a northern freeman without the power and the courage freely to speak my sentiments on every subject."[58]

But words, no matter how defiant, could not contain the tide of racial hostility and sectional appeasement that was now sweeping over major parts of the North. On January 17, 1838, the Pennsylvania convention voted by a large majority to amend the state constitution to bar all but "white freemen" from the polls. In protest, Stevens refused to sign the convention's revised constitution. Despite active mobilization by blacks and white abolitionists in the state in support of a "no" vote, however, Pennsylvanians ratified the draft constitution in a referendum ten months later.[59]

By then, Thaddeus Stevens seemed in most ways to have become as firm and outspoken an opponent of slavery as any abolitionist leader. But, like some other antislavery politicians such as William Seward, he was not yet ready to sign on with a political party defined first and foremost by its stand on that issue. In 1839, a wing of the abolitionist movement founded such a party, the Liberty

Party. The platform that it eventually adopted embodied the kind of de-nationalization of slavery strategy, aiming at "the absolute and unqualified divorce of the general government from slavery," that Thaddeus Stevens had already championed publicly. "The example and influence of national authority ought to be arrayed on the side of liberty and free labor," the platform urged. More concretely, it argued that "all attempts to hold men as property within the limits of exclusive national jurisdiction ought to be prohibited by law."[60]

Ohio's Salmon P. Chase, the Liberty platform's principal architect, knew of Stevens's antislavery reputation and asked the latter if he couldn't "bring the old Anti Masonic party of Pennsylvania on to the Liberty Platform." Although Chase was "not anticipating its immediate triumph," he did believe that a respectable Liberty Party showing at the polls would encourage others to rally to it in the future. Local Liberty Party supporter Jonathan Blanchard seconded Chase's request.[61]

Liberty Party members opposed voting for candidates who did not seek slavery's abolition. With abolitionist Gerrit Smith, they urged "the necessity of abolitionists to break off from" the Democratic and Whig parties entirely. Those national parties inevitably defended slavery, if only to retain their southern units—"for the South will enter none but pro-slavery parties."[62] Thaddeus Stevens disagreed with that stance. He did not believe that creating or joining an anti-slavery third party represented the way forward. He acknowledged to Rev. Blanchard that "my views and wishes accord with your own" concerning slavery and abolition. "The only question is as to the means likely to accomplish it." Stevens thought "that could be best done by declining, as yet, to organize a distinct political party" principally defined by the hostility to bondage that the two men shared. He held to that belief despite knowing "how often we have been cheated by the men of other parties" and "how few of them" who had made pre-election antislavery promises ever "prove[d] faithful after elected." But convinced that the Liberty Party could win few votes, Stevens stood back from it. He would continue for now in backing Whigs for public office—at the moment, army general Winfield Scott. If nominated and elected president, Stevens assumed, Scott would at least defend the rights of abolitionists and would do so, indeed, firmly "enough to make Slaveholders and their adherents hate him." So, Stevens concluded, in office Scott "will do more for our cause . . . than can be done by suffering defeat with a still more thorough anti-Slavery man."[63]

But while doubting the value of an independent antislavery party, Stevens continued his efforts on behalf of slaves in other ways. In Lancaster, he kept his eye on those who made a profession of tracking down fugitive slaves and of helping masters to recapture them. Stevens passed along what he thereby learned to fugitives and their friends, urging the former to make their way to Canada, where slavery had been outlawed by the British Empire in 1834.[64]

In moving from the dwindling Anti-Mason party to the Whigs, Stevens had gained access to a far bigger public stage. That gain, however, bore a price tag. In joining the Whigs, he became entangled in their mounting internal controversies and the power struggles that arose from them. Not least of those concerned the future of slavery.

CHAPTER THREE

Resisting Slavery's Expansion

1840–1850

The Whig Party that Thaddeus Stevens joined was anything but homogeneous politically. Although support for economic development united its members and supporters, profound issues divided them. Some Whigs cast in the Federalist mold were more aristocratic in their bearing and political assumptions, while others were more democratic-minded; some lamented the broadening of the suffrage that had occurred during the first decades of the century, while others embraced it. The most important intraparty dispute revolved around slavery, setting southern against northern Whigs but also pitting northern Whigs against one another.

In the South, Whig politicians competed with Democrats for the distinction of being slavery's best defenders. In the North, some Whig leaders were determined to conciliate slaveholders, while others were outright abolitionists. The Whigs of southern Pennsylvania included adherents of both the conciliationist and antislavery wings of the party. That fact complicated Stevens's position considerably. Although he did direct the Whigs' successful 1840 presidential campaign in his state, Stevens and his friends did not control the party's Lancaster County organization. More conservative Whigs predominated there.[1] That fact would become very clear as the sectional conflict escalated.

After the nullification crisis, the next major political event to touch the nerve of the slavery issue was Texas's application for statehood. In 1835, in-migrants from the United States who had settled in Mexico's Texas province rebelled against that country's national government. By early March 1836, Texas had become an independent slaveholding republic whose leaders sought statehood in the United States. Many in the free states, including Stevens, opposed annexation, dreading the addition of so large a slaveholding state. It would, they feared, extend the life of slavery in the country and strengthen slaveholder control over the federal government.

Unable or unwilling to defy that northern sentiment, Democratic president Martin Van Buren opposed annexation, too. In consequence, Van Buren became a pariah to southern Democrats, who in 1844 vetoed his nomination for another presidential term, instead nominating and successfully electing Tennessee slaveholder James K. Polk. While Van Buren and his allies steamed, a congressional majority accomplished Texas's admission to the Union as a state through a joint resolution in February 1845. The next year saw President Polk instigate war with Mexico in order to seize still more land from that country.[2]

The Whig Party as a whole, including one-term Illinois congressman Abraham Lincoln, opposed the war and demanded that no land be taken from Mexico as a result of it. Democrats generally supported the war but divided over what to do with the war's possible fruits. Already smarting under the southern whip, Van Buren and his allies in the North also recognized that a growing number of their constituents were souring on the Mexican War. Becoming identified with what those constituents had begun to see as a pro-slavery adventure, Van Buren warned his friends, would amount to "political suicide" for Democrats in the free states. His circle therefore opposed allowing slavery to exist in any lands that might now be torn from Mexico. Pennsylvania Democrat David Wilmot duly introduced a measure in the U.S. House of Representatives stipulating that "neither slavery nor involuntary servitude shall ever exist in any part" of whatever territory might be taken from Mexico during the war.[3]

Fourteen northern state legislatures endorsed this "Wilmot Proviso." The legislature of Stevens's Pennsylvania called on its representatives in the U.S. Congress "to vote against any measure whatever by which territory will accrue to the Union" unless slavery were "forever prohibited" therein. In the House of Representatives, a combination of northern Whigs and some northern Democrats passed the Wilmot Proviso in 1846. In the Senate, however, southerners and a handful of their northern allies were able to prevent the Proviso's adoption.[4]

Before long the seizure of Mexican land became an accomplished fact. In February 1848, the treaty that ended the war transferred the provinces of California and New Mexico to the United States. That made the original Whig stance of simply opposing annexations moot. The live question now became this: In the newly acquired territories, will there be slavery or not?

That question widened cracks in both major political parties. In 1848, some northern Democrats broke with their national party to join Liberty Party members (notably Ohio's Salmon P. Chase) and a number of antislavery northern Whigs and former Whigs (including Charles Francis Adams, Henry Wilson, and Charles Sumner, all of Massachusetts, and Joshua Giddings of Ohio) in launching a new political party, the Free Soil Party. These individuals had concluded that neither the Democratic nor the Whig Party would do what was necessary to bring about slavery's demise. "Our friends are quite certain now," Giddings summarized, "that the old organizations must be broken up and new associations formed." The national Whig Party had nominated General Zachary Taylor, a Louisianan raised in Kentucky, for president, with New York's Millard Fillmore as his running mate. Democrats nominated Michigan's Lewis Cass, an ardent champion of westward expansion. Neither ticket, proclaimed the new Free Soil Party, "can be supported by the opponents of slavery extension without a sacrifice of consistency, duty and self-respect." While acknowledging that the Constitution allowed states to legalize slavery within their own borders, Free Soilers demanded that the federal government oppose slavery's spread beyond its existing confines. There must be "no more slave states and no more slave territory."[5] When Martin Van Buren endorsed the Wilmot Proviso, the new party gave him its presidential nomination.

Van Buren came nowhere near winning the election that fall, but he and his campaign certainly made an impression. He received nearly three hundred thousand votes, nearly all in the free states but constituting more than 14 percent of all ballots cast there. That tally was almost three times bigger than the Liberty Party had ever garnered. Furthermore, Free Soil voters, alone or in coalition with others, sent a dozen men into the U.S. House of Representatives. In Ohio, the election of eight Free Soilers to the state legislature's lower house gave them the balance of power there, the leverage they needed to weaken legal discrimination against free blacks in that state and appoint Salmon P. Chase as a U.S. senator. In Massachusetts, similar developments sent Free Soil leader Charles Sumner to the U.S. Senate a few years later.[6]

But the Free Soil Party had no more success in recruiting Thaddeus Stevens than had the Liberty Party. Joining it seemed pointless to him. Since it was small and weak, he believed, its candidates "stand not a shadow of a chance" at the polls. The strengthening of Stevens's antislavery principles had thus outpaced the increase of his strategic foresight. Gaining office as an individual in order to do useful things seemed more important than joining or building a party that stood squarely for antislavery principles.[7]

Like many northern Whigs, including Seward and Lincoln, Stevens professed to believe that the Whig Party was already a free-soil party in effect, since its northern units backed the Wilmot Proviso. Indeed, Stevens told Lincoln shortly before the 1848 election, the very existence of a separate Free Soil party "puzzles us all," since "the whigs adopt it [the free-soil program] in full." That, however, was not true. Neither the public stance of individual northern Whigs nor even the platforms that some northern state units adopted transformed the national Whig organization into any kind of free-soil body. Stevens's lack of concern with building such a party at this point reflected his underestimation of what it would take to destroy slavery. And although he called antislavery "the cause" of the North, Stevens evidently did not yet see it as the one issue that, above all others, should *define* his national party's program. For him, as for many others, that recognition lay ahead.[8]

In the short term, events seemed to justify his adherence to the Whigs. In August 1848, the party's Lancaster County convention nominated him for a seat in the U.S. House of Representatives. He won that nomination by outpolling his main rival for it, a more conservative Whig, Abraham Herr Smith. During the election campaign that followed, friendly newspapers looked forward to watching Stevens display in Congress his famous gift for "witty repartee, his scorching sarcasm, his lofty eloquence, his great profundity, and his ponderous mind." He would doubtless employ those gifts on behalf especially of tariff protections and resisting "the extension of slavery into territory now free."[9]

The Democratic press predictably scorned candidate Stevens as *"the sworn foe of the South*—an abolitionist" who was a confirmed "agitator of sectional jealousies and divisions," a fomenter of "Strife, of Division, and of Hatred." Repeating the common southern charge that antislavery speech and writing encouraged slave revolts, Pennsylvania Democrats called Stevens "the foe of peace and safety of that portion of the American people, whose interests are threatened with violent assault." Stevens was determined, they added falsely, "not only to exclude Slavery from newly acquired territory—but, what is infinitely worse, [to] interfere with its existence where the Constitution has already planted it." The Democrats nominated a businessman and judge named Emanuel Schaeffer to fill that House seat.[10]

Lancaster County's unit of the Free Soil Party queried both the Whig and Democratic candidates about their views. Were they ready to exclude slavery from any place in the country where "Congress possesses Constitutional Jurisdiction over it," including the territories? Stevens replied "in the affirmative," promising in addition that he would "vote for no man for any office" who would oppose such exclusion. His Democratic opponent declared for the doctrine of "popular sovereignty," according to which not the U.S. Congress but the residents of any individual federal territory had the sole right to decide slavery's fate there. At the polls in the fall of 1848, Stevens defeated his Democratic opponent, Schaeffer, by a margin of almost two to one.[11]

Like some other northern Whigs, Stevens supported Zachary Taylor's presidential candidacy in that year, despite Taylor's being a slaveowner. Stevens did that on the general's promise that as president he would not veto the Wilmot Proviso should Congress as a whole eventually pass it. Stevens played a prominent role in Taylor's campaign in Pennsylvania while Lancaster's Free Soil Party members remained far more skeptical, questioning the antislavery credentials of "this owner of two hundred slaves" who had "yet to perform" the "first anti-slavery act of his life."[12] They campaigned instead for Martin Van Buren.

The country's voters sent Taylor to the White House. The most important development during his brief presidency was the fierce congressional controversy that erupted over slavery's future in the lands taken from Mexico and related matters. Before those debates ended, freshman congressman Thaddeus Stevens had made his name as a take-no-prisoners spokesman for the antislavery cause.

Taylor triumphed in 1848 partly by winning six states in his native South. But on January 21, 1850, he shocked southern Whigs by proposing that Congress skirt renewed sectional conflict by bringing New Mexico and California into the Union not as territories but as fully fledged states. Granting statehood immediately, he reasoned, would allow Congress to evade the thorny questions of slavery's proper status in a federal territory and especially the national government's right to legislate on that subject. By sidestepping those questions Taylor hoped to "avoid the creation of geographical parties," parties limited in their appeal and defined by their loyalty to different parts of the country.[13]

But rather than circumvent congressional conflict, Taylor's proposal helped to fuel it. It seemed clear that New Mexico and California would enter the Union as free states, an outcome anathema to slaveholders. On January 22, 1850, just one day after the president addressed Congress on that subject, North Carolina Whig Thomas L. Clingman declared that trying to appease the North with gambits like Taylor's was both hopeless and unacceptable. "A few months' travel in the interior of the North" had recently convinced him that "the old abolition societies have done a good deal to poison the popular mind" there, creating "a high degree of prejudice against us." Clingman went on to threaten that unless Congress adopted a territorial policy that satisfied the slave states, the South would "bring the Government to a dead halt."

A number of Clingman's allies went further. Georgia Whig Robert Toombs warned the House that if "you seek to drive us from the territories of California and New Mexico . . . and to abolish slavery in this District, thereby attempting to fix a national degradation upon half the States of this Confederacy, I am for disunion." Representatives of other southern states issued similar ultimatums.[14]

President Taylor added insult to injury in the South's eyes by appearing to side with New Mexico against the slave state of Texas in another dispute. Texans had staked a claim to much of New Mexico even prior to its annexation and were now threatening to send their state militia into that territory to enforce that claim. Taylor declared himself ready to deploy the U.S. army to defend New Mexico against any such invasion. That, in turn, led Georgia Whig Alexander Stephens to threaten civil war. In case of a military showdown, he promised, "freemen from Delaware to the Rio Grande" would "rally to the rescue" of Texas.[15]

In Congress, Whig Henry Clay and Illinois Democrat Stephen Douglas worked to fashion a multifaceted compromise to these and related disputes. With the encouragement of prominent Massachusetts Whig Daniel Webster, Clay outlined his "comprehensive scheme" on the Senate floor on January 29, 1850. First, like Taylor's plan, it would admit California into the Union as a state with the right to decide for itself whether or not to legalize slavery within its borders. Second, Clay, unlike Taylor, would organize the rest of the lands taken from Mexico into territories without specifying the status of slavery there. Instead, in accord with the principle of popular sovereignty, the white residents of each territory would decide that question for themselves. Third, Clay would keep slavery itself legal in the District of Columbia but put an end to the district's current role as a major interstate slave market. Henceforth it would be illegal to bring slaves into the district for the purpose of selling and delivering them elsewhere. Fourth, Clay would fix Texas's border with New Mexico to the advantage chiefly of the latter but in return hand Texas a large sum of federal money with which to pay off its pre-annexation public debt.[16]

A fifth part of Clay's plan would strengthen the hands of slaveowners pursuing escaping slaves. The U.S. Constitution already mandated the recapture of fugitives who fled into free states, and an act of February 1793 empowered an alleged owner or owner's agent "to seize or arrest such fugitive from labour" and then to bring the latter before a local "magistrate," justify the claim of ownership, and then take the accused fugitives back "to the state or territory from which he or she fled." The same law made it a crime punishable by a five-hundred-dollar fine to "knowingly and willingly obstruct or hinder" that process.[17] During the 1840s, however, a growing number of northern state legislatures had sought to obstruct enforcement of the 1793 law, and northern judges had proved undependable, too. Meanwhile, a network of antislavery activists, known as the Underground Railroad, helped to spirit fugitives into the North or on to Canada. Thaddeus Stevens supported and participated in that effort. Archaeological evidence unearthed during modern excavation of property that Stevens owned in Lancaster suggests that he harbored fugitives there.[18]

A new, tougher fugitive slave bill was intended to overcome such obstructionism. As finally crafted, it empowered federal marshals both to pursue accused runaways into free states and to compel residents there to join the posses. The new bill would also create a special force of federally appointed commissioners (expected to prove more dependable than northern judges) to preside over such cases. Like the law of 1793, it would deny accused fugitives the right to testify in their own defense. And the maximum penalty for harboring a fugitive or in any other way interfering with his or her rendition would increase from five hundred to a thousand dollars plus six months' imprisonment plus civil damages of a thousand dollars for each alleged slave enabled to escape custody.[19]

Clay acknowledged that, taken together, these measures represented "larger and more expansive concessions" on the North's part than the South's. But that, he said, was only fair, since the South had a much bigger stake in slavery's future than did the North. For the North, without slaves of its own, the fight concerned merely moral abstractions—"sentiment, sentiment, sentiment alone." For the South, however, it involved far weightier things—"property, the social fabric, life, and all that makes life desirable and happy." These words did little to endear this Whig "great compromiser" to many of his northern colleagues.[20]

Congress would debate this proposal and Clay's evaluation of its merits for the better part of a year. Southerners like Senators Jefferson Davis of Mississippi and Solomon Downs of Louisiana took the bull by the horns, touting the virtues of slavery. Because of "the interested, the kind, the affectionate care of the master," Davis declared, "cruelty . . . probably exists to a smaller extent" under slavery "than in any other relation of labor to capital." Expanding on that claim, Downs urged slavery's critics to "go on to the plantations" and spend time "among those negroes so much sympathized with." If they do, they will see that slaves were "the gayest, the happiest, the most contented, and the best fed people in the world." In fact, he continued, if they compared "the comforts and enjoyments of life" enjoyed by our slaves to those of northern workers, they would find that the conditions of the slaves are "superior." "They have no care for the future; everything is supplied to them; they have but moderate labor to perform; and when old age and sickness come upon them, certain provision is made for their support and comfort." And so it was, Downs chuckled, that we slave masters often observe "that our slaves are much happier than we are ourselves."[21]

These debates provoked Stevens's maiden speech in the House of Representatives on February 20. It was a characteristically blunt and forceful intervention. Thomas L. Clingman's threat to shut down Washington, Stevens said, revealed "a palpable conspiracy" among southern congressmen to "disorganize and dissolve" the national government. That threat amounted to "sedition," even "treason against the nation," and the Pennsylvania congressman doubted that there was "another legislative body in the world" where it "would not be followed by prosecution and punishment." But the sad fact was, Stevens grieved, that "in this glorious country . . . we can say anything within these walls or beyond them with impunity, unless it be to agitate in favor of human liberty." Only such a defense of human liberty, he added, was considered "aggression" in the U.S. Congress.[22]

Stevens then replied to Jefferson Davis and Solomon Downs with an abolitionist indictment of slavery. In the first place, he said, it harmed the country as a whole, undermined "the prosperity, the power, the permanency, and glory of this nation." A slavery-based society was also a poor foundation for a republican form of government. Elaborating on the venerable doctrine he had invoked fifteen years earlier at Pennsylvania's constitutional convention, Stevens asserted that "middling classes who own the soil, and work it with their own hands, are the main support of every free government." That was true because "those who defend and support the country must have a stake in the soil; must have an interest to protect and rights to defend." A viable republic must rest upon a foundation composed of independent small farmers, "an intelligent and industrious yeomanry" that was "equally removed from luxury and from poverty."[23]

But it was just that social class, Stevens claimed, that was small or absent in slavery-based societies. Such places "never can have a large number of industrious freemen," dominated as they are by members of "an untitled aristocracy" who "appropriate large tracts of territory to themselves, and thus prevent it from being thickly settled by freemen." As for the free but non-slaveholding people who do live there, Stevens continued, they "are the most worthless and miserable of mankind." They "feel that they are degraded and despised; and their minds and conduct generally conform to their condition." Such a society's real labor force was composed not of freemen but of slaves, a fact that not only undermined republican government but also stunted the economy, since slaves had no incentive to work hard or well and so "are idle and wasteful." "Men who are to receive none of the wages of their labor do not care to multiply its fruits," said Stevens. "Sloth, negligence, improvidence, are the consequence." And so "the land being neglected becomes poor and barren."[24]

To this point in his indictment, Stevens had emphasized slavery's injurious impact on the society as a whole, which many of slavery's more moderate critics also emphasized. But Stevens did not stop there. Like abolitionists and other radical enemies of slavery, Stevens denounced that institution for what he considered "still graver reasons," reasons reflecting his concern for the enslaved. He despised bondage, he said, because it was a form of "despotism," and he was "opposed to despotism throughout the world." Anticipating objections, Stevens explained his meaning. "That government is despotic where the rulers govern subjects by their own mere will—by degrees and laws emanating from their uncontrolled will, in the enactment and extension of which the ruled have no voice, and under which they have no rights, except at the will of the rulers."[25]

Stevens then went an audacious step further still. This description of despotism fit not only the southern states, he said, but also the United States as a whole. "In my judgment not only the slave States but the General Government, recognizing and aiding as it does slavery, is a despotism." Because "in this Government, the free white citizens" are the sole "rulers," and "all others are subjects." In fact, Stevens continued, those approximately "four millions of subjects lie under the most absolute and grinding despotism that the world ever saw." The American slave, he asserted, was worse off than the slaves of ancient Rome and Greece or the serfs of nineteenth-century Russia. For in this country "the subject has no rights, social, political, or personal. He has no voice in the laws which govern him. He can hold no property. His very wife and children are not his. His labor is another's. . . . He is governed, bought, sold, punished, executed, by laws to which he never gave his assent, and by rulers whom he never chose. He is . . . stripped of every right which God

and nature gave him, and which the high spirit of our revolution declared. . . ." The wretched condition of the nation's enslaved subjects
marked the country's free white citizens as "despots such as history
will brand and God abhors."[26]

But despite his own "unchangeable hostility to slavery in every
form, and in every place," Stevens once again vowed to "stand by all
the compromises of the Constitution, and carry them into faithful
effect." He would do so even though "some of these compromises
I greatly dislike, and were they now open for consideration, they
should never receive my assent." Accepting constitutional guarantees
for slavery where it already existed, however, did not and must not
require tolerating slavery's further expansion. That, on the contrary,
must be stoutly resisted, and Stevens predicted that such resistance
would trigger the great battle that loomed ahead between liberty
and servitude. That battle would be an epochal one indeed, not least
because all knew that restricting slavery to its present confines would
have tremendous consequences. Such restriction would eventually
doom bondage even within the states where it now existed. "Let
the disease spread, and although it will render the whole body lep-
rous and loathsome, yet it will still survive." But "confine this malady
within its present limits. Surround it with a cordon of freemen" so
"that it cannot spread, and in less than twenty-five years every slaveholding State in this Union will have on her statute books a law for
the gradual and final extinction of slavery."[27]

That geographical confinement would ultimately kill slavery was,
in fact, an opinion shared by those on both sides of the struggle.
Slave-based agriculture seemed to use up the soil and therefore to
continually require additional land. As the country's population as
a whole moved westward and created new states, furthermore, only
the creation of new slave states could sustain the masters' political
domination of Congress and the Electoral College. Allowing the territories and the states carved out of them to banish slavery, conversely,

would provide slaves contemplating escape with new sanctuaries toward which to flee. Stevens quoted complaints by both Virginia and Alabama congressmen that slavery's restriction to its current domain would lead inevitably to its death there. To Stevens, however, that outcome would be "one of the most agreeable consequences of the legitimate restriction of slavery"; the achievement of "universal freedom" would fulfill "the fondest wishes of every patriotic heart." Two hundred thousand copies of this speech were printed in pamphlet form and circulated nationally.[28]

Stevens must have anticipated that his scorching words would provoke slave-state rage. As he spoke them, southern congressmen gathered around his desk scowling, sneering, and cursing at him. An observer feared for Stevens's safety, mindful that in that era "southern gentlemen enforced their arguments with an appeal to the duel, and southern ruffians resorted to the bowie-knife and bludgeon." But Thaddeus Stevens showed no such concern, "apparently unconscious of the mutterings of the storm." On the contrary, he remained "as cool as if addressing a jury in his county court-house."[29]

And then, having flayed the slaveholders, Stevens turned his fire on the free states. Why, he asked, had slavery been allowed to survive in the United States so long? And what now enabled this barbaric system to threaten to spread even farther, meanwhile bullying the rest of the nation? The answer, he said, was to be found in the moral backsliding of the North. Its people, although numerically greater than the South's, had allowed the slaveowners to rule over them. Southern spokesmen proudly boasted of having controlled the federal government throughout most of the country's history. That claim, Stevens granted, was "both candid and true." But he could not hear it "without feeling the burning blush on my countenance, that the North with her overwhelming millions of free men, has for half a century been tame and servile enough to submit to this arrogant rule." And now, he noted, the South was once again using threats of obstruction and secession to cow northern congressmen. And southerners had good reason to expect that tactic to succeed. "You have too often intimidated Congress," Stevens acknowledged. "You have more than once frightened the tame North . . . and found 'dough faces' enough to be your tools."[30] The label "doughface" signified that the person had features so malleable that the South could rearrange them to suit it.

It was now the turn of those same doughfaces to bristle at Stevens's sallies. Representative Thomas Ross, a Pennsylvania Democrat, denounced Stevens as "a bad man" bereft of "even one patriotic impulse," someone whose words were "vulgar, indecent and unmanly." But what else was to be expected, Ross wondered, from someone so "degraded in feeling as to desire to raise the negro to social and political equality with the white man"?

But if fear for his physical safety did not silence Stevens, rhetoric like that would certainly not do so. Stevens poured still more scorn on northern doughfaces like Ross when the House turned to the proposed new fugitive slave bill. He began by assuring his colleagues that he had no desire to make "personal reproaches," not even against Ross, that "skunk across the way." Least of all would Stevens "reproach the South." On the contrary, he said, "I honor her courage and fidelity," because "even in a bad, a wicked cause, she shows a united front. All her sons are faithful to the cause of human bondage," all accept it as "their cause." Unfortunately, he lamented, "the North—the poor, timid, mercenary, driveling North—has no such united defenders of her cause, although it is the cause of human liberty." Shamefully, "even her own great men have turned her accusers," Stevens observed, clearly referring to Stephen A. Douglas, Daniel Webster, and their ilk. The North and its cause were "the victim of low ambition—an ambition which prefers self to country, personal aggrandizement to the high cause of human liberty. She is offered up a sacrifice to propitiate southern tyranny—to conciliate southern treason."[31]

Well, Stevens conceded, this combination of southern single-mindedness and northern groveling might be enough to enact the new fugitive slave law. But enforcing that law would not be so easy. The people of the free states, Stevens vowed, would never cooperate with a law that compels "all bystanders to aid in the capture of fugitives; to join the chase and run down the prey." That, he said, was simply "asking more than my constituents will ever grant." Like him, the Pennsylvanian continued, they "will strictly abide by the Constitution." They would, albeit with gritted teeth, refrain from interfering with slaveholders and their own agents as they hunted down desperate escapees. "But no law that tyranny can pass will ever induce them to join the hue and cry after the trembling wretch who has escaped from unjust bondage."[32]

Thaddeus Stevens's performance in Congress that season gratified antislavery-minded people. Rev. Jonathan Blanchard, reading Stevens's February 20 speech when it appeared in the abolitionist press, "implore[d] the blessings of the living and merciful God" upon the congressman. Blanchard thought that Stevens's was "the first thoroughly honest speech which has yet been delivered on that floor on the subject of slavery." He also believed that there had "never been a moment in the history of the great [antislavery] struggle in which any speech you could make would be read by so many persons and do so much good." Ohio's Joshua Giddings reported to Senator Charles Sumner that Stevens was an army unto himself. "He is one of the strong men of the nation. I entertain no doubt about his entire devotion to our cause." Stevens's Pennsylvania colleague Alexander McClure considered that speech and his others during the 1850 crisis "not only among the ablest but certainly the most impassioned of all his political deliverances."[33]

Those speeches signaled, too, a further hardening of Stevens's antislavery purpose. True, he still promised to respect compromises embedded in the Constitution, including its fugitive slave clause. But this commitment, he now declared, did not necessarily extend to all laws passed in the Constitution's name—and especially not to the Fugitive Slave Act of 1793, which granted alleged fugitives no jury trials and no right even to testify in their own behalf before the magistrates who would decide their fate. On June 10, 1850, Stevens called for repealing that "odious law." And he now condemned colonization as well. A proposal was then being floated, he had learned, to use federal funds to remove a large number of free blacks to some other country. It is unclear whether that plan involved involuntary colonization or the kind of voluntary emigration that he had endorsed in 1835. But in 1850 he scorned attempts to "exile her free people of color, and transport them from the land of their birth to the land of the stranger!" Such a proposal, he spat, was not even "fit to be made."[34]

Then, in early July 1850, President Zachary Taylor suddenly died, apparently of food poisoning, and New York Whig Millard Fillmore ascended to the presidency. Paradoxically, perhaps, that northerner bent further toward the South than had his southern predecessor. As Stevens's associate Alexander Hood foresaw, these unexpected developments would soon bring matters to a head. By the end of that month, the Fillmore White House had jettisoned Taylor's plan for California and New Mexico, throwing its support instead behind the measures then being advocated by pro-compromise forces in Congress.

Henry Clay had placed all his proposals into a single "omnibus" bill, thereby sealing its doom. Now Stephen Douglas broke Clay's bill down into five separate resolutions. The Senate adopted each of them in August; the House followed suit in September. Those resolutions passed on the basis of differently composed majorities. Most but not all northern Whigs voted against the fugitive slave law. Many of them also opposed the measures dealing with the new territories, wishing instead to have the federal government categorically outlaw slavery there. For mirror-opposite reasons, most South Carolinians, Mississippians, and other southerners also rejected the popular sovereignty formula for the territories. They wanted Congress simply to guarantee slavery's legality in all such places. The appearance of national agreement in 1850 thus only cloaked deepening actual political polarization. A measure of that polarization was the fact that of 230 members of the House of Representatives, only 28 voted for every one of the compromise bills. In the Senate, only four men did the same.[35]

The passage of the pro-slavery measures and the support that northern doughfaces like Douglas and Webster gave them left Stevens embittered. "It cannot be doubted," he told a Boston audience, "that the power of Slavery has been much increased and will increase, through the efforts of Mr. Webster and his friends." "The course of Liberty is hard to sustain in this republic," he complained to sympathetic Pennsylvania constituents, because our citizens appear unable to "understand why others than themselves should be free." But they should be asking themselves "what stronger right to freedom has the pale than the dark face." Instead they seemed simply to assume "that those who are weak[,] ignorant, and friendless, are for that reason, unworthy of protection, and are fit subjects of oppression." That assumption was widespread, he said once again, not only among southern but among so many northern whites as well. And there were, moreover, venal considerations at work.

Politicians from the free states uphold slavery "to purchase southern support" for their own projects and careers while "commercial communities who think more of a cent a yard profit on coarse cotton than human rights" stand by the slaveholders "to attract southern trade." The public was duped into going along with this by newspapers filled with "habitual falsehoods and perversions of facts." Stevens could only hope that "the people will ultimately see that laws which oppress the black man, and deprive him of the safeguards of Liberty, will eventually enslave the white man. That he who is but the tyrant of the African to-day will be the tyrant of the Anglo-Saxon hereafter."[36]

The 1850 legislative outcome that angered and depressed Stevens elated others. Leaders of both major parties hailed the passage of the Clay-Douglas measures not only as a solution to the specific political problems then posed but also as a lasting resolution of the North-South conflict as a whole. Clay had pioneered such optimistic predictions back in February when he promised that his plan's adoption would yield "peace and quiet for thirty years hereafter." In September 1850, Daniel Webster cheerfully greeted a group of congressional visitors with Shakespeare's words, "Now is the winter of our discontent made glorious summer. . . ." President Millard Fillmore cheered that the country had now "been rescued from the wide and boundless agitation that surrounded us." The passage of the Clay-Douglas measures, he proclaimed, represented "a settlement, in principle and substance—a final settlement—of the dangerous and exciting subjects which they embraced." Even Lincoln would pay homage to Clay's role in fashioning that deal. And Martin Van Buren, who had endorsed the compromise package as a whole, led followers out of the Free Soil Party and back into the ranks of the Democrats.[37]

The 1850 measures did indeed settle before the law the specific matters then at issue. But they did so in a way that satisfied the basic goals and grievances of neither North nor South. The enactment of those measures would not, consequently, prevent the re-eruption of multiple conflicts over slavery in the years ahead. In some important ways, on the contrary, they would guarantee such eruptions. Commenting on one part of that settlement, Stevens pronounced a prescient verdict on the whole: "[I]nstead of bringing repose, it will be

the cause of constant agitation and sedition. It will become the fruit-
ful mother of future rebellion, disunion, and civil war, and the final
ruin of the Republic."[38]

In the North, the popular sovereignty scheme and especially the
new fugitive slave law provoked sharp resentment. Many southern
planters and their political representatives, meanwhile, remained
deeply unhappy with Congress's failure simply to guarantee slavery's
legality in the territories. Mississippi's Jefferson Davis denounced it
as an "aggression upon the people of the South." Talk of slave-state
secession filled the air once again. Less combative southern leaders
urged their neighbors to remain within the Union and accept the
settlement—on condition that the North live up to those provisions
that *it* found repulsive, including the new fugitive slave law. That
advice prevailed, but the condition upon which it depended soon
proved unrealizable. [39]

CHAPTER FOUR

From Whig to Republican

1850–1856

Thaddeus Stevens's resistance to the Compromise of 1850 augured the end of his time in the Whig Party. Most Pennsylvania Whigs shared his dislike for that compromise, and Stevens initially received letters of encouragement and congratulations for his stand. But others in the party strongly supported the Clay-Douglas proposals. As Henry Wilson of Massachusetts later recalled, those more conservative Whigs considered "the slavery issue . . . to be full of menace." Viewing it through the lens of party interest and prizing national amity over political principle, they saw this divisive issue "as a disturbing and dangerous element, to be considered and disposed of" as quickly as possible. The Whigs of Lancaster County divided over the question, with the influential *Examiner and Herald* newspaper leading the pro-compromise chorus.[1]

Congress's enactment of the compromise measures turned the tide within the party against opposition. Numerous Whig congressmen who had previously objected now breathed a secret sigh of relief that at least the dangerous sectional crisis had passed. To continue litigating the issues of 1850, they believed, risked permanently alienating their southern colleagues and thereby destroying their national party. They intended instead to accept and abide by the settlement and get on with other business. This dynamic helped Whig conservatives in Thaddeus Stevens's home district to gain control of the party's 1851 county convention.[2]

Only a minority of Pennsylvania Whigs by now continued openly to defy the terms of the de facto compromise, but Thaddeus Stevens stood in the front ranks of those who did. He had assisted fugitives before 1850, and he continued to do so afterward. While he searched for legal grounds on which to block enforcement of the new fugitive slave law, he sent word to fugitives urging them not to surrender themselves but instead to flee the country. He followed that course even though it, like his adamant opposition to the 1850 compromise, imperiled his position in his party and therefore also his congressional seat.[3]

Stevens soon put his hostility to the new law into more public action. Despite the law's passage, slaves continued to escape from bondage, and some northerners, black and white, continued to assist them. In Boston, Syracuse, Detroit, and elsewhere free blacks and antislavery whites tried forcibly to rescue escapees from their pursuers, in some instances wounding and even killing the would-be slave-catchers. Thaddeus Stevens became involved in the most highly publicized of these dramas. In 1851, he served as the chief defense attorney in a case, *U.S. v. Hanway*, arising from the escape of Maryland slaves.[4]

In November 1849, four slaves fled from Edward Gorsuch's farm in Maryland's Baltimore County. In the late summer of 1851, Gorsuch heard that the young men had taken refuge in Lancaster County, Pennsylvania. Arming himself and collecting a group of relatives and friends, the slaveowner set out for Pennsylvania, "determined," as his son later recalled, "to have his property." In Philadelphia, Gorsuch obtained warrants under the new federal law for the capture of the four fugitives. He also added a U.S. marshal to his posse.[5]

What Gorsuch did not know was that black residents of Lancaster County had long since formed a self-defense network. Its members passed information back and forth across the Pennsylvania-Maryland border, assisted fugitives, and had already fought professional slave-catchers physically. As Gorsuch's posse now headed for Lancaster, members of this network identified it and sent word of its approach.

Before dawn on September 11, 1851, Gorsuch's party reached the Christiana, Pennsylvania, home of William Parker, himself an escaped slave who had become leader of the local black self-defense effort. Two of the Maryland fugitives and some other blacks were holed up inside the house. When Parker opened the front door, the marshal accompanying Gorsuch read aloud the federal warrants and advised the house's occupants to "give up at once," since he was empowered "to take you, dead or alive." Parker and his company defied the order, and the two sides exchanged gunfire. But Gorsuch remained determined. "My property I will have," he announced, "or I'll breakfast in hell." Other allies of Parker's, scores of them, now appeared on the scene, most of them black and many of them armed. Among the new arrivals were a third fugitive from Maryland, Noah Buley, and Parker's white neighbor, the miller Castner Hanway. The federal marshal asked Hanway and another white man for assistance, but they refused, instead urging both sides to avoid bloodshed. Encountering one of the fugitives, a man named Samuel Thompson, Gorsuch demanded that he surrender. In reply, Thompson and others set upon Gorsuch and killed him. When Gorsuch's son then advanced revolver in hand, Parker's brother-in-law shot him, too, nearly but not quite fatally. A third member of the posse was also shot multiple times. In the battle's aftermath, the four original Maryland fugitives managed to make their way to Canada; so did William Parker and some others. But in the racist hysteria that blew up, federal agents, local officials, and gangs of self-appointed vigilantes swept through the surrounding countryside, imposing a reign of terror on black residents.[6]

Meanwhile, the federal government charged that on that September morning, Castner Hanway and forty other men, thirty-eight of them black, "did wickedly and traitorously levy war against the United States." The specific acts of which they were accused ranged far and wide, including having produced and circulated "books, pamphlets, letters, declarations, resolutions, addresses, papers, and writings . . . containing . . . incitements . . . to resist, oppose, and prevent, by violence and intimidation, the execution, of the said laws." The charge of treason was itself an obvious overreach, and the claim that circulating antislavery tracts was itself treasonous was meant to intimidate abolitionists and opponents of the fugitive slave law more broadly. Daniel Webster, now Millard Fillmore's secretary of state, reportedly opined with approval that even if a guilty verdict could not be obtained, the trial itself would help discourage resistance to that law.[7]

Castner Hanway's trial began on November 24, with a Supreme Court justice, Pennsylvania's own Robert C. Grier, presiding. The prosecution team included not only the district attorney but also the attorney general of Maryland and Senator James Cooper, a Pennsylvania Whig. The chief counsel for the defense was Thaddeus Stevens. His team argued that Hanway had gone to William Parker's house that day under the impression that those besieging it were not a marshal and the holder of a legal warrant but rather (in Stevens's words) "a gang of professional kidnappers," "professional dealers in human flesh," who were bent on abducting Parker and spiriting him into slavery in the South. The defense had no trouble demonstrating that such abductions had indeed become common in southern Pennsylvania. That fact, said Stevens, explained "why a whole neighborhood might be ready upon a notice given . . . to go to a place" like the Parker home. Castner Hanway, Stevens continued, "went there with pure and laudable motives," and "what he did afterward . . . was honorable, humane, and noble."[8]

*   *   *

On December 11, Justice Grier charged the jury. He denounced abolitionism, complained about "infuriated fanatics and unprincipled
demagogues" who "counsel a bloody resistance to laws of the land,"
and agreed that the defendants were surely "guilty of aggravated riot
and murder." But Grier had to advise that what had transpired at the
Parker house did not really amount to treason. After that, the jury
needed only some fifteen minutes to bring in a verdict of not guilty.
That verdict foretold the end of the whole Christiana case. The rest
of those under federal indictment eventually went free. A charge
of interfering with execution of the fugitive slave law was brought
against only one person, a member of the local self-defense network,
and a jury found him, too, not guilty.[9]

This outcome infuriated southern political leaders. The governor
of Maryland, Gorsuch's home state, was particularly incensed. "Any
one must see, at a single glance," he warned his legislature, "that, if
this decision stands, the fugitive slave act is a mockery and a de-
lusion." Apparently in revenge for the dead slaveowner, a group of
men in Baltimore killed a Lancaster resident who had gone to that
city seeking a legal means to rescue a free black woman who had
been abducted from his farm. Conservative northerners were also
outraged and vented their anger upon Hanway's chief attorney. This
group included prominent Whigs in Lancaster County. One local
party member complained that Thaddeus Stevens had spent too
much time "defending those of his abolition brethren who were
implicated in the Christiana murder and riot scrape." Another be-
moaned Stevens's involvement in "the horrible tragedy recently enacted at Christiana, in which a respected citizen of another state was
cruelly murdered whilst in the peaceable pursuit of what the Constitution and law of the land have decided to be his property. . . ."
Lancaster's conservative Whig newspaper, the *Examiner and Herald*,

labeled slaveowner Edward Gorsuch's death "one of the most horrid murders ever perpetrated in this County or State" and laid the blame at the door of abolitionists and antislavery politicians like Stevens. Hanway and others, the editor said, "had been inflamed by Abolition harangues and incendiary speeches" in Congress "until they had come to look upon treason to the laws of their country as a moral duty, and upon murder as not a crime."[10]

The backlash against Stevens further weakened his position within the Whig Party. His stand against the 1850 compromise had already caused him trouble at home. True, Lancaster's Whigs had renominated him for his House seat in 1850. But they had done so, one claimed, only in accord with "long established usage," despite the fact that "his course in Congress was disapproved by nine-tenths of his constituents." That was probably an exaggeration; Stevens did, after all, win reelection that year. But Lancaster County's Whigs refused to send Stevens as a delegate to their party's 1851 state convention.[11]

Conservative domination of the county Whig convention led Stevens and some political allies (including Edward McPherson and Alexander Hood) to begin publishing a newspaper of their own in late November 1851, the *Independent Whig*, in the name of what they called authentic Whiggery. The conservative *Examiner and Herald* charged that "the most active friends of the new paper throughout the county are violent abolitionists, many of whom never voted for a Whig ticket in their lives," and that "the policy advocated by Mr. Stevens, if sustained by the Whigs of this county would at once separate them from the great Whig party of the country—from Clay, Webster, Fillmore, Scott," and others. The real question at issue, it insisted, was whether "the future policy of the Whig party of Lancaster . . . shall, or shall not . . . be shaped to suit the views of the abolitionists?"[12]

*   *   *

In anticipation of the 1852 elections, the Whig caucus in the U.S. House of Representatives met in the Capitol on December 1, 1851. Subsequent reports disagree about just who attended and precisely what transpired there. The most plausible account suggests that of the party's more than eighty House members, perhaps fifty to sixty took part, most of them northerners. A resolution presented there praised the 1850 compromise as "the most conciliatory, and the best for the entire country that could be obtained from the conflicting sectional interests and opinions." Therefore, it continued, the terms of the compromise "ought to be adhered to and carried into faithful execution as a final settlement in principle and substance of the dangerous and exciting subjects which they embrace."

Opponents tried to table (that is, to avoid voting on) the resolution, but that attempt failed by a vote of about two to one. Florida congressman Edward C. Cabell afterward reported that he and the other southern Whigs in attendance had "declared their determination to withdraw from the caucus, and no longer to act with the Whig party, if it failed to put itself on this national platform." When the caucus took a vote on the pro-Compromise resolution itself, an overwhelming majority supported it. At that point, a small number of northerners, including Stevens, walked out of the meeting. The conservative New York Whig congressman James Brooks nonetheless announced to the House as a whole that, as a result of the caucus's vote, his party's "breaches" had "been healed."[13]

The Whigs' 1852 national convention met in Baltimore during the second week of June. Its primary task was to select a presidential candidate. Many northern delegates favored Winfield Scott, while southerners preferred the incumbent, Millard Fillmore. At last, on the fifty-third ballot, the delegates chose Scott. William A. Graham of North Carolina, Fillmore's secretary of the navy, became Scott's running mate.

Alongside the clash over candidates lay lingering differences about the issues raised by the Mexican War. The convention adopted its party platform by a vote of 227 to 66. Regarding the 1850 compromise, it effectively repeated the stand that the party's congressional caucus had taken the previous December. The compromise measures, it held, specifically including the fugitive slave law, "are received and acquiesced in by the Whig Party of the United States as a settlement in principle and substance." The convention promised that "we will maintain them, and insist upon their strict enforcement," warning dissenters that "we deprecate all further agitation of the question thus settled, as dangerous to our peace; and will discountenance all efforts to continue or renew such agitation whenever, wherever, or however the attempt may be made."[14]

Shortly afterward, on Thursday, June 26, 1852, Stevens attended a Whig gathering in Lancaster city called to endorse Winfield Scott's nomination. The resolutions passed there cheered the 1850 compromise and praised the vice presidential nomination of William A. Graham as "a merited tribute of respect to the popular administration of President Fillmore, of whose cabinet he is a distinguished member." As for Millard Fillmore himself, the meeting added, he was due "the gratitude of his country for the calm, dignified and energetic manner in which he has discharged the responsible duties of his trying position." He was also due the gratitude "of the Whig Party, for his faithful and consistent adherence to its established policy." Stevens opposed those resolutions, and although slated to speak at this meeting, he ultimately declined to do so, claiming ill health.[15]

In rejecting the 1850 compromise measures and repudiating the Whig Party's acceptance of those measures, Stevens doomed his chances for renomination to his House seat. Conservative Lancaster County Whigs tore into him more furiously than ever. "In Congress he has disgraced himself and his county," wrote one, "by a course of the most frenzied abolitionism" and "judging from his late excesses and his former advocacy of *negro suffrage*" at the state constitutional convention back in the 1830s, "he will ride it to the very death." "Mr. Stevens seeks to convert the great Whig party into a faction of Abolitionists," wrote another, "and would sacrifice every interest of the country for the sake of aiding in the escape of runaway negroes!" A third complained that in Congress Stevens's advocacy of "negroism" had been so "ardent" that his occasional words in support of tariffs and Winfield Scott's candidacy had discredited those causes more than advanced them.[16]

The chief objection lodged against Stevens was that his policy would tear the national Whig Party apart. He was guilty, declared one local critic, of "an utter repudiation of all party and civil allegiance. He has deserted the Whig administration, seceded from the caucus of the party, and endeavored to sow the wildest dissension in its ranks."[17] No matter what Stevens said, another opponent swore, Lancaster's Whigs would not "withhold the right hand of fellowship from the gallant Whigs of Kentucky, Tennessee, N. Carolina, Maryland, Georgia and Louisiana, and be required to look upon Henry Clay as a political adversary."[18]

Facing the certain refusal of such Whigs to renominate him, Stevens sought instead to have an ally, Emanuel C. Reigart, nominated for his congressional seat. But local Whigs rejected Reigart, too, instead choosing a conservative named Isaac Hiester, who then won the fall election.[19]

Stevens now found himself in a corner. In the name of political realism, he had declined throughout the 1840s to join antislavery third parties, first the Liberty and then the Free Soil organizations. He had clung instead to the Whigs, expecting that their far greater electoral strength would yield more immediate returns for his favored causes, including antislavery. But now that same Whig Party, in the interests precisely of protecting its size and strength, was outlawing antislavery "agitation" within its ranks. And it was effectively banishing Stevens for refusing to go along with that policy. The gap between Stevens's values and aims, on the one side, and the Whig Party's perception of its own interests, on the other, had grown too large. His adherence to that party, which might once have seemed shrewd, did so no longer.

He needed a new political vehicle, and one was taking shape at the time. In the mid-1840s, Stevens and his allies had leaned on nativists to strengthen their hands politically. Emanuel C. Reigart, a former leader of Lancaster's Anti-Masons and a longtime Stevens ally, ran for Congress in 1846 and for governor in 1847 on "Native American" tickets. In the early 1850s, Stevens remained ready to ally with anti-immigrant, anti-Catholic forces for the sake of electoral advantage and willing to bend in their direction.[20] In this respect Stevens differed from Lincoln and especially from many who would later become radical Republicans. He was not noted for expressing anti-immigrant or anti-Catholic views. In 1830, indeed, he had opposed publication in an anti-Masonic newspaper of attacks upon any religion, lest it suggest "an intention of uniting *Church* and *State*."[21]

But it is also true that Stevens had never become a particular champion of immigrant rights. Perhaps he shared the opinion, especially widespread among New Englanders, that the Catholic Church, to which so many Irish and German immigrants belonged, was a bastion of political reaction and an enemy of republican government. The early Vermont constitution that promised religious freedom to all Protestant denominations, it is worth recalling, had not made the same promise to Catholics. Stevens may also have doubted the fitness of many immigrants to be responsible citizens. At Pennsylvania's constitutional convention in the 1830s, he had registered his suspicion of big cities and their residents. He adhered to that view long afterward. In the mid-1850s, Stevens would tell voters that it was up to "the yeomanry [that is, independent small farmers] of this State to ensure a triumph" for virtue at the polls, for if they "turn not out *en masse*, we shall be beaten by the cities." At mid-century, those cities were swiftly filling up with immigrants, and most of the newcomers aligned themselves with the Democratic Party. One of Stevens's future allies, the German American Carl Schurz, would lament that the Democrats' "strength . . . lies mainly in the populous cities, and consists largely of Irish and [the] uneducated mass of German immigrants." Here, then, was a purely partisan motive for linking up with nativists. Another was Stevens's awareness that nativist sentiment was strong in Pennsylvania, especially in the state's southeastern counties such as Lancaster.[22]

Allying with nativists would become still more attractive as Stevens's position in the Whig Party grew weaker and as popular support for Whigs eroded nationally. Northern Whigs' support for the Wilmot Proviso, Whig president Zachary Taylor's failure to take a solidly pro-slavery line regarding the lands taken from Mexico, and widespread northern resistance to the fugitive slave law—all of that alienated southern Whigs and divided the party in the North. Meanwhile, a spike in immigration engendered resentment among those Whig voters who judged their party insufficiently hostile to the newcomers. That resentment spurred defections from the Whigs and the explosive growth of a new nativist party, known formally as the American Party but more popularly as the Know Nothings.[23] Know Nothing lodges proliferated in Pennsylvania in 1852–53, and a large proportion of Whigs across southern Pennsylvania soon became Know Nothing supporters.[24]

The disintegration of the Whigs and the expansion of the new nativist party confronted antislavery politicians throughout the North with both a danger and an opportunity. On the one hand, they did not wish immigration to replace slavery as the primary political question of the day. On the other hand, they knew that some nativist voters opposed the further expansion of slavery. A number of antislavery politicians entertained hopes of reshaping the heterogeneous and still rather amorphous American Party into an antislavery organization—or hoped to win leadership of that party's antislavery-minded supporters and perhaps break them off from it. In that spirit, William Seward and his allies dispatched agents into the Know Nothing organization in New York State. In Massachusetts, Henry Wilson joined the Know Nothings with similar goals.[25]

Stevens allied with Know Nothings in Pennsylvania. He never either openly acknowledged or denied joining that party. Although two of its ex-members declared publicly that he had indeed become a member, Stevens evaded the claim. But his involvement in the nativist party's affairs nonetheless became obvious. When the American Party's county-level organization drew up an "Independent" electoral ticket in 1854, a Stevens associate, Anthony E. Roberts, ran for Congress on it, triumphing at the polls over both the conservative Whig incumbent, Isaac Hiester, and the Democratic candidate, Joseph Lefevre. Probably encouraging Stevens's attraction to that party was the fact that Pennsylvania's Know Nothings supported with great ardor the policies serving economic development that Stevens favored.[26]

But despite the visibility of his friends in Know-Nothingism's Lancaster County unit, neither Stevens nor those friends ever controlled it. Both there and at the state level, the Pennsylvania party proved to be an uneasy and unstable coalition of disparate elements, housing both straightforward nativists and forces more committed to antislavery. With some justice, the Democratic press called the state's American Party an "unholy alliance," and these two party factions—one primarily nativist and one primarily antislavery in purpose—struggled continuously over the content of the program. They may even have contested the nature and degree of the party's nativism. What is certain is that Stevens's allies in Lancaster's American Party tried persistently to push the issue of free soil to the forefront of its message, but without success.[27] Once again, as previously in the Whig Party, Stevens seemed to be stymied.

And then Democrat Stephen A. Douglas of Illinois sponsored a seemingly unrelated project that drastically transformed the political landscape to the advantage of slavery's enemies in the North. Douglas chaired the U.S. Senate's Committee on Territories and was a leading advocate of carrying white settlement westward. He was determined to facilitate settlement in those parts of the old Louisiana Purchase that were still unorganized politically and so without institutions of self-government. In early January 1854, Douglas introduced a bill designed to change that. It would transform that large, as-yet unorganized region into a new territory called Nebraska and authorize the creation of a territorial government there. The bill imported the popular sovereignty formula of 1850, specifying that the new territory's residents rather than the U.S. Congress would decide slavery's status there for themselves.[28]

Douglas's bill thus implicitly superseded the terms of the Missouri Compromise of 1820, which had banned slavery from this whole region. Douglas had inserted the popular sovereignty formula into his bill at least partly to appease southern congressmen; they had previously made it clear that no bill that did any less for them would pass. Having lost parity in the Senate when California entered the Union as a free state, southerners hoped now to regain their effective veto power in that body by creating one or more slave states out of what was left of the Louisiana Purchase. They also wished to make slavery in Missouri more secure by legalizing bondage in the neighboring new territory and thereby denying potential Missouri runaways a sanctuary there.

But silently overriding the Missouri Compromise did not satisfy the South's Senate leaders. They demanded an *explicit* revocation of the Missouri Compromise and, therewith, an explicit rejection of the doctrine that Congress had the legal right to exclude slavery from any territory. On January 23, 1854, Douglas complied, bringing in a new bill that explicitly repudiated the 1820 compromise. It also divided the region into two territories, Nebraska in the north and Kansas in the south. Many presumed that the Kansas territory, at least, would legalize slavery and that slavery once planted there would remain legal when Kansas eventually gained statehood.

The Senate passed Douglas's bill on March 3, 1854, and the House followed by a slim margin on May 22. The voting deeply divided both major parties. In the House, two-thirds of all northern congressmen opposed the bill, including all forty-five northern Whigs. Among northern Democratic congressmen, only a bare majority supported the bill, despite the fact that it had been written by a party leader and aggressively championed by a Democratic president, Franklin Pierce. Among southern congressmen, nearly all Democrats supported the bill while southern Whigs divided. President Pierce signed it into law within about a week of the House vote and later punished its opponents among northern Democrats by denying them party support and federal patronage.[29]

The Kansas-Nebraska Act struck a powerful blow against the political-party foundations of national unity. In nullifying what northerners had assumed since 1820 was a permanent compromise, it potentially opened to slavery a large swath of the continent closed to it since then. And it suggested that no compromise struck with the South would necessarily endure. A groundswell of anger at this new law arose in the free states. A friend expressed to Thaddeus Stevens a view widespread in the North, that this bill "constitutes a more insolent attempt of the slaveholding interest than any that had preceded it to render the United States a slaveholding government, and to set at defiance the principles of our national creed."[30]

Huge protest meetings seemingly everywhere denounced Douglas's bill, its sponsors, and its abettors. Most Whigs and many Democrats in the North were caught up in this popular eruption. In the fall of 1854, "anti-Nebraska" Democrats, Whigs, and Know Nothings came together in ad hoc electoral tickets that achieved great success at the polls in many free states. As the new law went into effect, meanwhile, would-be settlers entered Kansas from both the North and the South, with both sides determined to win the coming territorial elections. The fierce struggle soon burst into a guerrilla war that presaged the far bigger conflict yet to come.

Slavery's most militant and committed foes recognized in the Kansas-Nebraska uproar a major turning point in political life. For the first time, a very large proportion of northern voters, previously Whig or Democratic in affinity, were now identifying slavery's expansion as the principal issue on which to base voting choices. Determined to take advantage of this historic opportunity, antislavery forces strove to create not merely temporary election tickets but a fully fledged, potent, and durable political party united in hostility to slavery and determined to see it die. The extent and degree of popular outrage in the North for the first time made that party project appear not only necessary but feasible. That party, the new Republican Party, arose first in Wisconsin and Michigan in 1854. In the summer of 1855, Stevens and about a dozen other politically prominent Pennsylvanians set out to launch a unit of the new party in their state. They called upon those who, regardless of "former party distinctions," were now ready to follow them and "unite in a new organization to resist the further spread of slavery."[31]

Republicans held their first national convention in June 1856. Its platform denounced the repeal of the Missouri Compromise, branded slavery "a relic of barbarism," held that "all men are endowed with the inalienable right to life, liberty, and the pursuit of happiness," and insisted that the federal government's "primary object" must be "to secure these rights to all persons under its exclusive jurisdiction." Kansas must be admitted to the Union as a free state, and Congress must exclude slavery from all territories. The platform sought federal funds for the "improvement of rivers and harbors of a national character" and construction of "a railroad to the Pacific Ocean." The convention picked the western explorer John C. Fré-mont as its presidential candidate.[32]

The Democrats nominated an old acquaintance of Thaddeus Stevens—Pennsylvanian James Buchanan, whose doughface creden-tials were impeccable. "From my first entrance into the Senate of the United States until the present moment," Buchanan had trum-peted some years earlier, "my efforts have been devoted both in and out of that body, whenever the occasion required, to the mainte-nance of the constitutional rights of the South in opposition to all the projects of the abolitionists and quasi-abolitionists." The Know Nothing party chose ex-president Millard Fillmore to carry its ban-ner in 1856, arming him with a platform that stressed nativism and sectional conciliation. What was left of the Whig Party seconded Fill-more's nomination.[33]

The stakes could hardly be higher, as Stevens saw it. "The present crisis," he told a Lancaster crowd, "is more terrible than any since the Revolution" because "the very existence of your Republic is at stake."[34]

Republicans strove to pull toward themselves those nativist-minded voters who opposed the Kansas-Nebraska Act. To that end, organizers of the party's June 1856 national convention hoped to keep the party platform silent on the subject of immigrant rights. When a proposed draft proved explicitly to oppose "proscriptive leg-islation"—presumably including laws that radically lengthened the naturalization period, nativism's central demand—Stevens joined others in arguing strongly and successfully against that clause. The Republicans, he insisted, must not appear to be "in opposition to the largest party in Pennsylvania," that is, the Know Nothings. The final draft of the 1856 Republican national platform substituted vaguer language that ignored the issue of naturalization and confined itself to endorsing an "equality of rights" among those who were already citizens.[35]

In the general election that fall, Democrat James Buchanan won the presidency with 45 percent of the popular vote nationally and the electoral votes of every southern state except Maryland plus those of Illinois, Indiana, Pennsylvania, California, and New Jersey. Know Nothing candidate Millard Fillmore's support proved to concentrate disproportionately in the South. In the North, he attracted fewer than 14 percent of all ballots cast, less than a third of the Republican tally there, reflecting a striking decline in Know Nothing strength in the free states since 1854. In contrast, the campaign that the fledgling Republican Party mounted resulted in a stunning achievement. Although John C. Frémont received only a third of the popular votes nationwide, he received a plurality of those cast in the North, thereby garnering the electoral votes of eleven of the country's sixteen free states. Stevens considered that result a "victorious defeat."[36] In Lancaster County, his ally Anthony Roberts won reelection to the House of Representatives on the Republican ticket.

Still, Republicans had yet to find a way to capture the White House. In some key northern states, support for Fillmore deprived Frémont of the electoral votes he would have needed to win the presidency. And although in Pennsylvania favorite son Buchanan received an outright majority of the popular vote (Frémont got less than a third and Fillmore less than a fifth), Stevens remained convinced that in the state's southern tier, at least, "Americanism is the deepest feeling." He had labored during the campaign to form a fusion ticket at the state level between Republicans and Know Nothings, an undertaking in which he was only partially successful. A group of anti-Nebraska Know Nothings did break off from Fillmore's party and fuse with Republicans to form a state-based Union

Party, which placed Frémont at the top of its ticket. But a separate independent Know Nothing ticket remained in the field. And the Pennsylvania Republicans' attempt to woo rank-and-file nativist voters failed to attract enough of them to defeat the Democrats. Quite a few ex–Know Nothing voters in the Keystone State threw their support instead to Buchanan.[37]

The decade ending in 1856 had seen tremendous changes occur in the country's political life. Chief among the forces driving and shaping those changes was the struggle over slavery's future. In search of weapons with which to join and remain in the fray, Stevens had moved from one party to a second and then to a third. In the Republican Party he found one whose stated principles most closely aligned with his own. But as Frémont's failure to win the presidency demonstrated, that party had not yet found a path to national power. The search for such a path would absorb Stevens's energies during the next stage of his life.

CHAPTER FIVE

"If This Union Should Be Dissolved"

Stevens and the Road to War

History seemed to speed up after the 1856 election. Fateful events came tumbling one after another at a dizzying pace. The highest tribunal in the land declared unconstitutional any limits on slavery's spread throughout the territories. In Kansas, already bleeding internally from undeclared civil war, an unrepresentative legislature tried to impose a pro-slavery legal code on the territory. The president of the United States gave that move his blessing. In Virginia, a phalanx of antislavery terrorists assaulted a federal arsenal in hopes of freeing some slaves and sparking an insurrection by others. All of this undermined pro-compromise parties, accelerating the dissolution of the Know Nothings, dividing the Democrats and eventually splitting their party in two. This was the turbulent era in which Thaddeus Stevens returned personally to the political stage.

The nation's acceleration toward war began when the Supreme Court handed down its decision in the case known as *Scott v. Sandford*. Dred Scott was a slave owned by Dr. John Emerson, an army surgeon. In the 1830s Emerson moved Scott out of the slave state of Missouri into the free state of Illinois, then into the free territory of Wisconsin, and only then returned him to the South. Upon Emerson's death, attorneys for Scott filed a lawsuit seeking his freedom from Emerson's widow, Eliza Irene Sanford. Scott argued that he had become legally free by dwelling in a free state and then a free territory.

On March 6, 1857, Chief Justice Roger B. Taney, a Maryland Democrat, rejected Dred Scott's claim on behalf of a 7–2 Court majority dominated by southerners but including Associate Justice Robert C. Grier of Pennsylvania, the same man who had presided over the Christiana fugitive slave case five years earlier. Taney's opinion declared that Scott had no right to bring suit in the first place because black people had never been considered citizens—that, indeed, since the republic's founding they had "been regarded as beings of an inferior order, and altogether unfit to associate with the white race, either in social or political relations; and so far inferior, that they had no rights which the white man was bound to respect."[1]

Taney's version of history was inaccurate. Especially but not only in the republic's early decades, many free blacks had exercised a number of legal rights.[2] But if Taney's assertion *had* been well founded historically and legally, his verdict could have stopped with that assertion. If Scott was not entitled even to bring suit, no more need be said. Taney and his Court majority, however, wanted to use this case to settle the bigger, more explosive question of where a slave (and, by extension, the institution of slavery) might be carried geographically within the United States. So Taney went on to declare unconstitutional *any* law restricting the free movement of a U.S. citizen's private property, including human property, throughout the territories. Thus Congress had *never* had a right to limit slavery's expansion. By that standard, the Northwest Ordinances of 1787 and 1789, the 1820 Missouri Compromise, and all territorial laws outlawing slavery had always been null and void.

Six months after the *Dred Scott* ruling, an unrepresentative territorial legislature convened in the Kansas town of Lecompton. Preparing to apply for statehood, it drew up a constitution that legalized slavery there. The ratification referendum that followed did not offer voters the options of rejecting that constitution as a whole or of outlawing slavery in Kansas. Kansans were permitted to vote only on whether *additional* slaves could thereafter be brought into Kansas from the outside. Most settlers in Kansas, clearly opposed to slavery, refused to participate in the referendum, which therefore proceeded as the pro-slavery camp intended. Buchanan endorsed this Lecompton constitution, approved the referendum, and called upon Congress to admit Kansas as a slave state.[3]

The *Dred Scott* ruling, the Lecompton constitution, and Buchanan's endorsement of both pounded a wedge into the Democratic Party, alienating most northern Democrats from the administration and their party's southern wing. Buchanan had given his blessing to an obvious perversion of northern Democrats' favored formula for the territories: popular sovereignty. By denying to both Congress and territorial governments the right to outlaw slavery in any territory, the Supreme Court had rejected and nullified all popular-sovereignty plans.

All of that created a major problem for Stephen Douglas and other Democrats in the free states who knew that many of their constituents expected them to keep slavery out of the territories, even if without the outright federal ban that Republicans espoused. Those northern Democrats feared that their constituents would now abandon them. An Ohio Democrat anguished that if southern leaders of the party wanted to kill it in the northern states, they need only continue hanging "Lecompton" around their necks—and thereby "place the northern Democracy in the wrong, where it can be reproached and insulted, taunted and despised." If that happened, a Democrat in Stevens's own state warned, "we may soon add Pennsylvania to the domains of Northern fanaticism."[4]

Awareness of this peril spurred Stephen Douglas and like-minded northern Democrats to break openly with President Buchanan and reject the Lecompton constitution. Up for reelection to the Senate in 1858, Douglas also strove to reassure Illinoisans that they could keep the territories free regardless of the Supreme Court's ruling but without resorting to the federal ban that Republicans advocated. Ultimate power, he explained, still rested with a territory's electorate. Antislavery voters in any territory could make slavery impossible in practice simply by refusing to pass the kind of "affirmatory laws, and the necessary police regulations, patrol laws, and slave code" that slavery required.[5]

This doctrine, designed to placate northerners, made Douglas anathema in the South and to the Buchanan administration—proving yet again that no effective policy could satisfy both wings of the party. Over the next two years, pro-Douglas and pro-Buchanan forces warred upon each other, producing an informal but real split in the Democratic organization. One of the party's northern editors lamented that "upon no single issue is there adequate agreement for a common basis of action" within its party. In fact, he added, "there is no such entity as a Democratic party."[6]

This deep division among Democrats and the continuing disintegration of the American (Know Nothing) Party held out promise for Republicans. If they could win over disaffected pro-Douglas and/ or nativist voters, Republicans might well look forward to winning the White House in 1860. But opinions varied about how to do that. Should Republicans woo more conservative voters by compromising their antislavery principles, perhaps even warming to Stephen Douglas and popular sovereignty? Should they make greater concessions to nativism? Should they do both?

In the years between 1856 and 1860, Republicans including Charles Sumner, Joshua Giddings, William Seward, and Abraham Lincoln fought to keep or force anti-immigrant propositions out of their party's state and national platforms. Thaddeus Stevens did not join in that effort. In 1857, Pennsylvania's Republicans tried once again to work with some Know Nothings to create a fusion party, the "Union" party. They made this attempt rather halfheartedly, however; the fusion proved more formal than substantive. Republicans dominated the Union party's convention and, according to one of their delegates, strove there "to make the ticket as distinctively Republican as possible without slapping the Americans squarely in the face." The platform repeated the Republicans' 1856 demand that Congress bar slavery from the territories, and it nominated the free-soil leader David Wilmot for governor. The Union party gave some ground to nativism but not enough to satisfy that movement's hardcore supporters.[7]

When this ticket failed to win any more votes than Frémont had captured the year before, the state's Republicans changed course. In 1858 their candidates ran under the banner of a *new* fusion party, this one called the People's Party. It ditched 1857's demand to exclude slavery from all territories, replacing it with more circumspect language that criticized Buchanan's policy in Kansas without specifying what it would do there. To win conservative Whigs, it made additional concessions to nativist sentiment, promising to prevent the immigration of paupers, to strictly enforce existing naturalization procedures, and to crack down on voter fraud.[8]

In 1858, five years after leaving his seat in the House of Representatives, Thaddeus Stevens decided to seek reelection to it. He knew that he remained "ahead of the people in Anti-Slavery" in his district. He told Salmon P. Chase that, all across his own, southeastern part of the state, the people were "much less inclined to [R]epublicanism than in the North and West" and more committed to nativism. Aggravating Stevens's problem was the fact that the Republicans— while, unlike the Whigs, united by antipathy to slavery—had internal divisions of their own. In addition to abolition-minded radicals like Stevens, its ranks included a more conservative wing that now included the *Examiner and Herald*. With the Whigs' decline, that influential newspaper had drifted into the Republican Party, and in its editor's eyes Stevens remained a radical pariah.

Despite all these challenges, Stevens reckoned that a sharpening sectional conflict, the disarray of both the Know Nothings and the Democrats, and the shifting sentiments and loyalties of the northern public required and would enable him to gain office once again. That August he secured the Pennsylvania Union party's nomination for Congress from the state's Ninth Congressional District.[9]

In accepting that nomination and conducting his campaign, Stevens seems to have voiced no disagreement with the state party's overtures to nativists. But he refused to retreat on slavery. When other members of the state party cautiously lowered their voices on that subject, Stevens refused to follow suit. His acceptance speech stressed his moral revulsion toward slavery, specifically distancing himself from those "anti-Nebraska" politicians whose sole criticism of slavery was that it lowered the incomes of and undermined the respect due white workers. As a newspaper report noted, Stevens made clear that he hated slavery not only because it "was opposed to [the interests of] free white labor, but because slavery was *wrong*, oppressive, and barbaric." And although the Pennsylvania party had chosen that year to remain silent regarding its legality in the territories, Stevens once again broadcast his own views on that subject. True, he again acknowledged, Washington had no right simply to ban slavery within states. But Congress did enjoy "absolute control over the territories," and it should use that power "to keep it out of the territories forever." Critics had flayed him for such statements in the past, accusing him of being an abolitionist. Stevens now defied them. "If what he had just said made him an abolitionist," Stevens said, then "he was one."[10]

Stevens won handily in 1858. And all across his state, candidates atop the People's Party ticket soundly defeated their Democratic opponents, who were by now finding it difficult to turn out their long-time supporters. Eleven of the state's fifteen Democratic members of the U.S. House of Representatives went down to defeat. Across the country, Republicans gained a total of twenty-six seats in the House of Representatives and five in the Senate.[11] In the aftermath of Stevens's electoral success and perhaps emboldened by it, he doubled down on his democratic radicalism by publicly endorsing the right of women to vote and hold public office.[12]

A journalist described the Thaddeus Stevens who now returned to the House of Representatives: "He was sturdy, well built, with dark-blue and dull-looking eyes, overhanging brow, thin, stern lips, a smooth-shaven face." His oratorical style "was argumentative, sardonic, and grim." When speaking on the House floor, he rarely gestured theatrically with his arms as others often did; he simply clasped his hands before him. He kept his voice low but always audible, and his manner remained calm and deliberate, "dropping his sentences as though each one weighed a ton." He maintained that confident, unflappable mien even when he "launched his anathemas at his opponents," pronouncing those "as coolly as if he were bandying compliments." That combination of substantive aggressiveness and formal impassivity proved "particularly exasperating to his adversaries." An Ohio colleague, who did not much appreciate Stevens's manner, remembered it as being "bitter, quick as electricity, with a sarcastic, blasting wit."[13]

In mid-October 1859, New England–born abolitionist John Brown and a team of abolitionists launched an armed raid on the federal arsenal at Harpers Ferry, Virginia. In their ranks stood three of Brown's sons who had fought alongside him in the Kansas wars; three other Kansas veterans; five black men, two of whom were former slaves; and the white grandson of a slave owner. They planned to seize the arms stored at the arsenal, liberate nearby slaves, and then move farther south, raiding plantations and freeing additional slaves as they went. Those plans, however, speedily went awry. U.S. marines led by one Colonel Robert E. Lee shortly surrounded the raiders and riddled the building in which they had taken refuge, killing or mortally wounding several, including two of Brown's sons. Those survivors who did not manage to escape were captured. John Brown himself, severely wounded, was promptly jailed, tried, convicted, and sentenced to death by the state of Virginia.

While in jail, Brown was questioned by a group including Clement Vallandigham, a prominent doughface Democratic congressman from southern Ohio, and Senator James M. Mason of Virginia. After they failed to induce Brown to implicate additional northerners in his raid, Mason challenged Brown to justify his actions at Harpers Ferry. "Because you are guilty of a great wrong against God and humanity," the prisoner replied, it would "be perfectly right for anyone to interfere with you so far as to free those you willfully and wickedly hold in bondage." Brown had therefore done right, he held, and "others will do right who interfere with you at any time and at all times." Did Brown consider the raid a "religious" act? Yes, he responded; it was "the greatest service man can render to God." In taking up arms, Brown regarded himself as the instrument of Providence; to carry out Providence's dictates required violent methods in this case. Depending upon "moral suasion is hopeless," he judged. "I don't think the people of the slave States will ever consider the subject of slavery in its true light till some other argument is resorted to than moral suasion." And if his captors thought that his own execution would bring them peace, they should think again. "You may dispose of me very easily—I am nearly disposed of now," he said. "But this question is still [to] be settled, this negro question I mean; the end of that is not yet." So "you had better—all you people at the South—prepare yourselves for a settlement of this question."[14]

On November 2, Brown addressed the Virginia court that had just condemned him to death. His only crime, he said, was fighting for the rights of the downtrodden. Had he acted instead "in behalf of the rich, the powerful, the intelligent, the so-called great, or in behalf of any of their friends," those same deeds would have been judged "all right; and every man in this court would have deemed it an act worthy of reward rather than punishment." Instead he had tried to aid the "despised poor." Doing that, he believed, "was not wrong, but right."[15] One month later, on December 2, 1859, Virginia officials hanged John Brown. Six of his comrades in arms later followed him to the gallows.

The Harpers Ferry raid shook the country to its foundations politically. Democrats north and south blamed Republican condemnations of slavery for encouraging Brown's deeds. Republicans tried initially to put as much distance between themselves and Brown as possible. During the week that followed his execution, southerners in Congress accused Republicans of responsibility for the raid and once more threatened resistance up to and including disunion if their right to hold slaves were endangered. Thaddeus Stevens replied, as he had in 1850, that the South had been bullying weak-willed northerners this way for a long time—often enough, alas, with success. The published transcript of these exchanges on the House floor was evidently sanitized, but other contemporaneous accounts note that Stevens used coarse language to describe southern conduct. And according to Alexander McClure, Stevens also said that "John Brown deserved to be hung for being a hopeless fool," adding however that the man's foolishness lay in "attempt[ing] to capture Virginia with seventeen men." Surely, Stevens reportedly added, Brown should have realized "that it would require at least twenty-five."[16]

His words left his adversaries more than exasperated. Once again they physically threatened him on the House floor. Southern congressmen leapt from their seats, rushing angrily into the space around his desk. Mississippi congressman William Barksdale brandished a Bowie knife. No one regarded such threats as idle. Just a few years earlier a South Carolina congressman had used a walking stick to bludgeon Massachusetts's Charles Sumner into unconsciousness as he sat at his Senate desk. Stevens's colleagues were not about to tolerate a repeat performance. Republicans including the body builder and amateur boxer Roscoe Conkling of New York moved quickly to defend the Pennsylvanian. Amid this tumult, however, Stevens maintained his accustomed calm demeanor, and when order had been restored he dismissed the episode as "a mere momentary breeze," yet again confirming a colleague's appraisal that this was above all "a brave man." And within a week of John Brown's sentencing, Stevens was pressing for publication in booklet form of that man's powerful last letters, statements, and interviews. "I know nothing that would be more read," he said, "or do more good."[17]

When American voters went to the polls in November 1860, they participated in the most consequential presidential election in the country's history. It was a four-way contest. The Democratic Party had now formally split in two. Northern and southern Democrats fielded separate presidential tickets standing upon distinct political platforms. Conservative Whigs and Know Nothings, now rebranded as the Constitutional Union Party, put up a pro-compromise ticket.

In mid-May, the Republican national convention adopted a platform that rejected the legal foundation on which chattel slavery stood, denying that there existed an "unqualified property in persons."[18] The platform then declared that slavery was inherently illegal in any and all federal territories, demanded that the national government prevent its establishment there, and called upon Congress to admit Kansas as a free state. At the same time, it sought federal financing "for river and harbor improvements of a national character" and urged the national government "to render immediate and efficient aid" to the construction of a transcontinental railroad. "To encourage the development of the industrial interests of the whole country," the platform endorsed a protective tariff. Finally, the Republican Party demanded enactment of a bill to provide homesteads to small farmers and would-be farmers on federally owned land. The platform, in short, was a call to remove national political power from the hands of those pledged to the defense and extension of the slave-labor system and to transfer it instead to those determined to usher slavery toward extinction while actively aiding the growth and development of the North's type of diversified, free-labor capitalist economy.[19]

The 1860 Republican platform also took a strong stand in favor of immigrant rights. It included a plank opposing any laws, federal or state, "by which the rights of citizens hitherto accorded to immigrants from foreign lands shall be abridged or impaired." During the second half of the 1850s, the steadily increasing salience of the slavery issue induced a growing segment of the North's foreign-born population to transfer its loyalties from the Democratic to the Republican parties, a change especially apparent among recent immigrants from German-speaking parts of Europe. By 1860, the increased importance of this part of the Republican constituency had elevated a number of immigrant politicians into state-level party leadership. Their pressure, the hope of winning over still more such voters, and the dwindling political gravity of Know Nothingism all combined to induce the Republican national convention to adopt a forthrightly anti-nativist platform plank. Stevens, too, had by this time become aware that, in his words, "a large number of our foreign citizens are against Slavery."[20] That realization may explain why no evidence has surfaced that Stevens now opposed his party's anti-nativist stance.

The Republican convention made Abraham Lincoln its presidential candidate, and the Illinoisan seemed a shrewd choice. He had long and clearly condemned slavery on moral, economic, and political grounds. When supporters of the Wilmot Proviso attempted to bar slavery from lands taken from Mexico, Lincoln stood with them. In 1850, his fears for the Union led Lincoln to backtrack and applaud Clay's 1850 compromise measures. But the Kansas-Nebraska law four years later convinced him that slaveholders and their allies were determined to extend the slave-labor system and that to stop them antislavery citizens would have to take control of the federal government and put slavery itself "in the course of ultimate extinction."[21] That conviction led Lincoln into the leadership of Illinois's Republican organization, and in the years following the 1856 election he gained national attention. He consistently opposed retreat from the party's defining opposition to slavery's further expansion. He rejected the *Dred Scott* decision, questioned its finality, and denied that the U.S. Constitution recognized the right of property in human beings. He remained adamant about slavery's intrinsic evil and its threat to the Union, and he refused to be intimidated by southern threats of secession. "Let us have faith that right makes might," he told a New York City audience in 1860, "and in that faith, let us, to the end, dare to do our duty as we understand it."

But Lincoln also avoided the taint of radicalism. While advocating modification of the 1850 fugitive slave law to allow the accused the rights of due process, he declined to call for the law's outright repeal. And in his highly publicized debates with Stephen Douglas in 1858, he equivocated on the broader issue of white supremacy. In one speech he deplored "all this quibbling about this man and the other man—this race and that race and the other race being inferior, and therefore they must be placed in an inferior position." Black people should enjoy the "natural rights" to personal freedom and the fruits of their own labor. But he repeatedly denied the right of black people to be citizens, sit on juries, vote, or hold public office. And at one point, under pressure of Douglas's fierce race-baiting, Lincoln granted that the "physical difference between the white and black races . . . will for ever [*sic*] forbid the two races living together on terms of social and political quality." Instead "there must be the position of superior and inferior," with "the superior position assigned to the white race." Taken together, these positions made Lincoln an effective representative of the Republican Party's majority. [22]

Thaddeus Stevens delivered two major campaign speeches during the election year of 1860, one at its start and one toward its end. In late January he laid out before the House of Representatives what he took to be his party's core principles. Some boldness but also political caution shaped that presentation. "In my judgment," Stevens said, "Republicanism is founded in love of universal liberty, and in hostility to slavery and oppression throughout the world." Had his party "the legal right and the physical power" to do so, it would "abolish human servitude and overthrow despotism in every land" and certainly throughout the United States. But Republicans had neither the effective power to do the former nor the constitutional right to do the latter. In the United States, they could undertake only that portion of the larger project that the Constitution permitted. That document did give them the power, Stevens said, of "preventing the extension of slavery into free soil under the jurisdiction of the general government." That soil, he said, included the federal territories, navy yards, arsenals, and the District of Columbia. There, Stevens continued, Republicans "do claim the power to regulate and the right to abolish slavery." And in the federal territories, at least, they intended to exercise that power and that right. [23]

Notably, however, he did not call for abolishing slavery in the nation's capital district, a measure he had once endorsed. "The time has not yet arrived" for that, he now said, "nor do I see the period, for the present, when it will." Stevens offered no justification for that judgment, which differed not only from his own earlier stance but also from the position then being taken by other Republican radicals;

he merely noted that he stood on that subject with most of his party, which declined to call for abolition in the District of Columbia in its national election platform. Stevens displayed a similar circumspection in discussing the condition and fate of fugitive slaves. Unlike his national party and its presidential candidate, he did call once again for repeal of the 1850 Fugitive Slave Act. But he neither condemned all pursuit of fugitive slaves nor advocated publicly the obstruction of such pursuit. He professed, on the contrary, not to "object to a fair law, giving to the South the opportunity and the means of reclaiming their slaves." For that purpose, however, he declared the 1793 statute to be "sufficient." If he considered that law deficient, too—for failing to guarantee to alleged fugitives the right to testify in their own defense before being sentenced to captivity—he did not say so that day. In his cautious treatment of both of these subjects, Stevens may have been guided by a rather uncharacteristic concern not to have his party march too far ahead of the voters. Such concern likely explains his seeking the Republican Party's presidential nomination for the Supreme Court associate justice John McLean, a nonradical (but who had dissented from the verdict in *Dred Scott*).[24]

Stevens delivered his other major campaign oration of the year some nine months later, in late September, at a Republican mass meeting in New York City's Cooper Institute. Perhaps sensing by then that victory at the polls was imminent, he displayed on that occasion more of the candor and boldness for which he was famous. The coming electoral contest, he told his audience, was only the latest phase "in the long and persistent war between Liberty and Slavery; between Oppression and Freedom; a war which has existed, active or latent, ever since the first tyrant usurped the rights of others." And he laid into his opponents with gusto. Although he hoped to win over the "honest men" among supporters of the Whiggish new Constitutional Union Party, he poured scorn upon its "mercenary leaders" and those of its merchant members who "tremble when

Slavery frowns," who lived in fear of losing slaveholding customers, who therefore "smote the ground nine times with their foreheads in token of submission" to the South. And "if they have not eat[en] sufficient dirt," he predicted, just "let the required quantity be prescribed, and you may be sure they will forthwith set about it." To be sure, Stevens considered the northern Democratic Party much worse. In making that case, moreover, he expressed a far more open contempt for the pursuers of escaped slaves than he had earlier that same year. He quoted one northern Democrat's declaration that Republican officeholders would not enforce the fugitive slave law but that Democrats would certainly do so. "This I believe is true," Stevens said. "When a man who has been robbed of his liberty breaks the bonds of his oppressor, regains his natural rights, and is about to escape to a land of freedom, in the South you see bloodhounds" in hot pursuit, but "in the North[,] Democrats." He then wondered aloud which kind of slave-catcher was "the most respectable—the biped or the quadruped—the man or the dog?"[25]

The electorate's verdict in November 1860 was historic. The free states gave much stronger support to Stevens's party than they had in 1856. Where Republican presidential candidate John C. Frémont had received 45 percent of all ballots cast in the North, Abraham Lincoln now received fully 54 percent. What explained that dramatic surge in just four years? Undoubtedly it was the growing public conviction in the free states that slavery's indefinite survival, much less its further spread, constituted a mortal threat to the republic.

Republican strength proved greatest in New England and the upper Midwest, just as it had four years earlier. Stevens's native Vermont gave Republicans more than three-quarters of its popular votes.[26] But across the North, Lincoln also attracted many who had previously supported Know Nothing candidates, and this despite the Republican Party's explicit renunciation of nativism in its national platform. Slavery had by now shoved immigration off center stage, and compromise policies had lost much of their allure. So it was that the Constitutional Union Party, attempting to attract Millard Fillmore's 1856 constituency, in fact received just 13 percent of the popular vote nationally compared with Fillmore's 22 percent. Republicans won key northern states that they had lost in 1856. In both Illinois and Indiana, the Republicans' vote share rose from 40 percent to 51 percent. Even in New Jersey, whose electoral votes Lincoln split with Stephen A. Douglas, the Republican popular vote increased greatly, from below a third to nearly half. This pattern held good in Pennsylvania, too. Largely because of Know Nothing voters defecting to Lincoln, the Republicans' share of the vote there soared from 32 percent in 1856 to 56 percent in 1860. Alexander McClure reported at the time that although the state's Know Nothings "feel humiliated" by the national Republican platform's defense of immigrant rights "because it strikes directly at them," they had nonetheless "reluctantly swallowed the pill."[27]

Because Lincoln received almost no votes in any slave state, his free-state mandate translated into only 40 percent of the popular vote nationwide. In the four-way contest of that year, that constituted a national plurality but not, of course, a majority. The Electoral College, however, transformed that plurality *into* a majority. The next president of the United States would be a Republican.

Lincoln's triumph signified no routine alternation in office of parties and candidates espousing somewhat contrasting views and policies. It began instead a political revolution, initiating the transfer of the national government from the hands of slavery's defenders and collaborators into those of slavery's committed enemies. The southern elite understood that all too well. On the morrow of Lincoln's election, the *Richmond Examiner* sounded the alarm: "a party founded on the single sentiment . . . of hatred of African slavery, is now the controlling power" in Washington. That party's platform aimed to achieve the fundamental transformation of their section's economic foundation, even if gradually and peacefully. And in the planter leadership's eyes, the Republican threat to slavery's future posed not merely economic ruin but the end of their social, cultural, and political world. They agreed with a Natchez, Mississippi, lawyer, judge, and politician that slavery was the foundation on which all else rested, that slavery was "so incorporated into the existence of the slave holding States as social communities" that its extinction must mean also "the destruction of their social existence as Communities." They could only nod their heads when reading in the influential *Southern Literary Messenger* that for the South to surrender slavery would mean "destroying its civilization and progress, its safety and happiness, its very existence." A party that sought slavery's death was therefore (as a Tennessee newspaper accurately perceived) nothing less than "a revolutionary party." It was, an editor in Augusta, Georgia, wrote, "avowedly hostile to the rights, the honor, the interests, the peace, the safety, the tranquillity" of the southern section of the country. With such a party controlling the government's executive branch, a Richmond editor specified, federal power would now "be directed in hostility to the *property* of that section."[28]

As so often in the past, it was the planters of South Carolina who led the slaveholders' response. In early November 1860, its legislature branded Lincoln's election as "a hostile act" against the South and announced its intention to withdraw from the Union. On December 20, a special convention declared secession and made clear that its purpose was to protect the right to hold slaves.[29] By the end of the year, South Carolina's armed forces had occupied all federal property in Charleston and its harbor except Fort Sumter, and that fort was encircled and isolated. Then, in the early weeks of 1861, the remaining states of the lower South's cotton kingdom—Mississippi, Florida, Alabama, Georgia, Louisiana, and Texas—followed South Carolina out of the Union.

When it convened in December 1860, the lame-duck second session of the U.S. House of Representatives contained thirty-two members from the lower South. As the new year began, Stevens and the rest of the House watched as such men rose from their seats, delivered lengthy speeches of resignation, and stalked out of the chamber. On February 4, southern delegates met in Montgomery, Alabama, to found the Confederate States of America. As they had already done in South Carolina, bands of armed men in rebellious states seized United States property, including vessels, forts, weapons, post offices, customs houses, hospitals, a navy yard, and a mint. Throughout the lower South, as a result, the United States soon retained only a small handful of military installations in southern and western Florida and Charleston Harbor.[30]

Abraham Lincoln would not take office until early March 1861. Until then, James Buchanan would remain in the White House, and to him would fall responsibility for coping with the Union's breakup. Torn between his love of the Union and his ties to the slaveholding South (personified by a cabinet full of pro-slavery champions like Virginia's Henry A. Wise and Georgia's Howell Cobb), he dithered. As secessionists seized the nation's property in the South, he failed to respond. Delivering his last State of the Union address on December 3, 1860, Buchanan blamed the national crisis squarely on the North—and not merely upon northern Republicans but upon "the Northern people" as a whole. It was their "long-continued and intemperate interference . . . with the question of slavery," he insisted, that had brought the nation to the precipice. Their interference "has at length produced its natural effects." Exercising "malign influence on the slaves," the North had dangerously "inspired them with vague notions of freedom." As a result, "a sense of security no longer exists around the family altar" in the South. "This feeling of peace at home has given place to apprehensions of servile insurrections." Was it any wonder, Buchanan asked, that the slave states felt driven to take strong measures in self-defense?[31]

And yet, Buchanan acknowledged, there was no constitutional right of secession. Claiming that one existed was "wholly inconsistent with the history as well as the character of the Federal Constitution." Did that mean, then, that the federal government had a right to put down an armed rebellion against its legal authority? Well, no, the president continued. Like secession, "the power to make war against a State" was also "at variance with the whole spirit and intent of the Constitution." In short, the states had no right to secede, and the federal government had no right to prevent them from seceding.

Buchanan did take one feeble step on behalf of keeping the country intact. On January 5, he dispatched a single civilian merchant ship to bring supplies and reinforcements to besieged Fort Sumter. But as the *Star of the West* approached its destination four days later, South Carolina guns fired upon it. The unarmed vessel abandoned its mission and returned to its home port of New York City.

Here, surely, was a flagrant act of violent rebellion against the legally constituted national government. President Buchanan could have responded militarily. All over the North, voices called upon him to do so. But the president remained inert. As Stevens subsequently reminded the House, even though "our flag was insulted, and the unarmed vessel driven off, no effort has been made to avenge the insult." Buchanan's was a "tame, spiritless Administration," he spat. Privately, Stevens expressed his disgust in harsher terms. The president, he told his colleague Edward McPherson, "is a very traitor." Rumors circulated that the Pennsylvanian was planning Buchanan's impeachment.[32]

Stevens dismissed the president's attempt to blame the North for the national crisis. Coming from "a man who, during his whole political life, has been the slave of slavery," he said on January 29, that attempt was "not worth a moment's consideration." The North had not abrogated the rights of the South. Nor were such alleged abuses the real reason why slaveholders were now pulling the Union apart. Their real grievance was simply that "the North has taken from them the power of the Government, which they have held so long." But, he noted, the North had done that "according to the strictest forms and principles of the Constitution." Voters had merely done what they had every right to do; they had "elected the man of their choice President of the United States." In doing that, "no violence was used; no malpractice is charged; but the American people dared to disobey the commands of slavery; and this is proclaimed as just cause of secession and civil war." The sitting president's "impotent conclusion"—that the government was powerless to defend itself against what even Buchanan called an illegitimate and mortal attack—was simply absurd. Stevens demonstrated in detail and at some length that the Constitution did indeed empower the government "to defend and perpetuate the Union." Article II, section 3, he pointed out, "provides that the President shall take care that all the laws shall be faithfully executed," and "to enable him to do it," the Constitution "makes him commander-in-chief of the Army and Navy. To leave nothing in doubt, it gives Congress power to make all laws which shall be necessary and proper for carrying into execution all powers vested by this Constitution in the Government of the United States." In the face of those clear provisions, Stevens concluded, "it seems strange to hear that a great wrong may be committed against the Constitution, and no power exist to prevent or punish it. Posterity will wonder whether the statesmen of this age were fools or traitors." During his speech, scores of congressmen from the upper South, still in the Union, advanced upon Stevens again, cursing and threatening him. Yet again his allies rushed to protect him, forming what in infantry terms would be called a "square" defense, surrounding him with a four-sided human shield.[33]

As secession began and Abraham Lincoln prepared to replace

Buchanan in the White House, pressure once more mounted on Republicans to back away from their antislavery program, to save the Union by appeasing the South. As in the crisis of 1850, merchants in the nation's great commercial cities demanded such a retreat loudly and insistently. Safeguarding their commerce with the South trumped their abstract values. Politicians advanced various schemes for restoring peace between North and South. One proposal called for amending the U.S. Constitution to forbid any future amendments seeking to "abolish, or interfere" with slavery in the states. The Senate adopted just such an anti-amendments amendment with the necessary two-thirds vote. The House of Representatives also approved it, with a lopsided majority of 133 to 65. Many Republicans felt free to support such a measure on the grounds that their party had always forsworn direct federal interference with slavery in the states. In the same spirit, Lincoln later announced that he had "no objection" to this guarantee "being made express, and irrevocable." Forwarded to the states for ratification at the beginning of March, this proposed Thirteenth Amendment died only with the outbreak of war. Among the minority of congressmen who had steadfastly opposed this abortive amendment from the start, recalled Maine Republican James G. Blaine, "Thaddeus Stevens was at their head."[34]

Another proposed compromise went considerably further, explicitly permitting slavery to expand into some parts of the federal territories, thus rejecting the Republican Party's platform. Senator John J. Crittenden of Kentucky advanced the most popular of these proposals in the form of a series of constitutional amendments. At his plan's heart was the westward extension of the old Missouri Compromise line (at 36°30' latitude), outlawing slavery above that line while legalizing and permanently protecting it below it in all federal territories "now held" as well as in those that might be "hereafter acquired." That last phrase reflected enduring southern hopes of annexing additional land from Mexico, Central America, or the

Caribbean in which slavery could be legalized. (If any doubt existed about that intention, it disappeared when southern congressmen adamantly refused to delete the phrase from Crittenden's proposal.) Finally, all of Crittenden's proposed amendments were to be permanently in force, immune to repeal, once ratified.[35]

Most Republicans in Congress announced their refusal to back down. But there were exceptions, including Representative James T. Hale and Senator Simon Cameron; both of those Pennsylvanians expressed support for Crittenden's proposal. Lincoln was pressing his party's congressmen to concede nothing in the party's program, but his inner circle—especially his secretary of state designate, Senator William Seward—sent mixed signals. Seward had for some years been retreating from his radical reputation, and on January 12, he delivered a speech extolling the value of the Union, denying the constitutionality of secession, but also quailing at resisting secession by force. He did "not know," he confessed, "what the Union would be worth if saved by the use of the sword." To avoid having to face that question, Seward declared himself ready "to meet prejudice with conciliation, exaction with concession which surrenders no principle, and violence with the right hand of peace." Attending a large dinner party thrown by Stephen Douglas, he proposed a toast that prized national unity above and at the expense of all else: "Away with all parties, all platforms, all previous committals," he urged; away with "whatever else will stand in the way of restoration of the American Union." Republican senator John Sherman of Ohio suggested evading the question of Congress's power in territories by dividing existing territories into states that would decide slavery's status for themselves. Seward liked that general idea. He and Massachusetts Republican congressman Charles Francis Adams proposed that the New Mexico territory be promptly admitted into the Union as a slave state. On January 12, Lincoln signaled privately to Seward that he would not oppose such a step.[36]

On the House floor at the end of January, Thaddeus Stevens deplored the looming "dissolution of the Union" and declared himself ready, in order "to avert this catastrophe," to "go to the verge of principle"—but not beyond that verge. He had already declared himself against admitting any further slave states into the Union. More generally, he ranged himself firmly against any further concessions to slavery's expansion. He would not ask the northern people to submit to "humiliation, concessions, and compromises" in order "to appease the insurgents." He would not retreat from the ideals that had dictated the platform upon which Abraham Lincoln had been elected. "Rather than show repentance for the election of Mr. Lincoln, with all its consequences, I would see this Government crumble into a thousand atoms," he vowed. "If I cannot be a freeman, let me cease to exist."[37]

But Stevens was concerned about his colleagues. Although "on the record" most seemed to be standing firm, some sounded less resolute in private. "We have too many weak knees," he told Salmon P. Chase. And William Seward's public stance "has mortified and discouraged me" by seeming "to indicate that our platform and principles are to be sacrificed" in the name of "peace." Both Pennsylvania senators, Republican Simon Cameron and Democrat William Bigler, had publicly uttered pro-compromise sentiments. But neither man, Stevens assured Congress, "represented the principles of any considerable portion of the people of that State." Indeed, he considered it "a libel on the good name of her virtuous people to say that she would sacrifice her principles to obtain the favor of rebels," that they would "purchase peace by unprincipled concessions" to "insurgents with arms in their hands." If he thought otherwise, Stevens swore, he would leave that state for "some spot untainted by the coward breath of servility and meanness."[38]

*   *   *

There were good reasons to believe that most Pennsylvanians shared Stevens's rejection of retreat. In Harrisburg, Republican state legislators insisted that nothing "in our political condition demands concessions on our part"; nothing required abandoning the party's platform. Observers reported strong support for that stance across the state. Congratulatory messages reached Stevens from New England as well. Connecticut Presbyterian minister David Root assured Stevens that "the feeling of the great mass of Republicans, in all this region is intense, that there be no more concessions, no more compromises by our Representatives in Congress." Rev. Root wanted Republicans in Washington to stand by their party program "to the bitter end," and "if civil war comes, let it come." He congratulated Stevens for his readiness to "so decidedly & firmly discard, denounce & repudiate the idea of compromise," urging him to "do what you can to strengthen others who may be faltering." Across the North, Republican Party supporters conveyed the same message to their representatives and senators. The party's stalwarts and its rank and file pulled waverers back into line. The Crittenden plan failed to win congressional approval.[39]

What should be done now to stop disunion? Stevens did not immediately counsel resort to arms. The federal government, he told the House on January 29, should first employ other, nonlethal methods to force the seceding states back into their proper place in the Union. It should cut off mail service to the rebellious states, and it should continue from offshore to collect tariffs at Charleston Harbor and pocket the revenue. If this should prove impossible, the national government could use its navy to "prevent all vessels, foreign or domestic, from entering or leaving any of their ports."[40]

One way or another, however, this slaveholder attempt to dismantle the republic must be fought. "Those who counsel the Government to let them go, and destroy the national Union, are preaching moral treason," said Stevens. And if any rebels seriously believed that they could wield secession as a weapon with which to frighten the North into remodeling of the Union to suit slavery, they were deluding themselves. They could not "dissolve the Union now, and then reconstruct it on better terms" later. On the contrary, he warned them, after the lower South's secession the Union would surely become more, not less, antagonistic to slavery. The free states would see to that. "The present Constitution was formed in our [the North's] weakness. Some of its compromises were odious, and have become more so by the unexpected increase of slaves," whose numbers "were expected soon to run out" when the Constitution was written. But since then the strength and moral conscience of the North had increased. So if the current rebellion should eventually lead to some kind of redesign of the Union, no such pro-slavery concessions would be made this time. "If this Union should be dissolved, . . . if it should be torn to pieces by rebels, our next United States will contain no foot of ground on which a slave can tread, no breath of air which a slave can breathe." In such a union citizens would finally be able honestly to "boast of liberty," to "rise and expand to the full stature of untrammeled freemen." And any slave state that then stood outside such a union would speedily find itself in serious peril. Any of their slaves who managed to escape from bondage would find in a reconstituted United States a place of secure refuge. And with an antislavery United States to their north and other antislavery nations and Caribbean colonies to their south, those slave states "will be surrounded by freedom, with the civilized world scowling upon them." They would be in greater danger, in short, than they already were within the Union.

Stevens's warning that secession would tilt the Union further against slavery and accelerate slavery's extinction throughout North America anticipated important aspects of future developments. But in early 1861, Stevens was still focused on resisting the slaveowner attempt to break up the Union. That attempt must be resisted firmly.

Although the government should not draw the sword prematurely, he said, neither must it shrink from doing so if events finally required it. "Let there be no blood shed, until the last moment," but in the meantime "let no cowardly counsels unnerve the people." For if "at last" war proved unavoidable, let everyone be "ready to gird on his armor, and do his duty."[41]

CHAPTER SIX

Stevens's Civil War, Part I

For Victory Through Emancipation

Thaddeus Stevens was no longer a young man when the Civil War broke out; he had just turned sixty-nine years old. "To most men there comes, sooner or later, a period of inaction, inability for further progress," a fellow Republican congressman later observed. "This is the period of conservatism, and usually comes with gray hairs and failing eye-sight. It converses with the past and distrusts the future. Its look is backward and not forward." But, continued Representative Horace Maynard, "this period Mr. Stevens never reached." "The slaveholders' rebellion seemed to rejuvenate him and inspire him with superhuman strength."[1]

Indeed, the Civil War and its aftermath posed challenges that elicited Stevens's most consequential efforts. Appraising that conflict as a second American revolution, Stevens responded with great intellectual flexibility, repeatedly recalibrating his thinking about major issues, reevaluating old assumptions, and pressing new initiatives in the face of changing circumstances. He proved unusually able to grasp the nature of a given historical moment, to perceive that moment's implicit logic, to follow that logic to its conclusions, and to fight with all the considerable energy and skill at his command for the measures to which those conclusions pointed him, no matter how unprecedented or extreme they might appear. If in doing that Stevens sometimes felt the wind of history in his sails, he also worried that what he believed must be done would not be done, that the government and its leaders would fail to fulfill history's mandate. As a result, his words and deeds in the war and postwar years exhibited self-assurance and self-confidence but also impatience and frustration.

By the time, on March 4, 1861, that James Buchanan ceded the presidency and the national crisis to Abraham Lincoln, the seven states of the lower South had declared themselves out of the nation. Lincoln delivered a conciliatory inaugural address, but the rebellious states had no intention of either returning to the Union or permitting the U.S. government to maintain military installations on their soil. They demanded that the federal garrison abandon Fort Sumter in Charleston Harbor. When the government and the fort's commander refused, rebel artillery opened up on April 12, soon forcing Sumter's surrender. In response, on April 15 the president called upon all states to supply troops to suppress the armed rebellion.

Lincoln's call triggered secession by Virginia, North Carolina, Tennessee, and Arkansas. But the president could hardly have done otherwise. Representative William S. Holman of Indiana understood that. Holman, a Democrat, was a dogged opponent of the new administration. But even he publicly acknowledged that had Lincoln surrendered Sumter without resistance, "the fiery wrath of the people, whose trust he would have betrayed, would have driven him with irresistible fury from your capital." And had Lincoln's government not militarily resisted the country's armed dismemberment, "the storm of public indignation, irresistible as a sand storm on the Lybian desert, would have swept it away."[2]

Determined as Lincoln was to suppress the slaveholder rebellion, however, he did not at first seek to use the war to emancipate those in bondage. The military effort he oversaw aimed initially only to defend the Union, and Lincoln hoped that early battlefield successes would help keep that conflict brief and limited. Then, once Union forces had triumphed and reunited the country, Republicans could resume their prewar legislative campaign to place slavery on the road to "ultimate extinction" (in Lincoln's words) by surrounding it with free states and territories.[3]

Abolitionists and radical Republicans like Frederick Douglass and Thaddeus Stevens advanced a different diagnosis, prognosis, and prescription. Stevens early doubted, for one thing, that military triumph would come quickly or easily. He predicted instead that defeating so determined and able an enemy would require "a protracted and bloody war."[4] And success would come only by augmenting the military struggle with a frontal attack against slavery, the mainstay of southern society and its war effort. In Stevens's eyes, the two struggles were inseparable; the first could not be won without waging the second. He was among the first to champion the confiscation of slaves of Confederate partisans, to demand full legal freedom for those confiscated, to call for widening the scope of emancipation to embrace *all* slaves within the rebellious states, and then to press for the abolition of slavery throughout the United States as a whole.

As Stevens came to recognize, these measures would mean a radical transformation of southern society. Rather than retreat from those measures on that account, he ardently embraced them and explicitly championed the revolution that they constituted. It was obvious, he argued in the spring of 1863, "that ordinary means cannot quell this rebellion. Not even a succession of brilliant victories will end the war and prevent its recurrence. According to my poor judgment, the government must steel itself with sterner resolves, and prepare, if need be, for a revolution."[5]

The revolution that Stevens came to favor would center and exert its greatest influence in the southern states. At the start of 1861, four million human beings—one out of every three people in the South—were enslaved. During the years that followed, those millions would emerge from bondage into legal freedom. Their liberation would strip the South's ruling families of the principal source of their wealth. This second American revolution would also reshape national politics. It would deprive the southern elite of the control it had so long exercised over the federal government, transferring that control to the representatives of commercial, financial, and manufacturing interests based in the North.

But the fact that the Union war effort eventually yielded revolutionary consequences did not mean that the Republican Party as a whole consciously set out to *make* a revolution in 1861. This revolution, like many others, occurred because a conflict initially defined in more limited terms escalated in both methods and stakes.

With Lincoln's election, the Republican Party originally intended to begin reforming the Union by imposing measures at the federal level that would eventually induce southern states to recognize that slavery was doomed and therefore to abolish it within their own borders. Lincoln thought the process might take many decades. The slaveholders responded to that reform project with armed rebellion. That rebellion, and the war it spawned, changed not only the means with which the conflict was waged but its very significance, forcing open the door not to slavery's very gradual, eventual disappearance but to its uncompensated destruction within just a few years.

Still, wartime Republicans dismantled slavery only piecemeal—not promptly and thoroughly but through a succession of measures adopted over the course of almost two years. That process reflected changing Republican perceptions of the rebellion's extent, depth, and strength—of how long the war would last and what Union victory would necessitate. Stevens played a key role in leading both his party and the nation as a whole through those steps, highlighting the demands of an evolving situation, illuminating the necessary road forward, and prodding others to embark upon it.

Stevens became a pivotal figure in the wartime House of Representatives in early July 1861, when he assumed the chairmanship of its Ways and Means Committee. He had not been the Speaker of the House's first choice; two other men first declined that post in favor of other positions. But that committee wielded considerable legislative power, and the chairmanship made Stevens the top Republican floor leader in the House, equivalent to a modern majority leader. In that role, the Pennsylvanian would prove stern and severe in bringing laggards into line. A fellow congressman recalled sitting and talking in the House with Stevens on a morning when a bill to enfranchise black men in the nation's capital district was to come up for a vote. Another Pennsylvania Republican approached to ask Stevens to dilute the bill's strength. Stevens stared at the man "and with language much more emphatic than polite bade him go to his seat and vote for the bill or take the consequences of voting against it." The chastened congressman fell silent, retreated, and did as he was told.[6]

But Stevens was often too far in advance of his party simply to compel recalcitrant colleagues to do as he wished. In those cases, he and other radicals pointed the way forward for their fellow Republicans with the legislative initiatives that they introduced and the arguments made on their behalf. When those initiatives came under attack from northern Democrats, border-state unionists, and more conservative-minded members of the Republican Party, Stevens was often the quickest to respond. He thereby not only gave direction to less experienced and less perspicacious allies; he also raised spirits when theirs flagged. As a chronicle of the wartime Congress would later put it, "The timid became bold and the resolute made stronger in seeing the bravery with which he maintained his principles."[7]

Finally, Stevens exercised leadership not only within the Congress but in the country at large. Newspapers regularly published his speeches, many of which were also issued as pamphlets. In these ways and others, Stevens informed and influenced the Republican Party's rank and file. An Ohio "plain farmer" told Stevens that "your labors" were "duly appreciated" by his neighbors. An Iowa correspondent reported that Stevens's words and actions in behalf of "universal freedom" were popular in the "North West" and that mention of his name commonly elicited applause. A resident of Dublin, Indiana, congratulated Stevens on a House speech and asked for "a hundred or two [copies] to distribute in Indiana and Illinois." "I know of nothing," the Hoosier added, "which would contribute so much" to influencing public opinion. And winning over the public increased Stevens's influence in Congress. "Some of the papers call me 'the leader of the House,' Stevens told a journalist late in life. "I lead them, yes; but they never follow me or do as I want them until public opinion has sided with me."[8]

After adjourning in March 1861, Congress was not scheduled to meet again until December. But after Fort Sumter's fall, Lincoln called upon the Senate and House to reconvene in emergency session on July 4. When they did so, it became clear that the 1860 election and then the resignation of the rebellious states' delegates had placed both chambers in the hands of Republicans, giving them about a 60–40 majority in each. Thus empowered, Republican legislators began crafting laws to fit the Union for war. Armies had to be raised, officered, armed and equipped, trained, fed, sheltered, and transported. Warships had to be built, outfitted, and manned. Funds had to be found and appropriated for all those purposes. Within a few years, the Republican Congress would also pass a series of laws that gave to commercial and industrial development the kind of boost that advocates like Stevens had sought but which southerners and their northern allies had blocked for decades. These measures included support for construction of transportation facilities, banking, a national currency, land grant colleges, and tariffs. For northern farmers, it enacted a homestead law. Stevens and his Ways and Means Committee were at the center of much of that work.[9]

Another kind of war legislation, known as Confiscation Acts, would allow U.S. armies and navies penetrating the Confederacy to seize enemy property and slaves used in support of the rebellion. Many Republicans had warned the South before the war that secession would bring on slavery's swift destruction. Slaveholders who rebelled against the lawful national government would thereby pull themselves out from under the Constitution's protection. The federal government would then be free to strip those rebels of their slaves—if the slaves did not rise up and liberate themselves first. Republican Carl Schurz enunciated such a vision clearly in an August 1860 speech. Schurz was endeavoring to demonstrate that secession would be suicidal and that therefore threats to secede were hollow. Should "a Northern antislavery army" ever enter the South, he said, "the slaves [will] disappear" from the plantations—"and slavery with them." Any real attempt to withdraw from the Union, consequently, "would defeat the very objects for which it might be undertaken." Because the slaveholders knew that was true, Schurz assured his antislavery audience, "they cannot attempt it. . . . Slavery, which makes it uncomfortable [for them] to stay in the Union, makes it impossible for them to go out of it." Many other Republicans said similar things with similar purpose—to frighten southern whites away from secession while reassuring nervous Union partisans that secession would never occur.[10]

But threatening slavery's destruction in case of secession was one thing; carrying out such threats was another. When war erupted, most Republicans proved unready to initiate a sweeping emancipation. Recalling Schurz's words years later, the Republican radical Henry Wilson observed that although "the Republican presses and speakers everywhere" had "proclaimed like sentiments," most of them had in fact only "feebly comprehended the full significance" of the situation in which they found themselves, nor had they fully foreseen what consequences it would produce. Illinois Republican Isaac N. Arnold recalled more specifically "how reluctantly members [of Congress] touched slavery."[11]

The new president, too, hesitated to make good on prewar threats of slave confiscation. At least three practical considerations seemed to counsel that restraint. Lincoln knew that even in the country's free states, nearly half the 1860 electorate had voted not for him but for one of his three more conservative opponents. He would need the active support of as many of those non-Republican northerners as possible in order to win this war. Lincoln believed he could obtain and hold that support only if the Union war effort avoided any imputation of abolitionism.[12]

Second, the same kind of problem plagued the Union cause in the four slave states that remained in the Union after Sumter—Delaware, Maryland, Kentucky, and Missouri. Retaining those states, Lincoln thought, was crucial militarily. But there, he believed, a boldly antislavery war policy would cost him essential allies—would, in his own words, "alarm our Southern Union[ist] friends, and turn them against us."[13]

Third, many Republicans assumed or at least hoped that even in the Confederacy most whites, including many large slaveowners, were basically loyal to the United States. Even after a year of war, in fact, the Republican *New York Times* was still arguing that "the rebellion is not immediately the work of the Southern slaveholding class, nor of the masses of the Southern people. It is due to the intrigues, falsehoods and bad ambition of a class of political leaders, who precipitated a reluctant community into insurrection." If the

Union could wage war without excessively offending the Union's potential constituency inside the Confederacy, Lincoln and many others initially held, that "reluctant community" of loyal southern whites might yet reassert itself and pull their states back into the United States.[14]

These potent hopes, concerns, and cautions militated against an immediate full-scale assault upon slavery. For the Republican Party to overcome those hesitations, its leaders and members would need the practical experience that would make plainer what Frederick Douglass called the "logic of events," a logic that would reveal the necessity of wielding emancipation as a weapon. As Stevens's fellow congressman Albert Gallatin Riddle, of Ohio, said, "The war was to teach and enforce its own lesson in its own grim way." Changing Republican policy on slavery would also require the bold and persistent explication of the war's lessons by abolitionists and radical Republicans like Thaddeus Stevens.[15]

Carl Schurz himself later acknowledged the pragmatic, step-by-step manner in which Union policy had eventually evolved. "We went into the war for the purpose of maintaining the Union, and preserving our nationality." Even though all knew that "it was the slave-power which had attempted to break up the Union," the Union government did not at first plan to assault slavery. But "gradually, it became clear to every candid mind that slavery, untouched, constituted the strength of the rebellion; but that slavery, touched, would constitute its weakness."[16]

Slaves helped teach this lesson to the Union with their own bold actions, forcing themselves upon Union armies and providing them with many forms of invaluable assistance. In late May 1861, three slaves on the Virginia Peninsula evaded their owner and made their way to nearby Fort Monroe. That fort was one of the few installations that U.S. forces still occupied in a rebel state. The fort's garrison took in the fugitives. When a Confederate officer demanded that the fort's commander, General Benjamin Butler, return those fugitives, Butler refused. Instead he directed the fugitives to work under the supervision of his quartermaster. No abolitionist nor even a Republican, Butler simply thought it self-defeating to surrender such slave laborers to those already in arms against the U.S. government. A nation at war could rightfully seize the property of its enemies, he believed, especially property that those enemies employed against the nation itself. When Butler informed Washington of what he had done, U.S. General-in-Chief Winfield Scott and Secretary of War Simon Cameron gave their approval. Nearly a thousand more refugees before long entered Fort Monroe, and that figure doubled by the end of 1862. Thaddeus Stevens, his radical Republican colleagues, and abolitionists pressed the Union to see and understand what was unfolding before its eyes. The only way to defeat this stubborn rebellion, they argued, was to free the Confederacy's slaves.[17]

Benjamin Butler's ad hoc decision in May 1861 to give sanctuary to runaway slaves at Fort Monroe and the Union government's approval of that decision were important first steps toward a new policy. Another came five months later when the War Department authorized all army commanders to make use of fugitives who offered their services to Union armies. But that, too, fell far short of a general proclamation of freedom. Even as it took this limited step, "which insurrection makes unavoidable," the War Department stressed that it would otherwise avoid "all interference with the social systems or local institutions of every State." So it was that, in the same month, Union general Thomas W. Sherman assured South Carolinians that his army had "no desire to . . . interfere with any of your lawful rights or your social or local institutions" other than what the war made "unavoidable."

General John A. Dix made a less qualified promise to Virginians in November. His troops would "invade no rights of person or property. On the contrary, your laws, your institutions, your usages, will be scrupulously respected." To burnish his conservative credentials, Dix added that "special directions have been given not to interfere with the condition of any person held to domestic service," and he had ordered his subordinates "not to permit any such persons to come within their lines." The point of the order was that if slaves could not even enter Union lines, they could not be given sanctuary there.

In Confederate Tennessee, Union commander Don Carlos Buell recounted proudly in March 1862 that "several applications have been made to me by persons whose servants have been found in our camp" and that "in every instance that I know of the master has recovered his servant and taken him away." In both Tennessee and Louisiana, Union officers who refused to follow Buell's example were placed under arrest.[18]

Most congressional Republicans considered such protection of slaveholding intolerable. Illinois Republican Owen Lovejoy asked the House on July 9, 1861, to state its opinion that "it is no part of the duty of the soldiers of the United States to capture and return fugitive slaves." Thaddeus Stevens joined the large House majority that approved Lovejoy's motion. House members representing slaveowners who professed loyalty to the Union strove to shield the slave-labor system from the impact of the U.S. war effort. In July, Kentucky representative John J. Crittenden and Tennessee senator Andrew Johnson introduced a resolution into both houses of Congress. It promised that the Union was fighting solely "to defend and maintain the supremacy of the Constitution and to preserve the Union with all the dignity, equality, and rights of the several States unimpaired" and not for the purpose "of overthrowing or interfering with the rights of established institutions of those States" in rebellion.[19]

As members of Lincoln's party recognized, that resolution's authors introduced it in hopes of either committing Republicans to a socio-politically conservative war policy or (if Republicans voted "no") compelling them to confess openly to having an abolitionist agenda. In the event, few congressional Republicans voiced objection to the Crittenden-Johnson declaration. They were not waging war for the *purpose* of emancipating slaves but for the purpose of defending the integrity of the Union—although, they often added, emancipating some slaves might become a necessary *means* with which to accomplish that purpose.[20] During the last ten days of July, overwhelming majorities in both the Senate and the House passed the Crittenden-Johnson declaration. Only a handful of Republican radicals found such a pledge of non-abolitionist aims repugnant. To them, recalled George Julian of Indiana, that declaration seemed like an apology for the war effort and a repulsive groveling before slaveholders. With Julian and a handful of others, Thaddeus Stevens refused to vote for that resolution. Afterward, Republicans argued heatedly among themselves over the propriety of having voted yea or nay.[21]

Meanwhile, the Senate considered the first bill to authorize selective confiscation by Union armies of property used in support of the rebellion. Illinois Republican senator Lyman Trumbull brought the bill in from the Judiciary Committee, which he chaired. He also moved, as an individual, to add to the bill a provision that his committee had declined to endorse. His amendment would enable Union officers to seize not only property but also any enslaved person whose master put him to work "aiding or promoting any insurrection, or in resisting the laws of the United States" if that master had "permit[ted] or suffer[ed] him to be so employed." Trumbull proposed that such a master "forfeit his claim to such labor, and the person whose labor or service is thus claimed [i.e., the slave] shall be henceforth discharged therefrom."[22]

Formal debate on the bill and Trumbull's amendment began on July 22, 1861, one day after the Battle of Bull Run, which had ended in a full-scale rout of Union forces. Democratic senator James McDougall of California objected to confiscating slaves whose owners merely "suffered" their use by the Confederacy, since that would punish owners who had cooperated with the rebellion under duress. Trumbull immediately conceded the point and agreed to change the wording accordingly. The Senate then approved Trumbull's amendment by a vote of 33 to 6 and then adopted the bill as a whole.[23]

The Senate's easy passage of the amended bill reflected the recent growth among its Republican members of support for at least some slave confiscation. Just a few days earlier in the Judiciary Committee, Senator John C. Ten Eyck, a New Jersey Republican, had opposed including Trumbull's measure in the confiscation bill. But the United States' humiliation at Bull Run had since then helped to change minds like his by suggesting that initial Union hopes for a brief and easy war might well be too optimistic. Congressmen also learned that Confederates had made effective use of slave support labor in that battle and appeared likely to do so in the future, too. Senator Ten Eyck now executed an about-face, endorsing the confiscation policy that he had so recently rejected. His personal turnabout captured in microcosm the way that the war effort's requirements would lead the Republican Party step by step to escalate its attacks upon slavery. Military setbacks would militate in favor of employing additional weapons against the Confederacy. Military successes would push the Union in the same direction by plunging its armies deeper into the Confederacy and surrounding them with more slaves anxious to trade labor for freedom.[24]

The House of Representatives turned to the subject of confiscation on August 2, 1861. As it took up the Senate bill, Kentucky's John J. Crittenden protested that the Constitution forbade federal interference with slavery in the states. Kentucky Democrat Henry C. Burnett asked whether, under the terms of this bill, a slave confiscated would then be "entitle[d] to his freedom." When Republican John A. Bingham of Ohio replied in the affirmative, Burnett objected that the bill therefore amounted to "a wholesale emancipation of the slaves in the seceding or rebellious states." In response, Bingham assured him that the bill would affect only slaves directly serving the Confederate war effort.[25]

Some House Republicans balked at even such limited emancipation. Illinois's William Kellogg wanted to amend the bill so that a master's "claim to service" (that is, ownership) of slaves would not be "forfeited" but simply "confiscated" by the federal government. Kellogg seemingly hoped that his wording would remove any implication that confiscation amounted to a slave's true emancipation. New York Republican Alexander Diven wished to have confiscated slaves not freed but held and treated like Confederate soldiers taken as prisoners of war.[26]

When Stevens joined the debate, he objected sharply to Diven's suggestion. If confiscated slaves were classified as prisoners of war, they might later be sent back to their place of origin through a prisoner exchange deal. That such a person might thereby be returned to slavery repelled the Pennsylvanian. "God forbid that I should ever agree" that slaves once confiscated "should be restored again to their masters!" The seizure of any slaves by Union armies, Stevens insisted, must signify their full liberation. "One of the most glorious consequences of victory," he declared, would be "giving freedom to those who are oppressed." So "I, for one, shall never shrink from saying, when these slaves are once conquered by us, 'Go, and be free.'"[27]

But Stevens concentrated his fire that day upon Crittenden's claim that confiscation of slaves was unconstitutional. He had pointed out earlier, in his critique of Buchanan's last State of the Union message, that the Constitution did in fact require the president to "take Care that the Laws be faithfully executed." If confiscating slaves proved necessary to meet that obligation, it must be done. Moreover, he would argue subsequently, even his congressional opponents implicitly recognized the legitimacy of doing so, whether or not they acknowledged it. After all, he demanded of them, "whence do you derive the authority to kill the rebels? It is given by no express power in the Constitution." The only possible justification was that "you possess it as a means of the granted power to suppress insurrection," an extension of the president's constitutionally mandated duty to enforce the nation's laws. "When the Constitution is repudiated and set at defiance by an armed rebellion, too powerful to be quelled by peaceful means," he said, ". . . the Constitution itself grants to the President and Congress a supplemental power, which . . . must go on increasing and varying according to the increasing and varying necessities of the nation." In the present crisis, facing this specific threat, emancipation was the necessary and appropriate exercise of that power.[28]

Stevens added that, in fact, a right to confiscate slaves derived from a source superior to the Constitution. "Even if the Constitution were silent on this power," he held, but emancipation nonetheless "became inevitably necessary for the safety of the people, the first law of nature would" give the government that power. A law higher than the Constitution would permit—would, indeed, compel—the president to do whatever was necessary to assure the nation's survival. "*Salus populi*—the safety of the people—would become the supreme law—higher than all laws and all constitutions."[29] Seizing an enemy's property and slaves was necessary to suppress the planters' rebellion, and to Stevens that necessity made seizure legitimate.

He found support for that claim in a work titled *The Law of Nations*, a widely respected study by the eighteenth-century Swiss scholar Emer de Vattel that sought to explicate the nature of and logic underlying international law. Stevens invoked Vattel's assertion that "the entire nation is . . . obliged to perform the duty of self-preservation."[30] This obligation included seizing an enemy's property and its slaves during a war for national survival. In a fight for its very life, the United States was obliged to do whatever was necessary to triumph, and as it did so it must be guided not by the letter of the Constitution but by the demands of necessity.

Underlying this argument was a belief that an appropriate end dictates and justifies the means needed to achieve it. That claim was and is commonly vilified in the name of absolute moral standards of right and wrong that transcend time, place, and circumstance. But Stevens considered his own understanding of the relationship between ends and means to be irresistible and unassailable. Some worried that such reasoning and the precedents it justified could also rationalize tyranny. Stevens responded by directing attention back to the ends being sought in each case. That alone was the proper way to evaluate the legitimacy of the means being employed. Both the wartime Union government and the leaders of the rebellion claimed extraordinary, lethal powers. Must we honor both sets of claims? Of course not, Stevens replied. We uphold one claim and reject the other because of the very different ends that each actually served. In the Union's case, he said, extraordinary "power is granted for good," while in the Confederacy's case, such power is "seized for mischief." Those were the grounds on which to uphold the first and reject the second.[31]

Stevens was not here rejecting morality as a guide. But he held that whether an action was moral or immoral (good or mischievous) depended upon the end that it served, on the particular context in which the action occurred. In the context of a fight for national survival, the achievement of victory represented a higher good than any absolute right to life, much less the sanctity of private property. The government's seizure of slaves, necessary for the republic's preservation, became quite proper.[32] If loyal citizens were injured financially by such acts, he was willing to compensate them—although, he believed, there were "but few slaveholders that deserve our consideration." In these last few words, Stevens dismissed the notion that a substantial proportion of the slaveholding class was inwardly loyal to the United States.[33]

This line of thought informed Stevens's response to a series of questions. When antisecessionist trans-Appalachian counties broke off from Confederate Virginia and declared themselves to be a new state within the United States, the Lincoln administration employed tortured logic in ratifying that step. The Constitution required that any state approve its own dismemberment. Representatives of Virginia's unionist counties pretended to satisfy that requirement simply by declaring themselves to *be* the legitimate government of Virginia as a whole—and then voting to authorize that state's partition. Stevens dismissed this performance as farcical and the federal government's acceptance of it as sophistry. It is "but mockery to say that the Legislature of Virginia has ever consented to the division," he declared. In fact, the division of Virginia was justifiable only by "the laws of war. We may admit West Virginia as a new State, not by virtue of any provision of the Constitution but under our absolute power which the laws of war give us in the circumstances in which we are placed. I shall vote for this bill upon that theory, and upon that alone. I will not stultify myself by supposing that we have any warrant in the Constitution for this proceeding."[34]

On August 3, 1861, the Union's first Confiscation Act passed the House by a vote of 60 to 48. Most House Republicans voted in favor, but seven, including Alexander Diven, voted no. Another seven Republicans who were present on the House floor just before the yeas and nays were taken did not record a vote on this measure, having abstained or left the chamber. Lincoln signed the bill into law on August 6.[35]

That law was another milestone in the evolution of Republican wartime policy toward slavery. But even it was self-limiting, as Republicans such as John A. Bingham promised. Its framers aimed to touch no slave who was not directly used in support of Confederate armies, thereby leaving unchanged the condition of the slave population's vast majority. Some Republicans, such as Indiana's William McKee Dunn, asserted that since they were "for maintaining the authority of the Government," they were therefore also ready to declare that "if slavery stands in the way" of that effort, "slavery must get out of the way." But those Republicans also agreed with Dunn that any attempt to wage "a war upon slavery" itself and impose a "general emancipation of slaves" would be "as wild and chimerical a scheme as ever entered the brain of a madman." If that became government policy, Dunn averred, "our Union is forever gone, and there is no redemption for it."[36]

Dunn's more radical colleagues found such thinking wrongheaded. George Julian protested that the first Confiscation Act shielded those slaveholders within the Confederacy who "remained at home on their plantations in the business of feeding the rebel armies," in doing which they would therefore retain "the protection of both the loyal and the Confederate Governments." Thaddeus Stevens expressly looked forward to a more inclusive emancipation policy. He had concluded his remarks on August 2 by predicting that the narrow scope of the present bill would widen if the war proved lengthy, something he considered inevitable. "If this war is to continue," he said, "there will be a time when . . . every bondman in the South . . . shall be called upon to aid us in war against their masters, and to restore this Union."[37]

These words anticipated the terms of a Second Confiscation Act, which Congress would pass a year later. In the summer of 1861, however, not even Stevens was yet calling for the freeing of all slaves within the rebellious states, much less all slaves in the United States as a whole. Even the broader emancipation policy that he then wished for and anticipated would touch only those slaves "belonging to a rebel. . . . I confine it to them." Those masters who lived within the Confederacy but remained personally loyal to the United States would retain their slaves. Stevens saw farther down the road than did Lincoln or the Congress, but at that point not even he envisioned the road's end.[38]

In August 1861, a general commanding Union troops in a loyal slave state took steps that went beyond the terms of the new Confiscation Act. Pro-Confederate forces in Missouri were waging a ferocious guerrilla war against the Union. In response, U.S. general John C. Frémont proclaimed martial law there. He also ordered the execution of all captured guerrillas and the freeing of all slaves of Confederate sympathizers. Abraham Lincoln opposed those orders. While Benjamin Butler's seizure of slaves in rebel Virginia had conformed to the terms of the First Confiscation Act, passed shortly afterward, Frémont's actions did not. Unlike Virginia, Missouri formally adhered to the Union. And Frémont had sought to emancipate not only slaves *working for* the rebellion but *all* slaves owned by pro-Confederate masters. Lincoln feared that the general's action would undermine pro-Union sentiment throughout the loyal slave states, in particular the state of Kentucky, whose retention Lincoln regarded as militarily crucial. The president asked Frémont to revise his decrees to accord with the Confiscation Act. When Frémont declined to do so, the president himself publicly countermanded those decrees.[39] A few months later, Lincoln removed Frémont from command, ostensibly for other reasons.

Lincoln's treatment of Frémont irked Thaddeus Stevens and other Republican radicals. On the heels of Frémont's removal, they pressed Lincoln to act more aggressively against slavery. On December 2, 1861, Stevens brought a resolution into the House that "requested" that the president and all his commanders "declare free . . . all slaves who shall leave their masters, or who shall aid in quelling this rebellion." Such emancipation should apply to slaves owned by disloyal and loyal masters alike, although the latter should be compensated for their losses.[40]

Abolitionist Gerrit Smith congratulated Stevens for his resolute words and actions. So did many others from his own state and beyond. "*God Bless You Thaddeus Stevens*," wrote William W. Keith from western New York State. "Amid all the obloquy & insults of *pro-Slavers and Devils* you have dared to stand up a man." Uriah Bruner of Nebraska praised Stevens and suggested that if Congress failed to legislate emancipation, private citizens of the North should raise their own army of a hundred thousand men "and conduct the war to suit our own notions," and "liberate the slaves."[41]

President Lincoln's first annual message to Congress, presented just a day after Stevens called for a more expansive confiscation policy, sounded a very different note, cautioning against more sweeping emancipatory action. Congress had passed and he had signed a Confiscation Act, he noted. And "if a new law upon the same subject shall be proposed, its propriety will be duly considered." But for now, "in considering the policy to be adopted for suppressing the insurrection, I have been anxious and careful that the inevitable conflict" to preserve the Union "shall not degenerate into a violent and remorseless revolutionary struggle." He was determined not to assume "that radical and extreme measures, which may reach the loyal as well as the disloyal, are indispensable."[42]

When congressional Republicans caucused a week later, Stevens implicitly rejected Lincoln's restraining words. He sought instead to rally support for the measure that he had already introduced. Military victory was impossible so long as slaves continued to feed and otherwise sustain the enemy, he said, and the party's more radical members applauded him.

But Republican Alexander Diven of New York demurred, objecting to the caucus's even discussing Union war policy. All parties represented in Congress, he declared, were equally committed to the war effort, and any attempt by Republicans to formulate their own policy would unnecessarily and dangerously divide and weaken the Union cause. Behind the New Yorker's objection to the discussion lay a more specific rejection of Stevens's arguments and proposal. Diven opposed any emancipation decree as self-defeating; it would only make the Confederates fight harder. Indeed, he insisted, the caucus should seek no legislation not already proposed in the Republicans' prewar 1860 election platform. If adhered to literally, of course, such a guideline would dictate rescinding even the First Confiscation Act.[43]

The chasm yawning between Diven's position and Stevens's was thus very wide, and the debate that followed naturally enough became (as one reporter put it) "spirited." But it also became obvious that the political temper of the Congress was changing. On December 4, 1861, Indiana Democrat William S. Holman asked the House to "solemnly reaffirm" the Crittenden-Johnson resolution of July that had abjured any antislavery purpose on the part of the Union war effort. Stevens moved to table and thereby kill Holman's motion, and the House concurred, with three times as many Republicans sustaining Stevens as opposing him. As James G. Blaine noted, observers outside Congress "recognized and appreciated" the "wide divergence" between the way that most House Republicans responded to Crittenden-Johnson in December and the way they had reacted less than half a year earlier.[44]

That did not yet signify, however, a general readiness to escalate the Union's attack on slavery. As the House discussed an appropriations bill early the following year, Stevens tried to turn its attention back to his own proposed emancipation resolution. Neither the courage of the Union's soldiers nor the skills of its generals, he continued to stress, could guarantee a Union victory. "Their soldiers are as brave as yours," Stevens admonished his colleagues. "Nor have we abler generals than they." The key to victory was to be found elsewhere—in laying hands upon *all* of the rebels' slave laborers. It was not enough to seize only those directly supporting rebel armies. "So long as they [the rebels] are left the means of cultivating their fields through forced labor, you may expend the blood of tens of thousands of freemen and billions of money, year after year, without being any nearer the end." Even if "the black man never lifts a weapon" on the Confederacy's behalf, Stevens argued, "he is really the main-stay of the war" on the rebels' side. That crucial element of Confederate strength must be removed from the equation. Surely the feasibility of doing so was obvious. After all, "those who now furnish the [rebels'] means of war" are in reality "the natural enemies of slaveholders." It was precisely those people who could and "must be made our allies."[45]

In fact, those potential allies had already been demonstrating in action the value of such an alliance and how easily it would be to forge it. As Union forces captured pieces of the Confederacy's Atlantic coast starting in 1861, slaves escaped their masters and made their way toward the new arrivals. The same thing happened as various U.S. armies in 1861 and 1862 entered western Virginia, moved up the coastal Virginia Peninsula, drove southward down the Mississippi River valley into Tennessee and Mississippi, and up the same valley from New Orleans.

A Union officer in Murfreesboro, Tennessee, underlined the point by reporting that slaves were "the only friends we find." Union commanders found those friends very useful. Some brought with them wagons, horses, or food from their masters' larders. Others helped Union soldiers locate hidden weapons or foodstuffs or to identify the most militant Confederate partisans in an area. Some, an Ohio lieutenant noted, "carried information, and acted as scouts and guides on occasions when it would try the heart and nerve of their white companions." Brigadier General Daniel Sickles reported that in resisting pro-Confederate forces in Maryland, "the most valuable and reliable information of the enemy's movements" had come from "negroes who have come into our lines." Sickles had also employed such people as scouts or guides, "and they have uniformly . . . proved faithful" and in many instances had "proved to be persons of remarkable intelligence." In northern Alabama, Major General O. M. Mitchell reported that "the negroes are our only friends, and in two instances I owe my own safety to their faithfulness." Mitchell intended to have some of them serve as "watchful guards" on nearby plantations and he promised "protection" to any of them who furnished him with valuable intelligence. If Washington should prohibit such policies, the general added, "it would be impossible for me to hold my position."[46]

Thaddeus Stevens knew very well that many in the Union would nevertheless object vociferously to the emancipationist policy he advocated. "Prejudice may be shocked, weak minds startled, weak nerves may tremble." But the government must persevere. Stevens ridiculed the "puerile inconsistency" of those who would "send forth your sons and brothers to shoot and saber and bayonet the insurgents" but who "hesitate to break the bonds of their slaves." Addressing the same inconsistency on another occasion, Stevens recalled a tale from the war for independence in which a Patriot captain brought his company "in front of the British" but then "cried out, when they were about to shoot, 'For God's sake, don't fire, for don't you see it will only make them a great deal madder!'"[47]

Pro-slavery writers had always warned that if slaves were ever freed, they would turn bloodily upon their former masters. Stevens therefore anticipated that should the Union decree emancipation, northern doughfaces would doubtlessly "raise an outcry about the horrors of a servile insurrection." Stevens would later tell his nephew Alanson that "the slaves ought to be incited to insurrection and give the rebels a taste of real civil war." For now, he simply demanded to know "which is most to be abhorred, a rebellion of slaves fighting for their liberty, or a rebellion of freemen fighting to murder the nation?" He scorned those who "object to emancipation because it liberates the slaves of traitors! Tender-hearted Christians! Merciful statesmen! Benevolent philanthropists! If such men are statesmen, where are the idiots to be found?" Lamenting all such hand-wringing and legal quibbling, Stevens wished that he saw in the North the kind of "fiery zeal which impels the South." Those leading the Union "act from conscientious fidelity, under the cool dictates of honest judgment." But, sadly, "we feel nothing of that determined and invincible courage that was inspired in the Revolution by the grand idea of liberty, equality, and the rights of man."[48]

And now, having invoked the American Revolution, Stevens revealed a remarkable change in his view of revolutions in general. A considerably younger Thaddeus Stevens had denigrated the revolution in eighteenth-century France, holding it up as a negative example for the United States and using words like "jacobin" as epithets. But in 1862, led by new circumstances to urge fundamental transformation in his own country, Stevens wished aloud that "the ardor which inspired the French revolution" might find its like in the United States. The revolutionaries of France, like others elsewhere, he recalled with admiration, were "possessed and impelled by the glorious principles of freedom," an "idea which renders men unconquerable." The United States needed much more of just that kind of spirit. And such a spirit *would* arise, Stevens believed, only when the nation's citizens found themselves fighting for an equally inspiring cause. "Let the people know that this Government is fighting not only to enforce a sacred compact [that is, the Constitution], but to carry out to final perfection the principles of the Declaration of Independence . . . and the blood of every freeman would boil with enthusiasm, and his nerves be strengthened in this holy warfare."[49]

The resolution that Stevens introduced in December 1861 had called for freeing all slaves owned by Confederates and their sympathizers. Although that resolution did not specify clearly that it referred only to slaves in secessionist states, that seemed to be its intent. But he showed during the following month that he had raised his sights further. His January 1862 speech called for freeing all slaves throughout the United States: "Universal emancipation must be proclaimed to all." The Union must act to "extinguish slavery on this whole continent; to wipe out, so far as we are concerned, the most hateful and infernal blot that ever disgraced the escutcheon of man." His opponents would ask, Stevens anticipated, why we should emancipate all the slaves rather than just those owned by rebels. For one thing, he explained, "perjury, fraud, and falsehood" would make it very difficult to distinguish clearly between treasonous and loyal slaveholders. The disloyal might well claim to have been loyal all along. But there was a still more important reason for making emancipation universal. That was the only way to *preserve* the fruits of any military victory in this war, the only way to guarantee the *future* security of an eventually reunited republic. "Our object should be not only to end this terrible war now, but to prevent its recurrence." That required slavery's complete extirpation. Since "all must admit that slavery is the cause" of the war, they should also recognize that "so long as it exists we cannot have a solid Union." The unavoidable fact is that "the principles of our Republic are wholly incompatible with slavery. They cannot live together." If the federal government were to free even three-fourths of the slaves while leaving the rest in bondage, slavery as a legal institution would survive, and slavery "would soon again overrun the whole South," laying the foundation for yet another rebellion. So "you would have expended countless treasures and untold lives in vain." Therefore, "while you are quelling this insurrection at such fearful cost, remove the cause, that future generations may live in peace."[50]

This was a stirring speech. But when Stevens concluded, the House turned back to the appropriations bill that it had been previously debating. It did not act upon or even discuss his abolition initiative during the rest of that congressional session. And some three months later, in the spring of 1862, the president seemed to reaffirm his rejection of any broad-gauged emancipation policy. He did that in dealing with another Union general.

David Hunter commanded the Union's Department of the South, which meant that his writ nominally extended to all of South Carolina, Georgia, and northern Florida. At the end of April 1862, Hunter declared martial law throughout that jurisdiction. Then in May, asserting that "slavery and martial law in a free country are altogether incompatible," Hunter decreed freedom for all slaves throughout his department.[51]

Abolitionists, radical Republicans, and free blacks cheered. Northern Democrats and border-state politicians were furious. And on May 19, the White House repudiated Hunter's order. Lincoln would later explain his rejection of the emancipationist course favored by Frémont and Hunter by recalling that he "did not then think it an indispensable necessity." And the president objected on legal grounds as well. Frémont acted in a formally loyal state. Hunter had acted in a rebel state, but even there a general had no right to issue such a sweeping policy edict; only the president had that authority, and he had not ceded it to Hunter. Historians now recognize that this assertion of presidential prerogative reflected a softening of Lincoln's previous position on emancipation. He was now suggesting for the first time that the president of the United States did have the right to "declare the Slaves of any state or states, free." And behind closed doors, he had begun wondering whether he ought not, after all, make use of that power.[52]

The nature, extent, and significance of Lincoln's evolving thoughts, however, were not obvious to Stevens. During a House debate in July 1862, he opposed Lincoln's rescinding of General Hunter's decree and criticized the administration's war policy as too soft on the enemy and too susceptible to conservative pressure from border-state politicians. Although Stevens credited Lincoln with being "as honest a man as there is in the world," he also considered the president "too easy and amiable" and too easily "misled by the malign influence of Kentucky counselors" who urged appeasing putatively loyal slaveholders.[53]

*   *   *

As the logic of events asserted itself more and more forcefully, Congress adopted additional antislavery measures in the first half of 1862. In March it put teeth into its July 1861 objection to Union soldiers returning fugitive slaves to their owners. It now adopted a new article of war, a new legal rule governing the conduct of the armed forces. This article prohibited both army and navy personnel from "returning fugitives from service or labor, who may have escaped from any persons to whom such service or labor is claimed to be due." As supporters of this new article made clear, it made no exception for loyal slave masters nor for masters living in loyal states. And it mandated courts-martial and dismissal for any Union officer who violated its provisions. Although it did not repeal the fugitive slave law of 1850, this article ordered soldiers and sailors not to enforce it; Lincoln approved it on March 13.[54]

The following month saw Congress move to abolish slavery in the District of Columbia. Bills for that purpose had been introduced in both houses months earlier. The Senate gave its assent to such a bill on April 3, 1862. As recently as 1860, Congressman Thaddeus Stevens had abjured such a measure as untimely, possibly to abide by his party's decision not to place it in its electoral platform that year. But on this subject as on many others, new conditions required (or allowed) new policies.

Now firmly committed to D.C. abolition, Stevens pressed his House colleagues on April 10 and 11 to end the protracted debate, reject numerous dilatory amendments, and vote. The House finally passed the bill by a margin of 92 to 38. The majority included all Republicans voting. The new law immediately abolished slavery in the capital district, minimally compensating only loyal owners (three hundred dollars per slave, well below market prices in recent memory); it also appropriated moneys to finance emigration for former slaves who wished to leave the country.[55]

Lincoln was not entirely pleased with this bill. He signed it on

April 16, but in a message to Congress he alluded to "matters within and about this act, which might have taken a course or shape, more satisfactory to my jud[g]ment," although he declined "to specify them." The *New York Times*, then close enough to the president politically to be widely considered his house organ, was less reticent. It suggested that Lincoln would have preferred a bill that was "a little less hasty and radical," one that, for one thing, had implemented abolition in Washington gradually rather than immediately—and even then had done so only with the approval of the local white population.[56]

Three weeks later, on May 9, 1862, Owen Lovejoy introduced a bill in the House "to secure freedom to all persons within the exclusive jurisdiction of the Federal Government." He initially proposed to abolish slavery within the federal territories as well as "in all places whatsoever where the National Government has exclusive jurisdiction," including the nation's coastal waters and all federally owned forts, arsenals, and dockyards located within any of the states. Although opponents failed to table the bill, they continued to oppose it on legal and other grounds. And when Lovejoy tried to cut off debate and bring his bill to a vote, the House refused.[57]

Stevens was disgusted. Those who were "tender-footed upon the subject of slavery," he observed, "will ever seek any excuse for voting against this bill." They were "cunning in seeking out small and trivial objections, and magnifying them." He was equally dismissive of those "who are loud in their protestations of dislike of slavery, and yet when they come to a practical proposition for its abolition, . . . they meet us with all sorts of objections." Retreating before those objections, however, Lovejoy on May 12 withdrew his initial, more ambitious bill in favor of one that limited abolition to the federal territories. That bill did then pass the House, and three days later the Senate passed a slightly modified version, to which the House consented; Lincoln signed that bill into law.[58]

*   *   *

Stevens's cause encountered far greater trouble on the battlefield in 1862 than it did in Congress. True, success crowned nearly every initiative that Union armies took in the war's western theater (between the Appalachian Mountains and the Mississippi River), and the capture of New Orleans in the spring, followed by further penetration of southern Louisiana, was a major coup. But the story was very different in the eastern theater, which attracted much more public attention in both North and South. The spring and summer brought an unbroken string of serious Union defeats. In May and June in Virginia's Shenandoah Valley, General Thomas "Stonewall" Jackson outmaneuvered and outfought a series of Union forces that in total outnumbered his own. Union general George B. McClellan's Peninsula Campaign (from March through July) brought his huge army within a few miles of Richmond, seeming at that point to place victory in the war as a whole within that commander's grasp. But then, in the so-called Seven Days Battles, McClellan allowed himself to be frightened off by Robert E. Lee's smaller but more aggressive army. And in August, Lee defeated and inflicted heavy casualties on General John Pope's Army of Virginia in the Second Battle of Bull Run.

Stevens had predicted in August 1861 that to win the war the United States would need to broaden the scope of emancipation significantly beyond that of the First Confiscation Act. The moderate Republican *New York Times* was still rejecting such counsel the following spring. The North must "show that it is no design of this people to interfere with the municipal institutions of the Slave States" so that it can win "the respect of the Southern people." Congress must therefore "waste no more time upon confiscation bills." But for others, the bitterly disappointing and humiliating military defeats suffered by mid-1862 confirmed the wisdom of Stevens's warning. In July, Congress escalated its attack on Confederate slavery by passing a Second Confiscation Act. Where the first had addressed the condition only of those slaves directly employed in support of the Confederate war effort, this second bill declared that henceforth *any* slaves who came into Union hands and were owned by disloyal masters "shall be forever free of their servitude, and not again held as slaves." It also forbade U.S. soldiers to return any fugitives to their purported owners, on pain of expulsion from the ranks. Finally, the new law authorized the president to facilitate voluntary colonization—"the transportation, colonization, and settlement, in some tropical country beyond the limits of the United States, of such persons of the African race, made free by the provisions of this act, as may be willing to emigrate." As chair of the Ways and Means Committee, Stevens brought an appropriations bill into the House that included funding for colonization, and that bill passed.[59]

In the House, all Republican votes but one supported the Second Confiscation Act, which bill therefore passed by a wide margin. Stevens understood that this outcome reflected a substantial radicalization of his party's thinking since 1861. Just a year earlier, he observed, such a bill could not have passed—indeed, "a year ago not fifty [votes] could have been found" in favor of such a measure. The next day the Senate also passed the bill, with only two Republicans siding with the minority. Lincoln signed it into law on July 17.[60]

By now the president was reaching substantially the same conclusion about emancipation's necessity that Stevens had enunciated more than a year earlier. Lincoln informed his secretaries of state and the navy on Sunday, July 13, 1862, that the unanticipated strength of the slaveholders' rebellion had by now made a sweeping emancipation decree "a military necessity essential for the salvation of the Union." It had come down to this choice, he explained: either "we must free the slaves or be ourselves subdued."[61]

As the president embraced this view, he discarded a major consideration that had previously restrained him. Professedly loyal southern slaveowners, in both the Confederacy and the loyal border states, had failed to rally to the Union in the way that Lincoln had hoped. By the middle of 1862, he was therefore abandoning that hope and regretting the policy hesitations that it had fostered. Slaveowners in the border states, he complained in late July, "will do nothing for the government, nothing for themselves," other than resist attacks on slavery in the Confederacy for fear that such attacks would touch them as well. Accommodating those people in the past, Lincoln believed, had caused "the paralysis—the dead palsy—of the government in this whole struggle." It had, indeed, "paralyzed me more in this struggle than any other one thing."[62]

With these words, the president implicitly accepted Thaddeus Stevens's long-standing criticism of the way the White House had previously evaluated policy options. Now, in search of wartime allies, Lincoln was turning away from conservative advisors and critics and toward the freedpeople. On September 22, he delivered his preliminary Emancipation Proclamation, giving secessionist states until January 1 to return to the Union or see all their slaves declared "then, thenceforward, and forever free."[63]

Just a few weeks earlier, Stevens had nearly despaired of such an order ever being issued, lamenting that no one in the administration seemed to have "a sufficient grasp of mind, and sufficient moral courage, to treat this as a radical revolution, and remodel our institutions" accordingly. But when Lincoln boldly made good, on New Year's Day, on the threat contained in his preliminary proclamation, Stevens cheered him on, urging the proclamation's energetic enforcement and doing so with biblical images and language. "I believe," he declared, "there is a God, an avenging God, who is now punishing the sins of this nation for the wicked wrongs which for centuries we have inflicted on a blameless race." There was only one way to limit such heaven-sent punishment: the nation must "hasten to do justice" and thereby "stay the sword of the destroying angel."[64]

But even as he supported Lincoln's proclamation, Stevens judged it still insufficient. It would not free anyone in the four slave states still in the Union. It would not free slaves in those parts of the Confederacy that Lincoln had excluded from the proclamation's coverage. Finally, it would not make human enslavement as such illegal anywhere in the United States. Emancipating those who were currently enslaved did not outlaw slavery itself.

Once again, Stevens's views placed him far in advance of the nation. In the fall 1862 elections, Democrats gained thirty-four in the House of Representatives, governorships in two states, and control of state legislatures in two others.[65] Military defeats in the war's eastern theater sapped Republican voters' spirit, as Stevens had anticipated. And those defeats sharply reduced public confidence in Republican politicians, as Stevens's old friend and House colleague, Edward McPherson, noted before himself going down to defeat in Pennsylvania's Sixteenth Congressional District. But the electoral setbacks of that season also registered a backlash in the Union against the preliminary Emancipation Proclamation that Stevens had not foreseen.

Despite these political reverses, however, Stevens's party retained control of the House of Representatives through an alliance with a handful of independent unionist congressmen from the border states. And Stevens himself continued to enjoy the loyalty of his own constituents; even in that bad season for Republicans, Lancaster's voters returned him to Congress by a margin of nearly two to one.[66] This strong personal showing reflected the political bond that he had forged with his constituency and his local party organization. A decade earlier his antislavery radicalism had run afoul of Lancaster County's Whig organization and cost him his House seat. Stevens's experience since becoming a Republican congressman was different. Although important and sometimes bitter differences arose within the Republican Party, his high-profile expressions of the strongest sentiments and his championing of the strongest measures against slavery and even white supremacy more broadly would never again cost Stevens an election. He proved consistently able to convince most of his constituents that what he said and did was in their best interests over all. "In the course of my public life," he proudly declared at one point, "I have voted for unpopular measures and trusted to the good sense of the people whom I represented." And when I "explained to them" my reasoning, "they never rejected me on account of it."[67] That was an accurate description of his career as a Republican, at least. Two years later, voters once again returned him to the House with roughly two-thirds of all the ballots they cast.[68]

Nor did his party's losses elsewhere in 1862 deter Stevens from introducing a bill the following December to repeal the fugitive slave laws of both 1850 and 1793.[69] Other Republicans also brought in bills of their own on that subject. Not surprisingly, Democrats protested furiously. Repealing these measures, they raged, would violate the spirit and nullify the letter of the Constitution; it would be tantamount to abolishing slavery nationwide. If escaped slaves could not be returned, what security was left to slavery itself? A vote on these measures was repeatedly postponed, but in June 1864 Congress ratified such a bill, and Lincoln signed it into law.[70] That left the fugitive slave clause of the U.S. Constitution (article IV, section 2, clause 3) without an enforcing law.

Complaints that repealing fugitive slave laws would effectively accomplish abolition did nothing to discourage Stevens. He insisted in 1863 not only that all enslaved people be emancipated but that the institution of slavery itself be formally outlawed throughout the country. The distinction, once again, was an important one. "[T]here can be no security for the future without amending the Constitution so as to forever prohibit slavery in this republic," Stevens cautioned that April. Without such an amendment, it would be "in vain to emancipate every slave now." Because if enslavement itself remained legal, "the moment the States were re-admitted they would re-enslave every black man within their limits. Nothing in the Constitution would prevent them, as States, from dealing with them as they please."[71] Stevens was intimately familiar with such dangers. In his own part of Pennsylvania, bands of bounty hunters had long kidnapped legally free black residents and dragged them into Virginia and Maryland to be enslaved there. Stevens had highlighted that practice when serving as defense attorney in Lancaster County's prewar Castner Hanway trial.

On the battlefield, the year 1863 proved more favorable to the Union cause than had 1862. The Union's Army of the Potomac successfully halted Robert E. Lee's menacing raid into Pennsylvania. It was during that raid that Jubal Early destroyed Thaddeus Stevens's Caledonia Iron Works.[72] But Stevens's personal losses paled beside those that Lee's Army of Northern Virginia sustained in the Battle of Gettysburg. Almost simultaneously, in the war's western theater, Ulysses Grant's capture of Vicksburg and then Port Hudson finally placed the Mississippi River and its valley into Union hands. Containing some of the South's richest soil and largest plantations, that valley's loss to the Union delivered a stunning blow to slavery in Mississippi and Louisiana. Many of those slaveowners who remained on their land afterward saw black laborers refuse either to follow orders or to leave their premises when told to do so. "Most of them think, or pretend to think," complained one of the richest planters in the Natchez region, "that the plantation and every thing on it belongs to them." Other slaves simply abandoned their owners in huge numbers. And on plantations from which rebel masters had fled, former slaves often began farming the soil for their own benefit.[73]

Meanwhile, the democratic spirit driving Stevens's words and actions regarding slavery was revealing itself as well in his response to other issues. One of these was the treatment of Native Americans.

In the spring of 1860, prior to Lincoln's election, both Democratic and Republican congressmen called for stepped-up military action against Native Americans on the Texas and New Mexico frontier, justifying that call with reports that white settlers were being killed there. Thaddeus Stevens, in response, "wish[ed] the Indians had newspapers of their own," because "if they had, you would have horrible pictures of the cold-blooded murders of inoffensive Indians. You would have more terrible pictures than we have now revealed to us [of white casualties], and, I have no doubt, we would have the real reasons for these Indian troubles." That was so, he said, because "these troubles are oftenest caused by bad white men," and "nine tenths of the treaties which have been violated . . . have been violated by Christian white men, instead of savage Indians."[74]

Stevens's sympathies extended as well to the growing number of Chinese immigrants by then working in California. In 1862 that state's legislature imposed a special monthly tax upon those of them who took up almost any occupation other than agricultural laborer. And that June, California Republican congressman Aaron A. Sargent asked the U.S. Congress to raise the tariff on clean rice, a staple of the Chinese diet. Sargent made it clear that his purpose was to increase the burdens upon the state's Chinese immigrant population, whom he described as "a people of a strange tongue, vile habits, impossible of assimilation, and with customs difficult to penetrate," and who "swarm by thousands to our shores, like the frogs of Egypt." "We are overrun by these pagans," he exclaimed.[75]

As someone who had once worked closely with nativists, Thaddeus Stevens might have been expected to applaud such words and discriminatory measures. Instead, he indignantly condemned such mistreatment of "this class of people," treatment that has "disgraced the State of California." He reminded the House that "China has been much oppressed of late by the European nations," which had recently made war upon China because it refused "to consent to the importation of poisonous drugs that demoralize its society and destroy its people." Now that "a large number of Chinese have of late years migrated to the State of California to seek their fortunes," he asserted, "they have the right to go there; and I hold it to be in violation of every rule of law which should have [sway?] in a civilized country to discriminate against them." California's moves to persecute them "are wholly in conflict with the generous spirit of our free institutions. They are a mockery of the boast that this land is the asylum of the oppressed of all climes." In this instance, at least, Stevens's increasingly consistent championing of democratic principles led him to break with the nativist inclinations of his past. And the House of Representatives rejected Representative Sargent's proposal.[76]

Meanwhile, the Civil War raged on. Gettysburg and Vicksburg were major setbacks for the Confederacy, but they neither killed it nor guaranteed its eventual death. The slaveowners' rebellion remained alive, and its final defeat was by no means inevitable. From early in the war, Thaddeus Stevens had warned that destroying the Confederacy would require the Lincoln government to take extraordinary steps that went beyond even confiscation and emancipation of slaves. It would also require, at the very least, bringing black men into the Union's armies. In 1862 and 1863, Stevens and his radical allies redoubled their efforts to make that happen.

CHAPTER SEVEN

Stevens's Civil War, Part II

For Black Union Troops and Nationwide Abolition

Confiscation and emancipation naturally raised another major question—whether to employ freed slaves as soldiers. From the start of the war, black men in the North had been trying to don Union uniforms. And in the summer of 1861 Thaddeus Stevens foresaw the day when "every bondman in the South . . . shall be called upon to aid us in war against their masters, and to restore this Union."

But, following national policy in force since the 1790s, the government long rejected that idea and those initiatives. Most northerners were sure that black men could not make good soldiers; deep-seated racial ideology told them so. Nor did most white men wish to serve alongside black men in anything like the same status. That would insult their racial pride and presumably make it more difficult to recruit or keep whites in the ranks. Widespread initial expectations of an early Union victory made it easy to avoid reconsidering that policy. As a member of Lincoln's secretarial staff recalled, "so many of us, even of those opposed to slavery, found it hard to approve of what was doubtless so wise, so necessary a policy as the arming of the blacks." More than a year into the war, Lincoln assured an old friend that "none are to be armed" because "it would produce dangerous & fatal dissatisfaction in our army, and do more harm than good."[1]

Three factors eventually combined to change the president's mind. The first was the war's stubborn refusal to correspond with optimistic expectations about it. It became ever clearer that defeating the rebellion would take much more time and require far larger armies than most northerners had foreseen. As the need for numbers grew, the question naturally arose, where could the additional soldiers be found? The second factor was the pressure and example of free blacks and emancipated slaves. With the aid of a few bold Union officers, some black men demonstrated in action the value of changing Union policy. Third, Thaddeus Stevens and other radical Republicans in Congress pressed Lincoln's government to recognize and accept the logic of the situation, demanding that it not only accept black men into its armies but vigorously seek to recruit them.

As General Benjamin Butler's conduct at Fort Monroe back in 1861 portended, practical challenges to conservative policy toward slavery often arose from within the military. Although most members of the country's officer corps were politically conservative, some in the military machine did come to appreciate the war effort's requirements. At the beginning of December 1861, Lincoln's secretary of war, Simon Cameron, drafted a report that pointed toward a new policy. Cameron was far from a radical politically, but his responsibility to oversee the war effort had led him to face some hard truths. "It is clearly a right of the Government to arm slaves when it may become necessary as it is to take gunpowder from the enemy," his draft read in part. It followed for Cameron that it was not only a right but "may become the duty, of this Government to arm and equip them, and employ their services against the rebels, under proper military regulations, discipline, and command."[2]

Lincoln disapproved of those words, and he ordered his war secretary to drop them from the report's final version. Cameron did so, but by then he had already released the first draft to the press, and the *New York Times*, the *New York Tribune*, and many other northern newspapers published it. And in a December meeting of the Republican congressional caucus, as the *Tribune* also reported, Thaddeus Stevens declared that Cameron's "original report . . . deserved the approbation of every loyal citizen" because it alone "evinced correct notions about the true method of prosecuting the war."[3]

Although Lincoln soon removed Simon Cameron from office, the issue that the man had raised would not stay buried. On his own initiative, General David Hunter set out to arm liberated slaves in the Union's Department of the South in April 1862. He began the process of organizing a black regiment and reported success in doing so. But when word of his undertaking spread, border-state politicians and Democratic congressmen and newspapers fulminated against it. In the Senate, Delaware Democrat Willard Saulsbury denounced such attempts "to elevate the miserable nigger" and "put him in your army, and to put him in your navy." Even a reporter for the Republican *New York Times* fumed that "the enrollment of negroes in the military service in such States as South Carolina and Georgia, would, of course, mean nothing else than a determination to exterminate the white population in those States." Such a step would only infuriate and stiffen the resistance of Confederates. Southern whites might well accept defeat at the hands of white Union soldiers, the reporter thought. "But to expect them to submit quietly to the rule of their own slaves, armed by our Government and quartered in their midst, is an error, the folly of which is only exceeded by the devilish malignity that suggests it." Although the Republican Congress refused to condemn General Hunter, the Lincoln administration declined to defend him against Democrats' furious attacks or even to reply to Hunter's requests for the material means needed to proceed with his plans. Disheartened, the general dissolved his nascent regiment.[4]

Just as Thaddeus Stevens had praised Simon Cameron's draft

report, so did he now side with General Hunter. When Kentucky congressman Charles A. Wickliffe denounced Hunter and his works, Stevens responded that he, too, disliked "many things in the conduct of this war." But what he objected to were failures to deal with the Confederacy *more* sternly than the Lincoln government was doing. He had no objection at all to what Hunter attempted. On the contrary, he believed, the general had pointed to the only road forward. "I say that it is the duty of this Government to follow out the policy which has been inaugurated by the gallant and sagacious soldier who now commands our army in South Carolina." Nor would Stevens stop at arming those fugitives who happened to reach Union lines. He wanted a concerted campaign to seek out and recruit such potential black soldiers. "I am for sending the Army through the whole slave population of the South, and asking them to come from their masters, to take the weapons which we furnish, and to join us in this war of freedom against traitors and rebels." But, insisted a second Kentuckian, Robert Mallory, black men would not make good soldiers. "One shot of a cannon would disperse thirty thousand of them," he was sure. All that arming slaves would accomplish was the "indiscriminate slaughter of men, women, and children" at their hands. Stevens batted those claims away. Far from proving that blacks "are not capable of being made good soldiers and humane soldiers," he said, "history tells us that they make the best and most docile soldiers in the world." Rather than being "barbarians in nature," they were "a people as well calculated to be humanized as any other."[5]

More and more of Stevens's Republican colleagues were by now coming around to his view. A case in point was New York Republican congressman Alexander Diven. Having balked in the summer of 1861 even at confiscating slaves, he was just a year later regretting publicly that black men, slave and free alike, had not already been mustered into Union armies. And he now promised to introduce a bill to begin doing that. Diven's about-face obviously pleased Stevens, who added sardonically that he would have brought in such a bill himself but had refrained because, since he "was not a 'conservative,'" his bill "would have been called abolitionism" and so "would have been defeated." Other congressmen laughed—his fellow radicals, in appreciation; erstwhile opponents, perhaps in rueful acknowledgment.[6]

Within a few more months, Congress passed two pieces of legislation that empowered the president to bring black men into his armies. The Second Confiscation Act "authorized" Lincoln "to employ as many persons of African descent as he may deem necessary and proper for the suppression of this rebellion . . . and use them in such manner as he may judge best for the public welfare." The Militia Act of 1862 empowered the president more specifically to receive "persons of African descent" into the armed services, there to perform "any military or naval service for which they may be found competent." Such soldiers and sailors would be granted freedom, as would their family members, if their owners proved to be disloyal. The Senate passed the Militia Act by a vote of 28 to 9. The House rejected an attempt to table the Senate's bill by a vote of 77 to 30 and then passed it on July 16. Lincoln signed it the next day.[7]

These two laws permitted the president to enlist black soldiers, but they did not compel him to do so. And at first Lincoln was not so inclined. Weeks after the Militia Act's passage he told a group of visitors that while he would allow black men to perform support labor for military units, he would not permit them to become soldiers. But behind the scenes the president was wavering, and the old policy was beginning to disintegrate on the ground. From late August and into the fall, Union officers and partisans on the Kansas-Missouri border and in Union-occupied parts not only of South Carolina but of Louisiana as well began organizing infantry units composed of both black men who had been legally free even before the war and recently freed slaves.[8]

By the end of 1862, Lincoln had come around. On New Year's Day, his final Emancipation Proclamation called for inducting black men "into the armed service of the United States to garrison forts, positions, stations, and other places, and to man vessels of all sorts in said service." A few weeks later Stevens, concerned that Confederates who might capture black Union soldiers would abuse or kill them, introduced legislation stressing that a black recruit was a soldier like any other and entitled to the same treatment as any other at the hands of the enemy. It also authorized the U.S. president "to retaliate or interfere for his protection."[9]

Events in 1864–65 validated Lincoln's judgment that black troops would significantly strengthen the Union's armies. By the war's end, some 200,000 black men had served in the Union army or navy, the overwhelming majority of them recruited in slave states. Should we "lose the colored force," Lincoln warned conservative critics, we would be "powerless to save the Union." Keep that force, "and you can save the Union. Throw it away, and the Union goes with it."[10]

At first, most white officers assigned black soldiers solely to noncombat tasks. But the able and courageous performance of those who did come under fire led more Union commanders to put black troops into combat. As Stevens noted, "wherever they have been engaged, the uniform testimony is that they have been no less gallant, no less brave, no less faithful, than the white men who fought by their side." In the campaign that finally brought the war to an end, Ulysses Grant's forces in the spring of 1865 included fully thirty-three black regiments, whose members composed about one out of every eight Union soldiers in his command.[11]

Under the terms of the Militia Act, black soldiers initially received substantially lower pay than did white soldiers. It is testimony to the new recruits' self-respect that many of them objected forcefully to this discrimination. In April 1864 Congress took up a measure that would provide black soldiers with equal clothing, pay, rations, and equipment and make that retroactive to January 1, 1864. To Stevens, this was no more than elementary justice; Democrats who opposed the measure (such as Indiana's William S. Holman) were beneath contempt. The question before Congress, he said, was simply "whether the soldiers of the United States, who wear the livery of the Union, who march under the banner of the Union, . . . expose themselves in the battle and to death, shall be placed on an equality, or whether in that position and under that glorious flag we are to keep up the distinctions which have been the infamy and disgrace of the Union and the age, and which existed when slavery did." Surely by now only "a lover of slavery or a demagogue, will attempt to maintain the position that any of the soldiers who bear their arms in battle shall be treated as inferior to any other men who stand up by their side. I care not whether the soldiers are of Milesian, Teutonic, African, or Anglo Saxon descent." In fact, Stevens continued, if any soldiers deserved greater pay than others, "it ought to be that class of men whose perils are greatest when they go into our Army." The Confederates' official policy was to send captured black Union troops into slavery. Often enough, they simply killed black prisoners. "The black man knows," said Stevens, that "when he goes there that his dangers are greater than the white man's. He runs not only the risk of being killed in battle, but the certainty, if taken prisoner, of being slaughtered instead of being treated as a prisoner of war." Stevens took the opportunity to denounce racial prejudice generally, scoring preoccupation with "the accidental color of the skin or the shape of the face" instead of "the intellect and merit of the human beings with whom they are called upon to associate."[12]

Not surprisingly, Stevens's efforts on behalf of African Americans earned him gratitude and respect among them. William E. Matthews, a waiter and writer who led an African American literary society in

Baltimore, thanked Stevens for his role in opening the army to black enlistments. The black soldier Charles M. Blake was "grateful to you, Sir, for that abiding interest you have taken in the colored troops." James R. Gordon, a Philadelphia confectioner and equal rights activist, appreciated "the very kind feelings you have been pleased to have to [for] us, the colored people and our cause." The black abolitionist William E. Walker called Stevens "a true friend of the colored man," praising his "bold and manly advocacy of their rights—both in and out of Congress ever since 1850" and the fact that Stevens had "guarded *our interests* with more than a jealous and watchful eye."[13]

The recruitment of black troops into Union armies signaled an important *political* turn in the country's war effort. As revolutions deepen, as they become more radical in their methods and goals, the identity of their most active supporters commonly changes, too. So it was during the U.S.'s Civil War. Back in the spring of 1861, when the Lincoln administration was still defining its aims and methods more narrowly, the Union cause enjoyed strong backing across most of the North's political spectrum. But as the Republican government's attacks on slavery escalated, both the population and the Congress polarized. Even those northern Democrats who supported a war to preserve the Union (those known as "War Democrats") resisted emancipation and enlisting black soldiers. The even more conservative Democrats (the "Peace Democrats") sought an end to the conflict at almost any price, including the survival of slavery and perhaps even acceptance of secession. In his own state, Stevens claimed, "when the new volunteers were called for, Democratic leaders traveled everywhere and advised that no Democrat should volunteer, but stay at home and carry the election and regain power."[14]

Beginning in 1863, therefore, Lincoln's administration and armies began counting for success far more upon the efforts of African

Americans (soldiers as well as civilian support workers) than upon northern whites hostile to emancipation and black recruitment. This marked a key moment in the evolution of the Union war effort's base of popular support. Lincoln acknowledged that when he noted pointedly that an eventual Union triumph would owe far more to those "black men" who "with silent tongue, and clenched teeth, and steady eye, and well-poised bayonet, . . . have helped mankind on to this great consummation" than to those "white ones" within the Union who "with malignant heart, and deceitful speech, . . . strove to hinder it."[15]

In 1864, Ulysses Grant led the Union's Army of the Potomac in a bloody campaign against Robert E. Lee's Army of Northern Virginia. And William Tecumseh Sherman headed southward from his Tennessee base, aiming to seize the strategic city of Atlanta. Both Union armies made progress, but they did so slowly and, especially in Virginia, at great cost in life and limb. The painful pace and great bloodletting once again drove down morale in the North, so much so that Lincoln and his advisors that summer thought it likely that the Democratic Party's candidate for the Union presidency, ex-general George B. McClellan, would win the fall election.[16]

On his left flank, meanwhile, Lincoln faced attempts by some abolitionists and radical Republicans to replace him at the top of his party's ticket with either John C. Frémont or Salmon P. Chase. But Thaddeus Stevens, while still judging Lincoln's policy on emancipation too conservative, too hesitant, stood back from those intraparty maneuvers. He had suggested to Chase at one point that if Lincoln retained in his cabinet the assertively racist and rabidly anti-radical postmaster general, Montgomery Blair, it might indeed prove necessary to replace Lincoln himself. But in September 1864, the president requested and received Blair's resignation, and Stevens backed Lincoln's renomination and campaign. Although Mc-Clellan promised that if elected he would continue to war upon secession, he also repudiated emancipation as a weapon. And the platform that the Democratic convention adopted sought "immediate efforts" to arrange a cease-fire, promising that an eventual "convention of the States, or other peaceable means" would reunite the country "at the earliest practicable moment." Leading Confederates, following the Union election closely, understood that such a course would likely collapse the Union war effort. In this contest, Stevens decided that his stance toward Lincoln must be, in his own words, to "condemn privately" the president's shortcomings but "applaud publicly" his achievements.[17]

The Republicans' national convention met in Baltimore in June. It adopted a platform that called for amending the U.S. Constitution to abolish slavery throughout the country, an amendment for which abolitionists and radical Republicans had been calling since at least the spring of 1863. Lincoln had by now decided in favor of such an amendment, and in accepting his party's renomination, he endorsed it "in the joint names of Liberty and Union."[18]

Although Stevens backed Lincoln's renomination, he bridled at the Republican convention's decision to name Tennessean Andrew Johnson as Lincoln's running mate. When Alexander McClure spoke approvingly about Johnson to Stevens, the latter "turned his cold, gray eye upon me with an expression of profound contempt, and said: 'Can't you get a candidate for Vice President without going down into a damned rebel province for one?'"[19]

Despite his misgivings about Johnson, Stevens campaigned for the Republican ticket, warning voters that should they elect George McClellan, they would soon afterward discover that "the Republic has ceased to exist." But should they "re-elect the calm statesman who now presides over the nation, . . . he will lead you to an honorable peace and to permanent liberty." Military developments buoyed the Republican campaign. General Sherman captured Atlanta in September 1864. The end of Sherman's march through Georgia a few months later set the stage for another important development. Under pressure from congressional Republicans and the secretary of war, Sherman declared in January 1865 that a wide strip of land along the Atlantic coast stretching from Charleston to Jacksonville would be "reserved and set apart for the settlement of the negroes now made free." That order eventually gave about forty thousand freedpeople something vaguely termed "possessory title" to nearly half a million acres of land.[20]

Atlanta's fall significantly alleviated anxiety and war-weariness in the North, and on November 8, 1864, the Union's voters re-elected Abraham Lincoln by a substantial margin. In Pennsylvania's Lancaster County, the president received a larger majority of the votes than he had in 1860. A month earlier, Lancaster had returned Thaddeus Stevens to the House of Representatives by an even wider margin, awarding him almost two-thirds of all votes cast. Across the Union, the same congressional elections would increase the Republican delegation in the House by some 50 seats during the next congressional term, giving the president's party 70 percent of the seats in that chamber.[21]

The Senate did not await the Republicans' June convention, much less the next congressional term, before endorsing the nationwide abolition of slavery. On April 8, 1864, it passed the proposed Thirteenth Amendment by a vote of 38 to 6, far exceeding the two-thirds majority required for passage. All Republicans voted in favor; all negative votes came from Democrats. In the House of Representatives, too, a majority voted in favor a few months later. But the tally there fell short of the needed two-thirds mark.[22]

Thaddeus Stevens was unsparing in his condemnation of Democratic opposition. Emancipation was essential to Union victory, he repeated, if for no other reason than that God demanded it as a condition for his favor. "As I believe that a just God punishes national as well as individual sins," Stevens declared, "I cannot see how we can expect that the Destroying Angel will stay his hand until we obey the high behest 'to let the oppressed go free.'" It followed for him that responsibility for "the continued, misery and bloodshed which this nation shall endure" lay with those who were blocking the amendment.[23]

Success in the House came some seven months later. On the afternoon of January 31, 1865, Stevens rose to conclude the Republican case for abolition. Other House members immediately crowded around to hear his words while senators, Supreme Court justices, and other highly placed individuals filled the galleries and lobbies. The House then passed the Thirteenth Amendment in a vote of 119 to 56. When the result was announced, the chamber's floor and galleries erupted in cheers, tears, and ecstatic shouts of celebration. Months of both arm-twisting and bargaining had played their part in that outcome, but so had Republican gains during the 1864 congressional elections, likely changing the minds of some sitting Democratic representatives about which way the political winds were blowing. The Thirteenth Amendment then went to the state legislatures for approval.[24]

For the aging Stevens, Congress's endorsement of a step for which he had been fighting for so long could only have been gratifying. His health was declining, as was apparent to those around him. But "[i]f Providence should spare me a little longer," he sighed in the spring of 1864, until the day when "the foot of a slave can never again tread upon the soil of the Republic, I shall be content to accept any lot which may await me." Ohio Democrat George H. Pendleton accused Republicans in May 1864 of being a "revolutionary" party and demanded that they acknowledge it. "Admit you are in revolution; admit that you are revolutionists; admit that you do not desire to restore the old order; admit that you do not fight to restore the

Union. Take the responsibility of that position." Such a challenge held no terrors for Thaddeus Stevens, who extolled the "purifying fires of this revolution" and assured his listeners that "*revolution* it is." By early December 1865, the states had ratified the new constitutional amendment. Slavery was outlawed throughout the country.[25]

Some Republicans had begun talking as early as 1861 about how—through legal measures and by imposing what changes on the South—the warring states could be reunited. But only in 1863 did Republicans as a whole begin addressing the subject known by then as "reconstruction," the work of rebuilding the fragmented United States.[26] The major Union military victories of that year—Gettysburg and Vicksburg in July and Chattanooga, Tennessee, in November—strengthened confidence that victory would eventually come. That prospect required political leaders to ponder the questions of how a reconquered South would be governed, what changes might be made in its social and political life, and what the postwar nation as a whole would look like. Thaddeus Stevens was determined to answer those questions in ways that would advance the social and political revolution that he championed.

CHAPTER EIGHT

Stevens's Civil War, Part III

To Rebuild the Union

Since his youth, Thaddeus Stevens recalled one day, he had "fondly dreamed that when any fortunate chance should have broken up for a while the foundation of our institutions, and released us from obligations" to the slaveholders, then "the intelligent, pure and just men of this Republic . . . would have so remodeled all our institutions as to have freed them from every vestige of human oppression. Of inequality of rights, of the recognized degradation of the poor, and the superior caste of the rich." He had looked to the day when the United States would bring its laws and government into accord with the Declaration of Independence's assertion of human equality. To realize that dream now, Republicans would not only have to abolish slavery but also to "work a radical reorganization in Southern institutions, habits and manners" and "revolutionize their principles and feelings." As Union armies and navies fought their way into the Confederate states during the war, Stevens had reason to hope that the day had finally arrived.[1]

Union occupation of rebel territory confronted Washington with questions that would lay at the heart of what became known as Reconstruction: How would the Confederacy's defeat affect the South?

Who would govern there now? What government structures would arise? When and how should these states once again send representatives to the United States Congress and the Electoral College? What would happen to slavery in places not covered by the Emancipation Proclamation and, for that matter, those that *were* covered by it? As for those who had already gained freedom, what would be their legal status? The Supreme Court had ruled in 1857 that no black people were citizens or had any rights at all in this country. Which rights would they enjoy now? And what would become of the landholdings of the slaveholders, especially the planter aristocracy, some of which had already fallen into the federal government's hands? Who would own that land? Who would cultivate it and under what conditions? Answers to at least some of these questions could not await the end of the war.

Freedpeople and former slave masters presented opposing answers to those questions, as did Democrats and Republicans. Those differences would shape political identities, alliances, and conflicts for some time to come. Stevens would play a central role in the resulting struggles, struggles that would pit Republicans against Democrats as well as struggles that erupted within the Republican Party.

By the end of 1863, slavery was collapsing or at least badly eroding in the Mississippi River valley, most of eastern Arkansas, northern Alabama, northeastern Virginia, the Carolina coast, and parts of northern Virginia. The same was true in Tennessee and southern Louisiana, despite their exclusion from the Emancipation Proclamation. There, just as Lincoln had accurately predicted concerning the loyal border states, the "mere friction and abrasion . . . of the war" was grinding slavery down.[2]

Although mostly illiterate and previously forbidden to meet openly to share political opinions with one another, those recently

Thaddeus Stevens in a pensive mode. *LIBRARY OF CONGRESS*

An engraving, apparently by John Sartain.
LIBRARY OF CONGRESS

Thaddeus Stevens in his mid-forties. An engraving by John Sartain based on a portrait by Jacob Eicholtz.
LIBRARY OF CONGRESS

APPEAL

OF

FORTY THOUSAND CITIZENS,

THREATENED WITH

DISFRANCHISEMENT,

TO THE

PEOPLE OF PENNSYLVANIA.

PHILADELPHIA:
PRINTED BY MERRIHEW AND GUNN,
No. 7 Carter's Alley.
. . . . .
1838.

"Appeal of Forty Thousand Citizens Threatened with Disfranchisement" protesting the imminent decision by Pennsylvania's constitutional convention to restrict the vote to white males. *REPRODUCED WITH PERMISSION FROM THE HISTORICAL SOCIETY OF PENNSYLVANIA*

5

Lydia Hamilton Smith,
Stevens's housekeeper and
office manager after 1848.
WIKIPEDIA

6

"John Brown ascending the scaffold."
FRANK LESLIE'S ILLUSTRATED NEWSPAPER, LIBRARY OF CONGRESS

Former slave and abolitionist Frederick Douglass in 1870. He believed that the "inexorable logic of events" must lead the wartime Union to attack slavery. Thaddeus Stevens and Republican radicals articulated that logic in Congress. *LIBRARY OF CONGRESS*

8

Sketch by artist Alfred Waud of slaves abandoning their master's field and mounting plough horses to follow Union troops marching through the Confederacy. *LIBRARY OF CONGRESS*

9

Confederate General Jubal A. Early destroyed Stevens's Caledonia iron works during Robert E. Lee's raid into Pennsylvania in 1863. *LIBRARY OF CONGRESS*

"The Fifty-fifth Massachusetts Colored Regiment Singing John Brown's March in the Streets of Charleston." *HARPERS WEEKLY, LIBRARY OF CONGRESS*

Representative James Ashley of Ohio, an ally of Stevens's in the House of Representatives. *LIBRARY OF CONGRESS*

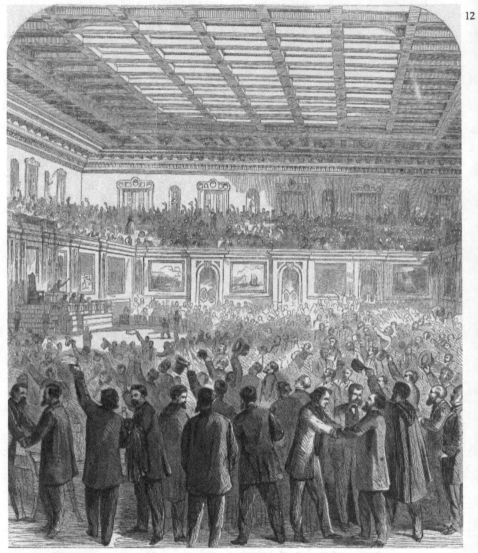

Cheers in the House of Representatives after it passed the 13th Amendment to the US Constitution that abolished slavery throughout the country,
January 1865. *HARPERS WEEKLY LIBRARY OF CONGRESS*

13

Representative John A. Bingham of Ohio, a leader of the Republican "moderates" during Reconstruction.
LIBRARY OF CONGRESS

14

Moderate Republican Senator William P. Fessenden of Maine.
NATIONAL ARCHIVES AND RECORDS ADMINISTRATION

15

Spectators cheer passage of the Civil Rights Bill of 1866 outside the galleries of the House of Representatives. *HARPERS WEEKLY LIBRARY OF CONGRESS*

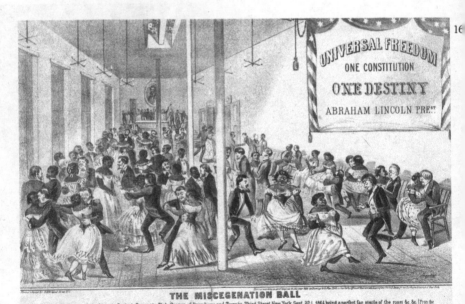

"The Miscegenation Ball." In 1864 the *New York World* published this racist cartoon lampooning the Lincoln campaign headquarters in New York City. *LIBRARY OF CONGRESS*

17

President Andrew Johnson allied with the South's elite to preserve white supremacy after the war. *LIBRARY OF CONGRESS*

18

PRESIDENT ANDREW JOHNSON PARDONING REBELS AT THE WHITE HOUSE.—[Sketched by Mr. Stanley Fox.]

"President Andrew Johnson pardoning rebels at the White House."
HARPERS WEEKLY LIBRARY OF CONGRESS

SCENES IN MEMPHIS, TENNESSEE, DURING THE RIOT—SHOOTING DOWN NEGROES ON THE MORNING OF MAY 2, 1866.—[SKETCHED BY A. R. W.]

"Shooting down Negroes" during the Memphis race riot, May 1866.
HARPERS WEEKLY LIBRARY OF CONGRESS

Henry J. Raymond, editor of the
New York Times and moderate
Republican congressman. He backed
Andrew Johnson longer than did
most of his party colleagues.
LIBRARY OF CONGRESS

IMPEACHMENT—THADDEUS STEVENS AND JOHN A. BINGHAM BEFORE THE SENATE.—Sketched by Theodore R. Davis.—[See Page 163.]

John A. Bingham and Thaddeus Stevens inform the Senate that the House of Representatives has voted to impeach Andrew Johnson.

HARPERS WEEKLY LIBRARY OF CONGRESS

22

The House of Representatives' impeachment managers in 1864. Stevens is in the front row, second from left, next to Benjamin Butler. John Bingham is seated in the same row on the far right. *NATIONAL ARCHIVES AND RECORDS ADMINISTRATION*

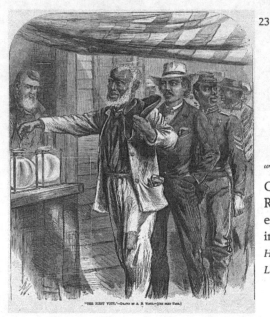

23

"The First Vote." Congressional Reconstruction enfranchised black men in the postwar South. *HARPERS WEEKLY LIBRARY OF CONGRESS*

24

Thaddeus Stevens in the Civil War era.
LIBRARY OF CONGRESS

25

Aged and infirm, Stevens had to be carried into the
Senate for Andrew Johnson's impeachment trial.
*L'ILLUSTRATION, JOURNAL UNIVERSEL (PARIS), COURTESY
JOSHUA BROWN*

Stevens's coffin lying in state in the US Capitol's rotunda near a statue of Lincoln. *NATIONAL ARCHIVES AND RECORDS ADMINISTRATION*

Inscription on Thaddeus Stevens's monument in the Shreiner-Concord Cemetery in Lancaster, Pennsylvania. *COURTESY ROSS HETRICK*

freed did not take long to articulate their hopes and plans. They had in fact been discussing the subject of slavery, its wrongs, and their aspirations for many years—in veiled form in religious words and practices, then more explicitly among themselves as Union armies advanced, and openly and in a great explosion of talk and planning once emancipation occurred. They did this in small groups, in large meetings, and then in formal state and national conventions.

At first, they raised cautious, relatively modest demands. In southern Louisiana, U.S. provost marshal John W. Ela reported in mid-1863 that black laborers were manifesting "a spirit of independence" and would "not endure the same treatment, the same customs, and rules—the same language—that they have heretofore quietly submitted to." They wanted to rebuild and obtain legal recognition for their families, which slavery had denigrated and dismembered. People who had regularly suffered whippings and other physical punishments now refused to allow employers to harm them or their family members or otherwise interfere in their family lives. Throughout Union-occupied parts of the South, meanwhile, black people were striving to obtain an education. When the first fugitives entered Fort Monroe in Virginia in 1861, a white official already found them anxious to learn to read. Wherever other officials went they encountered freedpeople "eager to obtain for themselves, but especially for their children, those privileges of education which have hitherto been jealously withheld from them."[3]

As slavery's advancing disintegration increased black people's optimism and self-confidence, they grew bolder in articulating aims and in acting to achieve them. That happened first of all on the farms and plantations where they lived and worked. Union provost marshal Ela watched "the negroes band together, and lay down their own rules, as to when, and how long they will work etc. etc. and the overseer loses all control over them." Planter complaints echoed Ela's observation. Freedpeople refused to work any longer under overseers in the hard-driven, regimented gangs common under slavery. In general, they would not labor as intensively as they had previously been driven to do, and they demanded shorter working days, shorter workweeks, and better food, shelter, and clothing. Families sought to relieve women from field labor performed under white supervision, both to shield them from predation and to allow them to spend more time in their cabins and caring for their children. Children, too, should be relieved of field labor so that they could help their mothers or attend school. Black people who all their lives had needed written passes in order to set foot outside their masters' premises now sought the same freedom that white people enjoyed to move about the countryside.[4]

Before long, black people also added legal and political goals to their demands. In October 1864, Frederick Douglass presided over a National Convention of Colored Men held in Syracuse, New York. One hundred fifty delegates attended from the District of Columbia and seventeen states, seven of them slave states. The convention demanded "the immediate and unconditional abolition of slavery," rejected colonization, and called for the extension to black people of "the rights of other citizens." Reminding the white public that "when the nation in her trial hour called her sable sons to arms, we gladly went to fight her battles," the delegates noted that while "we have fought and conquered," still we "have been denied the laurels of victory," excluded alike from schools, juries, and political life. They did not expect an end to racial discrimination "in social and domestic relations" but did insist "that in the matter of government, the object of which is the protection and security of human rights, prejudice should be allowed no voice whatever."[5]

This Syracuse convention launched a grassroots National Equal Rights League, dedicated to "recognition of the rights of the colored people of the nation as citizens," and that League soon spread into a number of states, north and south. It seems unlikely that significant number of freedpeople, as opposed to prewar free blacks, had been able to make their way to Syracuse. But southern units of the Equal Rights League were a different story. In January 1865, one of the Syracuse participants—James H. Ingraham, born into slavery, later a captain in a black Union regiment—chaired a State Convention of the Colored People of Louisiana. Delegates attended that convention from New Orleans as well as a number of rural parishes, and their ranks included freedpeople as well as antebellum free blacks. Those delegates created a Louisiana branch of the new League and endorsed an agenda similar to the one passed at Syracuse.[6]

By 1864, African Americans were calling specifically for voting rights. Two citizens of New Orleans met with Lincoln that March and urged him to endorse the enfranchisement of Louisiana's black males. The Syracuse convention called for "political equality," including both equality before the law and the right to vote. In January 1865, a Convention of the Colored Men of Ohio declared "that the safety of the Republic demands that, in the Territories, in the rebel States, when reorganized, and throughout the entire nation, colored men shall exercise the elective franchise, and be otherwise fully clothed with the rights of American citizens."[7]

Acutely conscious of slavery's breakdown in the border states and Union-occupied parts of the Confederacy and determined to counter the freedpeople's growing assertiveness, the southern white elite formulated its own aims in opposition. Having always regarded slavery as essential to profitable southern agriculture, landowners considered it impossible to proceed without restoring bondage or at least imposing something like it in its place.

Lieutenant Colonel George H. Hanks, the superintendent of Negro labor in the Union army's Department of the Gulf, reported in 1864 that planters there "yield to the idea of freedom only under compulsion. They submit to the terms dictated by the Government, because obliged to do so." But "the spirit of Slavery still lives among them." One group of Louisiana slaveowners thus promised to accept the coming of "free labor" if that freedom were strongly qualified—if the U.S. military would "compel the negroes to work" and to work "diligently and faithfully" for the whites. After all, argued planter W. W. Pugh of Assumption Parish, Louisiana, "coercion, & . . . fear of punishment . . . is essential to stimulate the idle and correct the vicious." Planters in Mississippi and Alabama sought the same kinds of accommodation. In the political sphere, leading members of that class sought to regain control of their state and local governments. Only that would enable them to exercise the power they craved over the black population.[8]

Abraham Lincoln's plans for the postwar South fluctuated significantly. That was true even of what he said about slavery's future. His Emancipation Proclamation had declared slaves in nearly all of the Confederacy to be free as of January 1, 1863. In attempting to organize loyal governments speedily in rebellious states, however, the president seemed for some time to hedge on that promise. At least twice during 1863, he signaled privately that if Confederate states opted to rejoin the Union they might free their slaves gradually rather than immediately.[9] He did that partly in hopes that offering a slow-motion emancipation process might encourage reunionist sentiment among rebels.

But as 1863 unfolded, the importance of black soldiers to the Union cause increased, the Union's military fortunes rose, and Lincoln returned to the principle of immediate emancipation. On December 8, he spelled out how he would treat Confederates who returned to the Union and on what terms they could "reinaugurate loyal state governments." The president offered "a full pardon" to all rebels who swore to "henceforth faithfully support, protect, and defend the Constitution of the United States and the Union of the

States thereunder" and to abide by all of the Union's wartime laws and edicts concerning slavery. Pardoned rebels would enjoy "restoration of all rights of property, *except as to slaves*." People freed during the war, he affirmed, must remain free. Any other policy, he said, would constitute "a cruel and astounding breach of faith." And Lincoln excluded from his offer of blanket pardon all members of the Confederacy's governmental, diplomatic, and military elite; those who had resigned seats in the U.S. Congress or commissions in the U.S. armed forces in order to join the rebellion; and those who had mistreated Union prisoners of war.[10]

Lincoln had always held that the rebellious states had never legally left the Union, even if they had forfeited temporarily certain rights within it. His December 1863 message specified conditions for restoring those states to full political standing. Once a tenth of a state's voters took the required oath, they could create what would "be recognized as the true government of the state," which would enjoy all the rights that such recognition implied. By the war's end, Lincoln had begun to nurture the beginnings of a few such governments. He did note that, as the Constitution specified, the power to decide whether to admit men sent to Congress from any states rested with the Congress itself.[11]

Considering that secession was an armed insurrection against the constitutional government—an insurrection immensely costly in blood and treasure—these were very lenient terms. And the 1863 proclamation contained two more concessions designed to attract secessionists back into the Union.

First, Lincoln offered new southern state governments the right to define freedpeople's legal status.[12] He promised not to oppose any "temporary arrangement" that such state governments might adopt concerning the condition of their "laboring, landless, and homeless class" of former slaves. While demanding recognition of black people's freedom from slavery and requiring that they be offered some education, Lincoln was offering not to oppose imposition upon them of what was known euphemistically throughout the Western Hemisphere as "apprenticeship." As all understood, that meant limiting the legal rights of ex-slaves and probably binding them to labor for others for some specified period of time. Oppressive conditions of that type had been imposed decades earlier on freed slaves in northern states and in the British Empire.

Personally, Lincoln acknowledged, he would rather see black laborers treated "precisely as I would treat the same number of free white people in the same relation and condition." But he would now mute that preference in hopes that his "acquiescence" in the wishes of "the deeply afflicted [white] people in those States" would speed their return to the United States. The Union army's conduct in the Mississippi valley seemed to affirm the sincerity of Lincoln's offer. There, Generals Benjamin Butler and Nathaniel Banks did outlaw whipping and require employers to pay wages to emancipated slaves. But they also assisted employers to discipline black workers, required workers to sign year-long contracts, and punished those who quit their employers before a contract term ended.[13]

In a second overture to rebels, Lincoln said that while ex-Confederates reentering the Union must swear to abide by the Union's wartime antislavery measures, they need honor that oath only "so long and so far as" those measures were "not repealed, modified, or held void by congress, or by decision of the supreme court." To prospective southern reunionists, these words suggested that they might yet avoid emancipation altogether.[14]

During the final months of his life, Lincoln's policy continued to evolve. Conciliatory gestures toward rebels mixed with heightened consideration for the plight of freedpeople. In early February 1865, he suggested to his cabinet that the federal government compensate rebellious masters for the loss of their slaves, abandoning that proposal only when cabinet members balked. In early April, the president permitted Confederate official John A. Campbell to call Virginia's Confederate state legislature into session for the purpose of formally surrendering to the Union. But Lincoln had no intention of permitting that rebel legislature to remain in session, much less in power, indefinitely. So when Campbell tried to use his gesture to accomplish just that, Lincoln shut the whole operation down. Meanwhile, he accepted General William T. Sherman's field order provisionally allotting much southern acreage to freedpeople. The president was also warming to the idea of limited suffrage for blacks. In March 1864, he suggested privately that Louisiana, once reintegrated into the Union, grant the vote to well-educated black men as well as to "those who have fought gallantly in our ranks." In the spring of 1865, in his last speech, Lincoln urged that course publicly.[15]

Thaddeus Stevens rejected Lincoln's reconstruction policies as far too lenient. He called for increasing and exerting the power of the federal government, for enforcing the subordination of rebels, and for guaranteeing not only personal freedom but equal legal rights to the emancipated. He showed no interest in offering concessions to the slaveholders. He surely concurred instead with Salmon P. Chase's insistence that, to win the war and rebuild the Union properly, "the Southern people whom we must conciliate are the black Americans, who till the soil, or load the boats, & cars, or pursue the handicrafts" along with whatever number of whites there who were genuinely willing to see genuinely free labor replace slavery.[16]

During the war, Stevens already advocated much that he would specify later in a presentation before a Lancaster audience. It was crucial to establish in the rebellious states, he believed, "governments . . . which shall be republican in form and principles." We must rid those states of "every vestige of human bondage" and make it impossible for slavery ever to arise there again. It was also necessary "to inflict condign punishment on the rebel belligerents, and so weaken their hands that they can never again endanger the Union." The federal government must grant and enforce equal rights for black southerners. In short, as he told an associate, the Republican Party must "treat this as a radical revolution."[17]

This agenda dictated Stevens's position regarding the rebel states' legal status. He sought a legal justification to do what the revolution he sought required, and he found that justification, once again, in the law of nations. The Constitution prevented the federal government from imposing such an agenda upon states so long as they remained within the Union. But all of the changes that he deemed essential in the South would become legally unassailable if Republicans would "accept the position to which they [the rebels] placed themselves," a position "severed from the Union; an independent government *de facto*, and an alien enemy to be dealt with according to the laws of war."[18]

Stevens thus joined James Ashley in the House of Representatives and Charles Sumner in the Senate in arguing that the rebel states had ceased to exist as properly self-governing political entities within the United States. They had instead become what they declared themselves to be, part of a foreign, enemy country. They had given up their previous constitutional rights within the United States. Once the Union defeated and occupied them, therefore, it could and should govern them as federal territories.[19]

Stevens elaborated in the spring of 1863. "The States in rebellion, who, . . . have declared themselves out of the Union, and have maintained such declaration by an armed force sufficient to make them separate *in fact*, and have established a separate and independent government *de facto*, are in the double condition of traitors and of a belligerent power." Therefore their "compacts with the United States are broken and dissolved, so that they can claim no protection under the Constitution of the United States or the laws thereof." Consequently "the United States may proceed against them untrammeled by any obligations but the laws of war; and that we may subdue them and hold them as conquered provinces." The legal doctrine that had allowed the government to fight the war with extraordinary means would also legitimate the extraordinary means necessary to secure the wartime victory afterward.[20]

Stevens thus disagreed sharply with Lincoln's belief that the rebellious states remained within the Union. The source of that difference, however, lay not in legal doctrine and nomenclature but practical policy—in his view of what had to be done next. He came as close as possible to saying as much in the fall of 1865. "No reform can be effected in the Southern States if they have never left the Union," he said. "But reformation *must* be effected; the foundation of their institutions, both political, municipal, and social, *must* be broken up and *relaid*." That could "only be done by treating and holding them as a conquered people. Then all things which we can desire to do, follow with logical and legitimate authority."[21]

But on this subject and others, Stevens, Sumner, and allied radicals did not speak for all congressional Republicans. The large contingent of moderates insisted on enforcing the Emancipation Proclamation and opposed attempts to restrict the freedom it declared. But they placed a higher value on restoring national unity than on further reshaping southern society, and they balked at breaching the bounds of legal tradition. They might be induced to support stronger measures if they judged them necessary to protect their core principles and interests, but they preferred not to do so. That disposition distinguished them sharply from Stevens and the radicals, for whom war and Reconstruction offered an opportunity to perfect the country and its institutions. Leading Republican moderates such as Maine's Senator William Pitt Fessenden, as a recent biography aptly notes, "had always regarded Reconstruction as a problem to be solved rather than an opportunity to be grasped."[22]

Differences about the meaning of emancipation became apparent as Congress debated the proposed Thirteenth Amendment to abolish slavery. Some supporters of the amendment, like unionist Senator John B. Henderson of Missouri, espoused a minimalist definition of emancipation. "We give him no right except his freedom," Henderson said of the former slave, "and leave the rest to the States."[23] But most Republicans, including Stevens, agreed with Illinois's Representative Isaac N. Arnold, who espoused a more expansive understanding of freedom, insisting that "liberty" meant "equality before the law."[24]

Stevens's belief that freedom must carry with it equal legal rights also carried the assumption that former slaves would continue to live in the postwar United States. So although he had earlier helped appropriate funds for voluntary colonization, he now forcefully condemned such undertakings. Colonization, he declared in May 1864, was both "unwise and cruel." Unwise, because "as a means of removing Africans from the country it was puerile," since "all the revenue of the United States would not pay for the transportation of one half of their annual increase." Cruel, because black Americans "were averse to removing them from their native land," and expatriating them against their will "would be as atrocious a crime as stealing them in Africa and reducing them to bondage" had been in the first place.[25]

The demand for equal civil rights for freedpeople outraged congressional Democrats. Eager to restore national life to something resembling its prewar condition, Democrats adopted the slogan "The Union as it was, the Constitution as it is." They opposed anything they regarded as punitive toward the South. And they remained firmly committed not only to white supremacy but also to the defense of slavery or a reasonable facsimile thereof.

On the House floor in early January 1865, accordingly, Ohio Democrat Samuel Cox called on Thaddeus Stevens to "give up his doctrine of negro equality" for the sake of restoring peace and national harmony. Stevens replied that he stood not for "equality in all things—simply equality before the laws." Cox understood, however, that equality before the laws was no small thing. It would mean not only freedom from enslavement but also equal treatment by the laws and in the courts—an end to discriminatory legislation and penalties and the rights to sue, testify, and sit on juries. Cox therefore pressed Stevens "to give up his idea of the equality of the black and white races before the law." To which Stevens tersely replied, "I won't do it."[26]

Congressmen who considered Lincoln's Reconstruction plan deficient wanted to guarantee more firmly the freedom and civil rights of black people and to raise the bar for rebel states seeking full rights within the Union. Early in 1864, Ohio's radical Republican senator Benjamin Wade and Maryland's representative Henry Winter Davis brought a bill into both houses of Congress that would not merely emancipate those currently enslaved but fully outlaw the institution of slavery. It also promised equal legal rights for all freedpeople once Reconstruction began—all rights, that is, except the rights to vote and to sit on juries. This Wade-Davis bill would also require that a clear majority of a rebellious states' white voters (not a mere tenth, as Lincoln had stipulated) pledge to support the U.S. Constitution. And only those would be permitted to elect representatives to the states' constitutional conventions who swore not simply future loyalty but also never to have voluntarily aided the Confederacy.[27]

This was not enough for Thaddeus Stevens. Even the Wade-Davis bill "does not . . . meet the evil" because, like Lincoln's plan, "it partially acknowledges the rebel States to have rights under the Constitution, which I deny." He introduced a substitute bill on April 29, 1864, that took the ground that Representative James Ashley had staked out, proposing to govern all ex-rebel states as federal territories. But Democrats as well as numerous Republicans rejected his bill, claiming that the rebellious states had never left the Union because the Constitution denied them the right to do so. That argument left Stevens dumbfounded. Of course the Constitution forbade them to secede! That is why "in going out they committed a crime for which we are now punishing them with fire and sword." But it was absurd to claim that outlawing an act made its commission impossible—to say, in other words, that crimes generally could not occur. He reminded his critics that "the law forbids a man to rob or murder, and yet robbery and murder exist." In Stevens's eyes, his Republican critics were men "of great constitutional learning, but whose nerves are constructed of such delicate fibres that the shock of a bold idea throws them into convulsions." More bluntly, he later told a journalist that they had "no bone in their backs, and no blood in their veins."[28]

In early May, Henry Winter Davis tried to reconcile Stevens and his allies to his own bill by adding a preamble taken from Stevens's measure. That preamble denied that residents of any rebellious state should "be represented in Congress" or, indeed, "take any part in the political government of the Union." But a majority in the House, unwilling to make this concession to the radicals, rejected that proposed preamble by a vote of 76 to 57. Seventeen Republicans joined Democrats to defeat it and another four abstained. The Wade-Davis bill without the preamble then passed the House by a nearly identical vote, from which Thaddeus Stevens abstained. The Senate added its assent to the Wade-Davis bill two months later.[29]

The Wade-Davis bill that Stevens judged inadequate Lincoln found excessive. When it reached his desk, he chose to kill it with a pocket veto (which occurs when a president withholds a signature from a bill passed during the final ten days of a congressional session). He objected to the bill's dismissal of the fledgling state governments that he was then cultivating in Louisiana and Arkansas. He also denied that Congress had a constitutional right by itself to outlaw slavery in any state.

The president still did not grasp, Stevens groaned, "the rights of war and the law of nations." He didn't understand that in a war threatening the republic's existence, the requirements of winning that war rather than the letter of the Constitution must dictate *both* the government's war program *and* what needed to be done after victory to "prevent its recurrence."[30]

In Stevens's view, finally, ending the southern elite's threat to the republic required breaking that elite's economic power. Born and raised in a Vermont proud of rejecting landlord rule and canceling the property rights of both pro-British Loyalists and New Yorkers, Stevens had called during the war's first year for "confiscating the property of the rebels" in order to "pay the cost of this rebellion." Within another year he had sought confiscation for more explicitly political purposes, proposing that "a military tribunal" be attached to Union armies to seize and sell rebel lands "to the highest bidder." Not only would moneys thereby raised pay off the national debt but the process would also replace traitors on that soil with "bold and loyal settlers" who, "with arms in their hands, shall take resident possession by themselves, or their tenants, and be ready to defend it against all comers."

Stevens objected to the Wade-Davis bill in April 1864 largely because he feared that, by implying that the seceded states remained within the Union, it would impede such land seizure and resale. The nation could by right take *all* the property of rebels, he insisted, because they had stepped outside the Union's constitutional framework. But he took care to aim confiscation at only "the most guilty" of the rebels, the Confederate elite. Those people must not be "allow[ed] to return with their estates untouched." The measure that Stevens tried to substitute for the Wade-Davis bill called for seizing landed estates in the ex-Confederacy greater than one hundred acres in size and all property worth at least one thousand dollars. Such measures would evolve into one of the most controversial proposals that Thaddeus Stevens ever put forward.[31]

The war's end and the crushing of the rebellion in the spring of 1865 transformed issues that had involved only parts of the South into ones that suddenly involved all of it. Simultaneously, every question about the South's future that arose during the war would now move to the center of the nation's political stage. In the dramas that unfolded there, Thaddeus Stevens would again play a leading role.

CHAPTER NINE

"In the Midst of a Revolution"

Stevens and Postwar Reconstruction

The Confederacy's collapse took Thaddeus Stevens by surprise. He had predicted in early February 1865 that the rebellion would continue for another year or so.[1] But two months later, Union troops broke through rebel defenses around Richmond and Petersburg, Virginia, propelling Robert E. Lee's army westward in a desperate escape attempt that soon ended in surrender at Appomattox Court House. A month after that, Union soldiers captured Jefferson Davis and his escort as they fled southward. The war was effectively over.

The Union's victory settled major questions. The United States would not be divided into two separate and hostile countries. Millions of enslaved human beings would now be legally free. But the Confederacy's destruction posed as immediate, unresolved issues all the other questions about the postwar world that had first surfaced during the war. Abraham Lincoln's murder and Andrew Johnson's accession to the presidency transformed differences over those questions into an unprecedented constitutional confrontation.

Before the war, Johnson had been a Democratic senator from Tennessee. Born in that state's eastern hill country to a family with little property, he had managed over time to prosper and acquire a handful of slaves. But Johnson resented the power that the major planters wielded in the South. He opposed secession in 1865 and remained in his Senate seat when his state declared itself out of the Union. That firm and consistent unionism subsequently led Lincoln to appoint Johnson military governor of Union-occupied Tennessee and then to accept him onto the 1864 Republican ticket.

Johnson had accepted the Union's emancipation policies, and as postwar president he at first seemed ready to deal firmly with the Confederate elite. Consequently the North at first placed great confidence in the new president, and even radical Republicans anticipated a good relationship with him. But before long Johnson revealed quite different inclinations, moving to return the rebellious states as soon as possible to their prewar position and to secure the whites' control over the freedpeople.

Johnson detailed his program (which he called "restoration," a term he preferred to "reconstruction") in proclamations issued in the spring of 1865, while Congress was in its normal nine-month recess, which stretched from March to December. That recess covered the whole pivotal period from before Lee's surrender through the aftermath of state-level elections in the fall. His decrees offered amnesty to almost all white southerners who would swear future loyalty to the Union. Johnson did exclude members of the social and political elite from this offer, but they could petition him for individual pardons. Those amnestied or pardoned would obtain not only their personal freedom, voting rights, and the right to hold office but also the return of all nonslave property.

Meanwhile, the White House would establish provisional civilian governments in seven states, requiring them to nullify the ordinances of secession, repudiate Confederate-era state debts, abolish slavery within their own borders, and ratify the prospective Thirteenth Amendment. Those provisional governments were to hold elections to state constitutional conventions and state legislatures. Only whites deemed loyal to the U.S. government would vote.[2] Johnson advised but did not require that such new state governments enfranchise the estimated 10 percent or so of their black populations thought likely to pass certain property and literacy standards.

Johnson claimed that his policy was identical to Lincoln's, and as initially stated there was some formal similarity. Stevens rejected the equation. Lincoln had specifically denied wishing to impose any specific Reconstruction plan, Stevens recalled, and had acknowledged Congress's right to decide which states' delegations to admit into its chambers and which to exclude. In contrast, Johnson insisted upon his own plan and tried to coerce Congress into accepting it. Stevens might also have noted that Lincoln had not offered individual pardons to Confederate leaders he had excluded from the offer of general amnesty.

Stevens might have noted, too, the very different ways in which Lincoln's and Johnson's policies evolved over time. Over the course of the war, Lincoln had displayed a growing respect for black people and came increasingly to embrace their rights as citizens. During the postwar period, Johnson moved in the opposite direction. Despite proclaiming himself the tribune of the South's white small farmers and grandiosely promising to be a "Moses" for the freedpeople, he drew steadily closer to the southern elite while evincing ever-greater contempt for African Americans. Although suggesting quietly that ex-Confederate states grant voting rights to some black men, for example, he publicly scorned the idea of black people participating in politics. He declared in December 1867 that historically "negroes have shown less capacity for government than any other race of people." There was a "great difference between the two races in physical, mental, and moral characteristics," he added, and for that reason whites and blacks would surely remain divided in values and goals. And "if the inferior [race] obtains the ascendency over the other, it will . . . create such a tyranny as this continent has never yet witnessed." When congressional Republicans tried nonetheless to enfranchise freedmen, Johnson warned darkly that "of all the dangers which our nation has yet encountered, none are equal to those which must result from the success of the effort now making to Africanize the half of our country." Why, then, had Johnson counseled enfranchising some black men? In order, as he intimated privately, to "completely disarm . . . the radicals, who are wild upon negro franchise."[3]

Republican representative George Julian, who had sat with Johnson on a congressional committee during the war, concluded that the Tennessean was "as decided a hater of the negro . . . as the rebels from whom he had separated." Frederick Douglass deduced as much by observing the vice president–elect during the inauguration ceremony of March 1865. As Douglass watched, "Mr. Lincoln touched Mr. Johnson and pointed me out to him. The first expression which came to his face, and which I think was the true index of his heart, was one of bitter contempt and aversion." "Whatever Andrew Johnson may be," Douglass told a companion, "he is no friend of our race." The differences between Lincoln and Johnson also determined the distinct ways in which each viewed Republican radicals. Lincoln found them unrealistic, impatient, annoying, unmanageable, even "utterly lawless." But he believed that their hearts were in the right place—that, as he put it to his secretary, "after all their faces are set Zionwards." To Johnson, radicals were villains, pure and simple.[4]

The southern elite soon recognized Johnson's presence in the White House as a godsend.[5] Ex-Confederate leader Howell Cobb advised friends "to yield to our destiny with the best possible grace—recognize as fixed fact the abolition of slavery—conform in all respects to the new state of things." They should "take the amnesty oath when permitted to do it" or "apply for special pardons." This would then allow them to achieve a most-cherished goal, "the early restoration of our state and civil government."[6] Most did just that, flooding Johnson's desk with requests for pardons that Johnson granted by the thousand.[7]

The president's conciliatory conduct lifted the spirits and boosted the self-confidence of planters. Different sections of that class and its advocates had reacted differently in the immediate aftermath of military defeat. Some exuded continued defiance. Others were demoralized and feared the most severe punishment. "When their armies were dispersed," Thaddeus Stevens later recalled of them, they would "gladly" have accepted severe surrender terms if only their lives were spared. But when Andrew Johnson signaled that their treatment would be far milder than they had feared, they began once again to raise their heads. A mood of defeatism gave way to renewed assertiveness.[8]

Eyewitness testimony to that effect was plentiful. John Minor Botts, a well-known Whig congressman in prewar Virginia, landed in a Confederate jail because of his open unionism during the conflict. "At the time of the surrender of General Lee's army and the restoration of peace," Botts later recalled, rebel leaders "seemed to have been entirely subdued. . . . They felt exceedingly apprehensive for the security of their property, as well as for the security of their lives; and a more humble, unpretending set of gentlemen I never saw than they were at that time." All that had changed, however, with Andrew Johnson's forgiveness of ex-Confederate leaders. "From the time that Mr. Johnson commenced his indiscriminate system of pardoning all who made application," Botts recounted, the southern elite "became bold, insolent, and defiant," and since then "the spirit of disloyalty and disaffection has gone on increasing day by day, and hour by hour, until among the leaders generally there is as much disaffection and disloyalty as there was at any time during the war, and a hundredfold more than there was immediately after the evacuation and surrender of the army." Reports reaching Stevens's mailbox confirmed that account.[9]

Stevens protested Johnson's restoration policy from the spring of 1865, while Congress was still in recess. The new president had no constitutional power to restore a rebellious state to its place in the Union or to recognize such a state's government, he said. Those powers belonged to Congress. Johnson should call the national legislature back into session to address those matters. Otherwise, as he diplomatically put it, the president risked "allow[ing] many to think that the executive was approaching usurpation" of Congress's rightful powers.[10] In early July, Stevens wrote Johnson again, warning that no leading Republican "approves of your policy," that on the contrary all "believe that 'Restoration' as announced by you will destroy our party" and "greatly injure the country." Meanwhile Stevens strove to enlist other Republicans in the cause of "arresting the ruinous course of the President." In mid-August, he persuaded his party's state convention in Pennsylvania to oppose restoring political rights to any rebel state until it proved ready to guarantee to all "the inalienable right to life, liberty, and the pursuit of happiness" and to insist that the sole power to restore rebel states to the Union lay with the Congress.[11]

President Johnson brushed aside such opposition. By mid-December 1865, he was proclaiming his policies successful; eight of the "insurrectionary states," the president announced, had satisfactorily "reorganized their respective State governments" and were now showing obedience to the federal government and its laws "with more willingness and greater promptitude than under the circumstances could reasonably have been anticipated." Not only that, but "in nearly all of [those states] measures have been adopted or are now pending, to confer upon freedmen rights and privileges which are essential to their comfort, protection, and security."[12]

Neither Republican radicals nor moderates found it easy to take that appraisal seriously. The fall of 1865 had seen white southern voters elect ex-Confederate officials to office everywhere. Former rebel military officers now proudly wore their uniforms in the Louisiana state legislature. In North Carolina, Jonathan Worth, who had served as state treasurer during the war, became governor. Both South Carolina and Mississippi elected unpardoned Confederate generals, Wade Hampton and Benjamin G. Humphreys, as their governors. Johnson pardoned both men after their election. South Carolina declined to repudiate the debts of its Confederate-era state government, and Mississippi refused to ratify the Thirteenth Amendment. Southern delegations being sent to the Thirty-Ninth U.S. Congress included the Confederacy's vice president, six cabinet officers, fifty-eight members of the Confederate congress, four Confederate generals, and five colonels. Not even Andrew Johnson could miss the animus driving such conduct. "There seem in many of the elections," he acknowledged privately, "something like defiance."[13]

Wealthy southerners and their political representatives soon revealed definite plans for using their reacquired political power. They aimed first and foremost to maintain or regain their plantations. As for who would work that land, some initially hoped that slavery itself might somehow survive—if, for example, the states should refuse to approve the Thirteenth Amendment. That hope died with the amendment's ratification at the end of 1865. But how, then, would southern landowners find the kind of labor force that they believed profitability required, people who could be induced to do an extraordinary amount of work at comparatively small cost to the landowners? It had been an article of faith among southern proprietors since the seventeenth century that only compulsory labor, enforced by law, would answer that need. A northern reporter touring the postwar South found that opinion as strong as ever. Planters "have no sort of conception of free labor. They do not comprehend any law for controlling laborers, save the law of force." Ex-Confederates said as much in so many words. "No planter," an Alabaman affirmed in July 1865, "sees any way by the present lights to make useful laborers out of free negroes."[14]

By the year's end the South's elite had accepted the end of slavery because it had no other choice. But if planters and their allies had their way, formal abolition would constitute the outer boundary of change. Samuel Thomas, a Union colonel serving in Mississippi and northeastern Louisiana, reported that although whites now recognized that they could no longer own individual black people, "they still have an ingrained feeling that the blacks *at large* belong to the whites *at large*." If permitted, they would return black people to a condition as close as possible to slavery. To do that they would, as a conservative New Orleans newspaper anticipated, create a new labor system "prescribed and enforced by the state."[15]

Black landlessness was a precondition for that program's success. It seemed essential, that is, not only to keep plantation lands in planters' hands but also to make it impossible for blacks to obtain *any* decent land to farm, so that they would have no alternative to working for the whites. As the same Colonel Thomas explained, "The whites know that if the negro is not allowed to acquire property or become a landholder he must return to plantation labor and work for wages that will barely support himself and his family; and they feel that this kind of slavery is better than none at all."[16]

Preventing blacks from owning land was but the first step down the road to renewed subordination. The next was to deny to landless blacks the personal rights that might enable them as hired laborers to command higher wages, shorter hours, and better working conditions, or to leave field work altogether. Southern state governments elected under Johnson's aegis began to pass legislation inspired by the planters' agenda. New laws, known collectively as "black codes," aimed to create a malleable and dependent black labor force. Those codes acknowledged the end of slavery and stipulated freedpeople's right to own some forms of property, make contracts, obtain legal marriages, and gain limited access to the courts. More telling were the provisions that denied freedpeople a host of other rights and freedoms.

Details varied from state to state, but most of these codes included the same basic elements. Denying that African Americans were citizens, states passed laws that sharply limited or flatly withheld many of the rights associated with citizenship—to serve on juries, to own land or guns, to select one's place of residence and occupation, and even to pick one's employers and negotiate terms. Many localities forbade blacks to take any jobs but field labor and domestic service. Several state codes imposed lengthy hours of labor and work duties and specified the servile demeanor expected. Freedpeople judged to be without appropriate types of employment could be arrested, jailed, and fined. If unable to pay that fine, they would be hired out to an employer who assumed responsibility for the fine and deducted it from the workers' wages.

The black codes laid special claim to the bodies of children, depriving parents of the legal means to defend their families. A North Carolina law enabled officials to remove black children from their families and "apprentice" them to someone else "when the parents . . . do not habitually employ their time in some honest, industrious occupation." When courts did place such children with other adults, they typically chose a child's former owner rather than family and friends of the child's parents.[17]

The effect of the black codes thus was to define a black person's status in the postwar South as that of an impoverished, permanently landless laborer with a minimum of legal rights, living in a state of semi-slavery/semi-freedom. It seemed obvious to Stevens that these discriminatory and "oppressive laws" aimed to "crush to death the hated freedmen." But Andrew Johnson made no attempt to have those laws rescinded or even modified.[18]

While southern state and local governments took aim at freedpeople's rights, bands of whites enraged by defeat and emancipation assaulted them physically. Stevens heard from a former Union officer still living in North Carolina that "the Southern people are Especially bitter against the negro (though afraid of him) because he has been made free—Sometimes threatening loudly what they will do with him when his friends the Yankee troops have been removed." The officer added that "all classes unite in abusing the Negro by word of mouth, and so far as they dare do so, by deeds of personal violence." County and municipal officials, claiming to act in self-defense against alleged black violence, formed armed militia companies and patrol groups to identify, intimidate, beat, and kill local black leaders. Guns in hand, they stripped black families of weapons and other property, whipping, maiming, shooting, and hanging those who resisted them or in some other way offended whites' sensibilities.[19]

In late 1863, when the war's outcome was still in doubt, Lincoln had felt obliged to try to lure rebel states back into the Union with a promise to allow them to impose special restrictions on freedpeople. Two years later—with the war won, with the felt need to bribe rebels into reunion therefore gone, and with black people having played so important a role in the Union's victory—the Republican Party was no longer willing to tolerate such glaring violations of its ideal of "free labor." It certainly would not abide Confederate leaders resuming control of southern political life. As Republican moderate James G. Blaine reflected, "If the Southern men had intended . . . to inflame the public opinion of the North against them, they would have proceeded precisely as they did." The black codes of 1865–66, the neo-Confederate state governments that enacted them, and the antiblack violence of the war's aftermath therefore pushed steadily growing numbers of Republicans to oppose Johnson's policies and open a new phase in the Reconstruction process.[20]

The House of Representatives and Senate reconvened in early December 1865, and the first question posed for Republicans was whether to admit or exclude the men who claimed to represent the ex-Confederate states. To seat them, Republicans feared, might return control of Congress and the White House to an alliance of northern and southern Democrats. That, Stevens warned, would mean surrendering all of the hard-won gains of war and ensure "the oppression of the freedmen . . . and the re-establishment of slavery."[21]

On Saturday, December 2, the Republican caucus in the House of Representatives decided unanimously to have Congress create a joint congressional committee that would investigate conditions in the states of the ex-Confederacy and determine which if any of them "are entitled to be represented in either house of Congress." Until that committee submitted its findings and Congress acted upon them, it added, "no member shall be received into either House" from the rebel states.

Two days later, as the Thirty-Ninth Congress convened, Edward McPherson, the new House clerk who had long been close to Stevens, called the roll of its members. In accordance with the Republican caucus's decision, he refused to read off the names of those claiming seats from the ex-Confederate states. After helping McPherson brush aside protests by House Democrats, Stevens presented his caucus's call for a joint committee, and on December 13 Congress agreed to form one. Its fifteen members included Stevens, who led the House's contingent. The moderate Republican senator William P. Fessenden became committee chairman.[22]

With the rebel states barred from Congress, Republicans held 70 percent of the seats in the U.S. Senate and 75 percent in the House.

Stevens aimed to use his party's legislative power to advance radical changes already under way in southern society. The nation now finds itself, he said in July 1866, "in the midst of a revolution." The task now was to proceed with "perfecting a revolution" already in progress. Stevens granted that the people of the North had not deliberately embarked upon such a path when they elected Lincoln and then went to war to save the Union. Indeed, he conceded, had they been asked directly to choose it back then, "possibly the people would not have inaugurated this revolution." But now that a treasonous rebellion had "forced upon them" a revolutionary course in sheer self-defense, he hoped that the people would carry that revolution through to its necessary conclusion.[23]

But Stevens and his closest allies did not control Congress, because they did not control the Republican delegation. By one estimate, only one out of every three House Republicans in 1865 was a radical; in the Senate, the proportion was one out of five. Neither did radicals dominate the Joint Committee on Reconstruction. Unable to dictate Congress's legislative agenda, therefore, they would have to depend upon the merits of their proposals, the failure of moderate alternatives, and the instructive power of events taking place in the South to demonstrate the necessity of their proposals to fellow Republicans. More often than many expected, that is exactly what happened.

The same dynamic that during the war had pushed the Republican Party to repeatedly escalate its attacks upon slavery now led it to promise protection of black people's rights. The power of Frederick Douglass's "inexorable logic of events" was once again on display. But that logic did not always prove potent enough to empower the radicals. Moderates could and did often resist it, digging in their heels and frustrating Stevens's efforts. Reconstruction in the Johnson years would be shaped by the way that developments in the country at large affected the shifting balance of forces in Washington between

Republican radicals and the White House, with Republican moderates holding the middle.[24]

For the moment, the black codes and the neo-Confederate officials who imposed them pulled Republican radicals and moderates together. On February 20, 1866, Stevens brought a resolution from the Joint Committee on Reconstruction into the House that barred anyone from the rebel states from being seated in either chamber until Congress specifically judged those states "entitled to such representation." Over furious Democratic protests and attempts to obstruct, delay, and force adjournment, the House adopted that resolution. The Senate concurred on March 2. Of Republicans in both houses, all but a handful of die-hard Johnson loyalists voted in favor.[25]

Meanwhile, the House and Senate addressed themselves to the future of the Freedmen's Bureau. Congress had created the Bureau in March 1865 as a temporary agency that would provide some material assistance to destitute former slaves, oversee contractual relations between them and prospective employers, and manage confiscated and abandoned lands. In the first months of 1866, both houses of Congress voted to extend the Bureau's life and expand its powers, now mandating it to provide military protection to freedpeople denied equal rights before the law in ex-rebel states and giving it jurisdiction in those cases.

Johnson vetoed the Freedmen's Bureau extension bill on February 19, claiming that its provisions were unnecessary since slavery "has been already effectually and finally abrogated throughout the whole country." Such a law, he also charged, would infringe upon the rights of white southerners. And by providing food, clothing, and shelter to destitute freedpeople, the Bureau would tell blacks that they did not need to work for a living, thereby weakening both "their character and their prosperity."

Johnson justified his veto with another assertion, one that carried the most sweeping implications. Lawmakers must not pass such important legislation, he insisted, while they continued to exclude representatives of formerly Confederate states from their midst. By vetoing the bill on that ground, Johnson was employing presidential power to infringe upon the internal affairs of the Congress, using the veto to force legislators to admit representatives of rebel states or risk his striking down every congressional bill concerning Reconstruction. Congress narrowly failed to override this veto, but that summer it passed a second Freedmen's Bureau bill. When Johnson vetoed it, too, congressional Republicans did override him. [26]

And in February and March of 1866, both houses passed a momentous civil rights bill. Designed to specify the nature and extent of the freedom granted in the Thirteenth Amendment, this legislation broke sharply and in a number of ways with previously dominant conceptions of constitutional federalism, dramatically increasing the role of the national government in protecting individual rights. It declared that all people born or naturalized throughout the United States were citizens of the country, thus challenging the Supreme Court's 1857 *Dred Scott* decision. (Only excluded were "Indans, not taxed," who were considered to belong to their own tribal sovereignties.) The bill required that all laws and all criminal penalties apply in the same way to all citizens. Although it did not grant black men the right to vote, it did give them property rights and equal access to the courts. Anyone trying to abrogate those rights would now be guilty of a misdemeanor punishable by a fine of up to a thousand dollars or a year in prison. The federal government would enforce those rights, and those accused of violating them would find themselves in federal, not state, courts. [27]

Johnson vetoed that civil rights bill on March 27, 1866, denouncing it as a violation of constitutional federalism, an invasion of the rights of states. He objected substantively to this attempt to legislate "a perfect equality of the white and colored races," since recently freed slaves could not possibly "possess the requisite qualifications to entitle them to all the privileges and immunities of citizenship of the United States." He also objected on more frankly racist grounds. It was impermissible to outlaw "discrimination between different races" because such discrimination was quite appropriate. In any case, he added, the protections that the bill afforded to black people were unnecessary. It "may safely be assumed," the president declared in the teeth of the black codes and widespread antiblack violence, that existing state and federal laws already "are sufficient to give protection and benefits" to the freedpeople. Nor was it "likely," he assured the nation, that southern states would pass discriminatory laws. On the contrary, with slavery now abolished "there will be a new adjustment" in the South between white and black, an adjustment "which both are deeply interested in making harmonious" and so both will surely cooperate to "satisfactorily work out the problem."[28]

That message's divorce from reality was stunning, once again driving Republican moderates to join radicals in opposition. On April 6, 1866, the Senate voted to override the veto of the civil rights bill, with all but four Republicans and one independent unionist voting to do that. Three days later, the House voted to override as well, with only one northern Republican (Henry Raymond) and six border-state unionists joining Democrats in Johnson's support. And so the bill became law.[29]

That summer, the Joint Committee on Reconstruction described the conditions in the South that justified such a measure. The committee's radical and moderate Republican members agreed that although rebel armies had been defeated and dispersed, the spirit of rebellion remained powerful and widespread in the ex-Confederate states; both African Americans and pro-Union whites there lived in peril. Furthermore, the committee said, those state governments had never been properly created following the Confederacy's collapse, nor were they truly republican in form. Affirming the nation's right and responsibility to prevent disloyal people from regaining control of the federal government and its resources, the committee called upon Congress to seat no representatives from rebel states until they provided "such constitutional or other guarantees as will tend to secure the civil rights of all citizens of the Republic" within their borders.[30]

Enactment of the civil rights bill constituted an important step forward for the cause of legal equality in the South. But everyone in Washington knew that a law passed by Congress, even over a presidential veto, could still be ruled unconstitutional by the Supreme Court or rescinded by later Congresses. To avoid future reversal, Republicans moved to enshrine the contents of the Civil Rights Act in the U.S. Constitution. Stevens had called for doing that as early as December 1865, proposing a constitutional amendment guaranteeing that "all national and State laws shall be equally applicable to every citizen, and no discrimination shall be made on account of race and color." On April 30, 1866, Stevens brought the Joint Committee on Reconstruction's version of an amendment into the House of Representatives.[31]

Congressional debate on that subject began about a week later. The amendment eventually adopted included multiple provisions. It prohibited paying state debts incurred under the Confederacy or compensating anyone for the emancipation of his or her slaves. Far more important, it altered the Constitution's stand concerning the nature and inclusiveness of citizenship, the role and power of the federal government in protecting citizens' rights, and the basis for allocating congressional power among the various states.

The amendment extended citizenship in both the country and their states of residence to "all persons born or naturalized in the United States, and subject to the jurisdiction thereof." It did thereby overturn the *Dred Scott* decision. The amendment also forbade states to "make or enforce any law which shall abridge the privileges or immunities of citizens" or to "deprive any person of life, liberty, or property, without due process of law" or to deprive them of "the equal protection of the laws."[32]

The proposed amendment went beyond the Civil Rights Act to address the structure and functioning of government. It barred from state or national office all men who had previously sworn allegiance to the U.S. Constitution, as either military or political officials, but had gone over to the rebellion. And it changed the way that the size of any state's delegation in the House of Representatives (and therefore the Electoral College, too) would be calculated.

The Constitution originally based the size of a state's House delegation on "the whole Number of free Persons" plus "three fifths of all other Persons" (that is, slaves) living therein. In the antebellum era, that so-called three-fifths clause had thus given southern white citizens disproportionate representation in the House and the Electoral College. Emancipation now threatened to increase that power. Unless something were done about it, a southern state would now benefit from the *full* number of its black residents even though blacks could not vote in that state. Ironically, thus, the extinction of the three-fifths clause would strengthen the political hand of freedpeople's former masters.

Congress could have solved this problem by placing enfranchisement of southern black men in the proposed constitutional amendment, as a number of radical Republicans urged. That would have allowed Republicans to fill many of the additional House seats created by the three-fifths clause's demise. But not enough Republicans were as yet willing to infringe upon a state's long-standing prerogative to set qualifications for voting. Nor were many Republican leaders ready to challenge the strongly racist views still rife not only in the South but in the North as well.[33]

So the Joint Committee on Reconstruction presented the House with an alternative solution that sought to accomplish black enfranchisement in the South indirectly. By the terms of the constitutional amendment that it initially proposed, if even *one* black man were denied the vote on a racial basis, *no* black people would be counted in fixing the size of that state's House delegation. Stevens had expected that fear of so politically debilitating a punishment would compel southern states to give the vote to black men "at no distant period." But because more conservative Republicans in the Senate found this provision too severe, the Joint Committee subsequently reported out a weaker version of the amendment providing that a state's House delegation be reduced only in *proportion* to the number of adult male citizens specifically barred from the polls.[34]

Stevens acknowledged the shortcomings of the proposed amendment on May 8, 1866. It was "not all that the committee desired," he said, and it "falls far short of my wishes." He had long believed that the founding fathers "had been compelled to postpone the principles of their great Declaration [of Independence], and wait for their full establishment till a more propitious time." That time, Stevens thought, should by now have arrived. Unfortunately, he had been compelled to recognize, the halfway measure being considered was "all that can be obtained in the present state of public opinion" because "the public mind has been educated in error for a century" and was therefore unreceptive to guaranteeing fully equal rights to all men.[35] "Believing, then, that this is the best proposition that can be made effectual," Stevens explained, "I accept it." To allow it instead to die would have "postponed the protection of the colored race perhaps for ages." He would not "throw away a great good because it is not perfect. I will take all I can get in the cause of humanity and leave it to be perfected by better men in better times."[36]

As these words demonstrate, Stevens did not—contrary to his reputation in some quarters—reject compromise in general. He offered a textbook lesson in *how* to accept a necessary compromise without abandoning or concealing one's own political position and preferences and so without disorienting one's allies and supporters. He agreed to this less-than-ideal "short step" toward black suffrage because he had no way of achieving a superior measure. But he made clear to everyone both his views as well as the limitations of the compromise he felt compelled to accept. By refusing to pretend that the amendment was better than it was, he prepared allies and supporters to renew the fight when conditions allowed.

The House passed this proposed Fourteenth Amendment on May 10, 1866, by an overwhelming majority, sparking applause on the floor and cheers from the public galleries. Wisconsin Democrat Charles Eldridge snarled an objection to this demonstration "by the 'niggerheads' in the galleries." The galleries responded with hisses, but the Speaker of the House declared that such demonstrations were indeed inappropriate. Stevens then inquired, with tongue in cheek, whether it was "in order for members on the floor to disturb those in the galleries." Amid laughter, the Speaker admonished House members that they "should not insult the spectators."[37]

The House version of the new amendment would bar Confederate loyalists from voting for members of Congress or presidential electors until 1870. When the Senate took it up, it removed that provision, excluding rebel leaders not from suffrage but only from holding public office. The House acceded to that change. Stevens warned that failing to disfranchise Confederate loyalists while "loyal men of color" remained vote-less endangered the republic's future. But he accepted this modified amendment, since despite "the omission of many better things," it did include "much positive good." In one respect, in fact, it was stronger than the House's version, because while the initial attempt to disfranchise ex-Confederates had applied only to national elections, the amendment's final wording effectively excluded the white South's traditional leadership from *all* public office. In any case, Stevens dared not wait any longer before adopting this admittedly "imperfect" amendment, lest further Republican backsliding yield some even less satisfactory measure or none at all. We must, he concluded, "take what we can get now, and hope for better things in further legislation."[38]

This fourteenth constitutional amendment went to the states for ratification, where a sufficient number approved it by July 1868 for its formal adoption. With Johnson's encouragement, however, ex-Confederate state legislatures decisively rejected it. The single exception was Tennessee, where local Republicans had already fashioned a new state government, outlawed slavery within state borders, disfranchised rebels, moved to protect the civil rights of blacks, and canceled the state's Confederate-era debt. Voting to ratify the amendment in July 1866, Tennessee jumped to the front of the line of states seeking readmission to Congress.

Ohio's John Bingham promptly moved that Congress return that state "to her former proper, practical relations to the Union" and seat its representatives in both houses. The House and Senate concurred on July 23. A handful of congressional radicals opposed that resolution because Tennessee still withheld the suffrage from former slaves. But Thaddeus Stevens voted for it, although without enthusiasm, probably in part for fear that firm opposition would damage his party in the crucial showdown with Johnson that loomed ahead in the congressional elections that autumn. But the question of whether, by admitting the Tennesseans, Congress was promising other rebel states the same reward, should they simply ratify the Fourteenth Amendment, became a bone of contention between Republican moderates and radicals.[39]

If the congressional elections scheduled made Stevens uncharacteristically nervous, it was because he understood how much rode upon their outcome. They would inevitably serve as a referendum on the Fourteenth Amendment and the merits of Johnson's "restoration" policy. And if Republicans suffered defeat at the polls, the radicals' hand would surely be weakened within their party.

Stevens's apparent skittishness helps explain not only his acceptance of Tennessee's readmission to Congress that summer despite its denying the vote to black men but also his rather shamefaced private qualms about Frederick Douglass's visibility at a September convention of southern Republicans. Stevens knew, he confided to Representative William Kelley, that "it does not become radicals like us to particularly object" to the black abolitionist's prominence there, but he could not help fearing it would inflame "the old prejudice" in the northern public and thereby "lose us some votes."[40]

During the 1866 congressional election campaign, Johnson took to the stump to denounce the Fourteenth Amendment and pillory Republican radicals. On a speaking tour that fall, hecklers baited him in one locale after another, which stoked the president's invective. He had already charged publicly that Thaddeus Stevens was "opposed to the fundamental principles" of the U.S. government and was "laboring to destroy them." Before the tour ended, he was demanding to know why Stevens should not be hanged as a traitor.[41]

The question now was, how would Union voters respond to the conflicting rhetoric and programs of Republicans and Democrats, of the White House and Congress?

CHAPTER TEN

"Perfecting a Revolution"

The Ballot, the Land, and Impeachment

T he results of the 1866 congressional elections proved Thaddeus Stevens's apparent nervousness to be unfounded. Andrew Johnson's opposition to the Fourteenth Amendment had alienated even conservative Republicans, and his incendiary rhetoric helped clarify for the Union public how high were the stakes and how stark were the alternatives it faced. In the North, the verdict was unmistakable. Republican congressional candidates added to their already big majorities in both houses. In the House of Representatives, the party's radical wing grew slightly. Republicans achieved similar victories at the state level, winning governorships and state-legislature majorities everywhere in the North as well as West Virginia, Missouri, and Tennessee. Even so conservative a Republican congressman as Henry J. Raymond, until recently a staunch Johnson ally, understood the popular vote's meaning. The people, he saw, had repudiated Johnson's "restoration" program as well as presidential control of the reconstruction process, endorsing instead congressional authority and the Fourteenth Amendment.[1]

Republican gains put the wind into radicals' sails. Acknowledging that he had been "rather conservative last winter," Stevens publicly resolved to become "radical" once again in future. "The people," Stevens declared in early January 1867, "have once more nobly done their duty. May I ask, without offense, will Congress have the courage to do its duty? Or will it be deterred by the clamor of ignorance, bigotry, and despotism from perfecting a revolution?" Much remained to be done. Although the prospective Fourteenth Amendment did threaten southern white influence in Washington, it contained no practical mechanism with which to protect black people and loyal whites inside the South.[2]

Stevens had introduced a Reconstruction bill to address that problem in July 1866, and the House began formal consideration in January 1867. It was imperative, Stevens said, to protect loyal residents of rebel states "from the barbarians who are now daily murdering them" and who were "daily putting into secret graves not only hundreds but thousands of the colored people." From freedpeople and white southern unionists came a stream of letters recounting discrimination, intimidation, and violence by vengeful whites both in and out of public office.[3] Raising Stevens's sense of urgency further was a late 1866 Supreme Court decision. In *Ex parte Milligan* the Court ruled that a military tribunal could not convict someone of a crime where civilian courts were functioning. That decision seemed to threaten the army's ability to enforce law and order in the states of the former Confederacy. Surely it was now more crucial than ever to create new governments in those states. Otherwise, Stevens warned, "all our blood and treasure will have been spent in vain."[4]

To create the new southern governments that Stevens envisioned, his bill would require each of the rebel states to hold constitutional conventions that spring. All adult males would be eligible both to vote and to serve as delegates except those who had held political or military office in or had otherwise voluntarily sworn allegiance to the Confederacy. Those men, the bill stated, had forfeited their

U.S. citizenship. Balloting for state convention delegates, moreover, would take place under judicial supervision and army protection. Delegates chosen would draw up new state constitutions that must respect the rights of all citizens regardless of "language, race, or former condition." Those new state constitutions would go before the public and, if ratified, would come to Congress for review. Only after Congress approved such a constitution would a state become "entitled to the rights, privileges, and immunities of a State within the Union." If in the future any of the states concerned should withdraw its guarantees of legal equality, that state would once again "lose its right to be represented in Congress."

Stevens's original bill allowed existing state governments in the meantime to continue functioning de facto, but alarm expressed by other radicals led Stevens promptly to drop that provision. And when Representative Rufus Spalding of Ohio warned that blacks would likely be "shot down like so many dogs" when they tried to vote, Stevens accepted an amendment that would strengthen federal protection of black voters by placing the states involved under martial law and suspending habeas corpus there.[5]

In support of his bill, Stevens delivered a full-throated call for extending political rights to the freedpeople. Yes, he said, "we have broken the material shackles of four million slaves." And "we have imposed upon them the privileges of fighting our battles, of dying in defence of freedom, and of bearing their equal portion of the taxes." But what did their legal freedom amount to when whites remained free to assault and kill black people without restraint by local or state governments? "We have unchained them from the stake so as to allow them locomotion," he said, but only "provided they do not walk in paths trod by white men." And while Congress had given freedpeople the "privilege of attending church," they could safely exercise that privilege only "if they can do so without offending the sight of their former masters." "By what civil weapon," Stevens demanded, "have we enabled them to defend themselves against oppression and injustice?"[6]

The House debated Stevens's bill for weeks. Then John A. Bingham moved to send it for review to the Joint Committee on Reconstruction. Bingham, a longtime enemy of slavery, did believe that abolition must guarantee equality before the law and citizenship. But he was also one of the strongest advocates of a speedy return of Confederate states to full rights within the Union. He evidently sought to return Stevens's bill to committee in hopes of thereby burying it, given the radicals' lack of a majority in that committee. Stevens and his allies said as much. When Bingham denied that intention, the angry Pennsylvanian muttered that "in all this contest about reconstruction, I do not propose either to take his counsel, recognize his authority, or believe a word he says." But a House majority composed of Democrats and moderate Republicans approved Bingham's motion to send the proposed bill to committee. Stevens appeared to be stymied.[7]

Once again, however, the logic of events intervened and imposed itself upon Republicans' thinking. Violence against freedpeople and southern white unionists along with the open defiance of Congress by both Johnson and southern states drove growing numbers of moderates toward firmer measures. In the spring and early summer of 1866, white crowds rioted against blacks in Charleston and Norfolk. In May of that year, white police and black Union army veterans clashed in Memphis and exchanged gunfire, after which whites surged into black neighborhoods, assaulting men, women, and children, killing forty-six, injuring seventy-five others, and destroying more than ninety homes. On the floor of the House of Representatives, Stevens lashed out at those urging hasty national reconciliation. They should cease "their siren song of peace and good will until they can stop my ears to the screams and groans of the dying victims at Memphis."

Worse was yet to come. In New Orleans at the end of July, Republicans attempted to convene a state constitutional convention to enfranchise blacks. Whites, including police recruited from the ranks of former Confederate soldiers, set upon delegates and their supporters, killing about fifty, wounding two hundred more, and putting homes, churches, and schools to the torch. Nor did the violence then relent.[8]

The conduct of Senator George H. Williams of Oregon captured the impact of such events upon many non-radical Republicans. Williams had previously expressed moderate views, but on February 4, 1867, he introduced a bill to impose army rule upon all states of the ex-Confederacy save Tennessee (which, as noted, Congress had readmitted to full rights in the Union the previous July).[9] Stevens rallied to Williams's bill. The Joint Committee approved it and asked Stevens to bring it into the House of Representatives. Stevens did so on February 6. With Bingham's backing, Republican moderate James G. Blaine sought to tag on a guaranteed route for rebel states back into full standing. His amendment promised those states that if they voted for the Fourteenth Amendment, brought their own laws into conformity with it, and enacted universal manhood suffrage, their delegates would be seated in Congress. He then moved to send the Williams bill and his own amendment to the House's Judiciary Committee for review.[10]

Shifting sentiments among House Republicans allowed Stevens to scotch Blaine's maneuver on February 13 with a powerful speech in the House pointing to the pro-Confederate violence in the South. "For the past few months," he reproached his party, "Congress has been sitting here, and while the South has been bleeding at every pore, Congress has done nothing to protect the loyal people there, white or black, either in their persons, in their liberty, or in their property." Having insisted to the president that Congress alone had the right to intervene in those states, we now "sit by and move no hand, we sit by and raise no voice to effect what we declare to be the duty of Congress." To burden the proposed Reconstruction bill with a guaranteed path for ex-Confederate states to gain readmission to Congress, Stevens warned, "would be an entire surrender of those States into the hands of the rebels." Observing his party "about to destroy itself" and about to deserve destruction through a "great dereliction of duty" that would forever damn it in the annals of history had plunged him, he confessed, into "a moral depression."[11]

His words struck home. Although more than twenty Republicans voted against the Reconstruction bill or abstained, enough moderates now joined their radical colleagues to prevent sending the bill to committee and then to approve the un-amended bill by a big margin. "Heaven rules as yet," sighed Stevens, "and there are gods above."[12] But his hosannas proved premature. In the Senate, Republican moderates succeeded in attaching to the bill the amendment that Blaine and Bingham had failed to add in the House.

Both houses finally agreed on a common version of the bill on February 20, 1867, and Stevens declared himself satisfied with it. That bill grouped the ex-Confederate states into five districts administered by the army. Military commanders would be assigned to each district along with "sufficient military force to enable such officer to perform his duties and enforce his authority." It would be the duty of those soldiers "to protect all persons in their rights of person and property, to suppress insurrection, disorder, and violence, and to punish, or cause to be punished, all disturbers of the public peace and criminals," and they could overrule any attempt by state authorities to interfere. To hear such cases, commanders could create military tribunals whenever they judged it necessary. And although the Johnson-sponsored state governments would survive and function, the federal government could "abolish, modify, control, or supersede" any of them if necessary. Nor might anyone serve in such provisional state governments who in the past had served in the U.S. Congress, its military, or in any state office and then gone over to the Confederacy.

In hopes of prolonging federal control of the rebel states, Stevens had opposed any fixed formula for how they might regain their pre-war rights and powers. But the standard for doing so inserted into the bill against his wishes was an exacting one. Each state must hold a convention to draft a new constitution. Black men must participate in the election of delegates, but no one barred from holding office by the proposed Fourteenth Amendment could vote for delegates or serve as a delegate to a state's constitutional convention. The constitutions emerging from those conventions must enfranchise black men, and new state legislatures arising on that basis must ratify the Fourteenth Amendment. Only once such an interracial electorate as well as the U.S. Congress had approved such a new state constitution, and only once that amendment had been incorporated into the U.S. Constitution, could a state's delegates take their seats in Congress and the state itself resume full self-government. Stevens again felt constrained to accept this bill, though he jeered at Republican moderates' obstructionism and inconsistency. They had voted for this bill only "after trying every side wind and expedient to cripple or defeat" it. He expected no better in the future.[13]

Although weaker than Stevens wished, this Reconstruction bill repelled the president, who immediately vetoed it. The measure, Johnson declared, was unnecessary, unjust, unconstitutional, and "utterly destructive to those great principles of liberty and humanity for which our ancestors . . . have shed so much blood and expended so much treasure." Congress overrode his veto the same day, taking another major step in upending the antebellum order in the South. Illinois congressman Shelby Cullom pointed to the dynamic once again at work. "The men who have been struggling so hard to destroy this country were and still are the instruments, however wicked, by which we are driven to give the black man justice, whether we will or no," he observed. It was precisely "by the unholy persistence of rebels that slavery was at last overthrown. Their contempt of the constitutional amendment now before the country will place in the hands of every colored man of the South the ballot."[14]

Passage of this Reconstruction Act buoyed the South's black population and encouraged its ongoing fight for its rights. Black workers in various industries went on strike demanding better conditions. Public conveyances faced demands that they integrate their vehicles. Everywhere freedpeople held meetings, many protected by armed guards, to learn how and to decide for whom to vote. Those southern white unionists who had come to look upon black voters as irreplaceable allies against the old elite also cheered the new law and Stevens's role in its passage.[15]

The fact is, however, that Thaddeus Stevens had not stood in the vanguard on the question of black voting. He was not one of the first in Congress to urge enfranchising freedmen. He vacillated. In September 1865, he explicitly abjured addressing the issue until some later date. In December, however, he told the House that "without the right of suffrage in the late slave States . . . I believe the slaves had far better been left in bondage." In January 1866, he opposed granting the vote to former slaves until the federal government had provided them with adequate guarantees of all their rights—until "this Congress has done the great work of regenerating the Constitution and laws of this country according to the principles of the Declaration of Independence." In July, as noted, he parted company with Charles Sumner and some other congressional radicals by voting to admit Tennessee's representatives to Congress in spite of that state's denial of the vote to black men. A few days later, he pressed for giving the vote to former slaves, feeling "pangs of self-condemnation" for Congress's failure as yet to do so. Freedmen "must have the ballot or they will continue, virtually, to be slaves."[16]

Why this equivocation? Stevens had insisted upon color-blind voting rights in Pennsylvania fully three decades earlier. He once again upheld that principle during the war, when Congress addressed the subject of voting rights in the District of Columbia, where the Constitution gave Congress a direct governing power. In January 1866, the House passed a bill enfranchising black men in the capital district. Although ten House Republicans and five border-state unionists had joined the opposition to it, the bill's passage there provoked cheering both in the galleries and on the floor, cheering that the Speaker seemed for some time unable to silence. Following the Republican gains in the 1866 elections, the Senate passed such a bill in mid-December, and the House concurred, this time with only two Republicans and seven border-state unionists joining Democrats in opposition. Johnson vetoed that bill a few weeks later, rehearsing the arguments that congressional Democrats had raised earlier. Black people were unable "to comprehend the duties and responsibilities which pertain to suffrage," nor did they need the vote "to protect either their interests or their rights." The Senate overrode his veto on the same day that Johnson issued it, and the House followed suit a day later. Stevens also supported a bill to enact color-blind suffrage in the federal territories that the House passed on May 15, 1866, and to which the Senate assented on January 10, 1867. Johnson withheld his signature from that bill, but since he did that before the last ten days of the congressional session, the bill became law.[17]

So Thaddeus Stevens did press for black suffrage in his own state and in other places where the national government exercised clear constitutional authority. Why, then, did he wait longer before consistently championing black voting rights within the rebel states?

He did that at least in part for fear that associating a measure so "unpopular" in the North as color-blind male suffrage with other

Reconstruction measures that he considered more important and effective—especially prolonging direct federal control over the rebel states—would jeopardize the whole undertaking. He may also have worried that the freedmen, as an uneducated, propertyless, and impoverished class, might become political putty in the hands of their wealthy employers. His early training in and continued adherence to ancient republican beliefs, those that had fed his qualms in the 1830s about fully universal male suffrage in Pennsylvania, probably reinforced such concerns. As William Kelley later summarized Stevens's view, both "a landed aristocracy and a landless class" were "dangerous in a republic."[18]

Stevens preferred to maintain the ex-Confederate states in the status of federal territories for an extended period—"for some years." His party's majority, however, like Lincoln, rejected territorialization, eventually settling instead on a doctrine known as "the grasp of war." That doctrine held that the laws of war gave the federal government the right to suspend certain rights of states that were making war upon it. Its most important difference with Stevens's program was practical rather than theoretical—it was intended to emphasize the partial and temporary nature of Washington's power in those states.[19]

Once the Republican Party refused to prolong direct federal rule in the rebel states, Stevens had little choice but to depend upon a black electorate to prevent those states from falling back into Democratic (that is, ex-secessionist) hands. In 1866, state-level elections in the South drove that necessity home when voters placed Confederate sympathizers in office. And perhaps the Republicans' sweep of elections in the free states that same year reassured Stevens that enfranchising southern freedmen would not cost Republicans northern votes.[20]

In January 1867, Stevens announced himself "for negro suffrage in every rebel state." Only on that basis would loyal governments arise there; otherwise "loyal men, black and white, will be oppressed,

exiled, or murdered," and those states "are sure to be ruled by traitors" who would "send a solid rebel representative delegation to
Congress, and cast a solid rebel electoral vote" for the presidency,
thereby placing control of the government in their hands and the
hands of their northern allies. That was unacceptable. Moreover, Stevens asked, "Have not loyal blacks quite as good a right to choose
rulers and make laws as rebel whites?"[21]

And once again Stevens criticized laggards in his own party—
those "who admit the justice and ultimate utility of granting impartial suffrage to all men" but who "think it is impolitic." They reminded
him of how "an ancient philosopher" responded to an opponent who
"admitted that what he required was just but deemed it impolitic."
The philosopher, Stevens recounted, asked the man, "Do you believe
in Hades?" "I would say," Stevens continued, "to those . . . who admit
the justice of human equality before the law but doubt its policy:
'Do you believe in hell?'" To be sure, he might just as easily have
reproached himself for equivocation. And he did later that month. In
voting to admit Tennessee's delegates to Congress, he now confessed,
he had "shut my eyes" to that "outrage in the constitution of Tennessee" that excluded blacks from the suffrage. He vowed never to do
such a thing again.[22]

In accordance with the Reconstruction Act's provisions, the states
of the ex-Confederacy held constitutional conventions. Black men
there voted in great numbers in the fall of 1867, while most eligible
adult white men in the South refused to participate. As a result, Republican delegates dominated those conventions, and the constitutions they produced declared legal and political equality for blacks;
created the South's first public school system; outlawed imprisonment for debt, and whipping as a criminal punishment; reduced the
number of crimes punishable by death; and did away with regressive

mechanisms and policies such as property requirements for both holding office and sitting on juries. General elections eventually held under those constitutions also put Republicans in southern governors' mansions and in control of state legislatures.[23]

Black men welcomed the chance to enter the political arena. Although some freedpeople made substantial educational gains during the first years of freedom, most were still illiterate. They learned how to act politically by doing so. An elderly freedman in Georgia observed, "Every creature has got an instinct. The calf goes to the cow to suck, the bee to the hive. We's a poor, humble, degraded people, but we know our friends. We'd walk fifteen miles in war time to find out about the battle; we can walk fifteen miles and more to find how to vote." That they nearly always decided to vote for Republicans is not surprising. As a group of freedmen in Asheville, North Carolina, explained, since congressional Republicans "have evidenced their determination to exhaust every effort to secure to us all the blessings of freedom, we recognize in them and their supporters our best friends and doubt the sincereity [sic] of all pre tended [sic] friends who oppose their general policy."

Still, the new black voters made it clear that they would not become pawns or rubber stamps for Republican leaders. When they attended mass meetings held for that party's candidates, they specified what they needed and expected. An unsympathetic white writer later reported that "at their gatherings all have something to say, and all are up at once. They have a free flow of language, and their older men exhibit a practical, get-at-the-facts disposition." That writer added that although "the negroes have been accused of being easily led by [Republican] demagogues," it seemed to him instead that "they really rule the demagogues, not the demagogues them." Because just "let the politicians do anything which is distasteful, and opponents spring up in every quarter. They are extremely jealous of any one's assuming to dictate to them."[24]

Results of congressional elections in 1867 differed by region. Black voters empowered Republicans in the South, but elsewhere outcomes weakened the party. In state and local elections across the North, the size of the Republican vote shrank dramatically compared with a year before. A variety of local issues influenced that outcome, but most observers saw it as a reaction against black enfranchisement in the South. Republicans did not lose control of Congress, but party moderates blamed radicals for the electoral setback and determined to rein them in. The moderate leader William P. Fessenden was happy to see that "influential journals" were attributing the outcome "to a general disgust with the leadership of Stevens and his drive." And Ohio radical Benjamin Wade predicted grimly that among his party colleagues the results would "make the timorous more timorous."[25]

The Republicans' 1867 electoral setbacks in the North and the backlash against radicalism within the party made it harder than ever for Stevens and his co-thinkers to resist the readmission of additional rebel states to Congress. But he had no more reason than ever to trust the political proclivities of most southern white voters. So he tried to couple readmission with multiple safeguards.

The Joint Committee on Reconstruction had gone out of existence when the Thirty-Ninth Congress adjourned in March 1867. When the new House convened that December, it created its own Reconstruction committee and placed Stevens in the chair. In March 1868, that committee offered to restore full rights to Alabama, but only on several conditions—"that the right of suffrage of citizens of the United States shall never be denied or abridged in said State on account of race, color, or previous condition of slavery"; that those Alabamans barred by the Fourteenth Amendment from public office also be disfranchised; and that Congress be empowered to annul any state law or amendment to that state's constitution that violated these terms.[26]

John A. Bingham opposed those conditions as an attack upon constitutional principles and moved to delete them from the bill. Stevens responded angrily that to do so would serve only "the interest of slavery," but the House carried Bingham's amendment by a vote of 71 to 39. (Requests that the official record make clear who voted how on that change were refused.) Still trying to ensure the permanence of black voting rights, Stevens sought to add a provision to the bill enabling Congress to rescind Alabama's full statehood status if it subsequently reneged on its commitment to universal male suffrage.

The House rejected his initiative. Shortly afterward, it so thoroughly amended the original bill as to postpone entirely Alabama's readmission. But by summer the two houses had agreed, over Stevens's objection, to readmit not only Alabama but also Arkansas, North and South Carolina, Louisiana, Georgia, and Florida, all on the condition that they simply promise to make equal voting rights permanent. In doing that, Congress omitted Stevens's original provision disfranchising Confederate leaders. Neither did Congress give itself the right to annul future discriminatory state laws or amendments to state constitutions, thus denying the federal government another method of ensuring the survival of universal male suffrage in those states. With his original terms for readmission replaced by far weaker ones, Stevens abstained from voting on the measure. Once it passed nonetheless, only Mississippi, Texas, and Virginia remained without normal state rights.[27]

Until the summer of 1867, Stevens had avoided the subject of black voting rights in states outside the former Confederacy—that is, in the North and the four border states. But by August of that year, at the latest, he had altered course, deciding that universal male suffrage must prevail throughout the country, North and South. He admonished the governor of Indiana, once a law student of his in Gettysburg, that the rights enshrined in "the Declaration of Independence *must* come to pass in all its parts" and "universal suffrage is one of them."

While some Republicans concluded from their electoral setbacks in 1867 that it was time for the party to pull in its horns, Stevens argued that "radicalism is the only thing now that will save and rescue us." By the spring of 1868 he was pressing the point on the House floor. The time had at last arrived, he declared, when "demagogues who talk to us about differences of races must be ashamed and skulk from the face of the world." The nation must recognize "universal and impartial suffrage as the only foundation upon which Government can stand. . . . When you attempt to depart from it you cease to be men and become tyrants, deserving the execration of the human race. We have reached a point in the history of this nation when we can adopt that great and glorious principle." Stevens and some other radicals found legal justification for doing so in Congress's earlier approval of the Fourteenth Amendment. By agreeing to punish states for restricting the suffrage (by reducing their congressional representation), he argued, the House and Senate had implicitly recognized that voting was a right inherent in (male) citizenship.[28]

Stevens's plan for reconstructing the South did not stop at legal and political change. The region's economic and social structure must be transformed as well. Central to such renovation was seizure of the rebel planters' landed property and its distribution among former slaves in the form of small farms. That would create a more egalitarian society. It would also give black voters the economic independence they would need in order to resist political intimidation by white employers.

Slaves and freedpeople fought for land even in the midst of the war. They began working the soil owned by rebels who had fled before Union armies. That occurred in parts of Virginia, North

Carolina, Georgia, Louisiana, and a number of points along the Mississippi River.[29] And the American Freedmen's Inquiry Commission discovered the strength of the freedpeople's yearning for farms of their own.

Created in March 1863 to investigate the condition of emancipated slaves, the AFIC submitted its preliminary assessment in June of that year. "The chief object of ambition" among blacks, it reported, was "to own property, especially to possess land, if it be only a few acres." Freedpeople believed that centuries of arduous but unpaid work by themselves and their ancestors had earned them the right to become independent small farmers. They should no longer labor for others on other people's land—on "dis bery land," as one freedman said it in his Gullah dialect, "dat is rich wid de sweat ob we face and de blood ob we back." Confiscated plantations, they held, should be carved up into modest-size farms and given to them. The national convention of black men that met in Syracuse in October 1864 claimed "our fair share of the public domain," regardless of whether the nation had acquired that soil "by purchase, treaty, confiscation, or military conquest."

A petition from the South Carolina sea islands explained what denying that ambition would mean. Remaining landless, it said, would leave freedpeople "working as in former time" for former masters "and subject to thier [sic] will as then." The Confederacy's defeat encouraged hopes that land would indeed accompany freedom. Enactment of the 1867 Reconstruction Act both reinforced such hopes and encouraged freedpeople to demand that those hopes be realized. A South Carolina politician now saw "a great deal more danger of 'Cuffee' than Thad Stevens taking over lands."[30]

The Second Confiscation Act of 1862 had given Abraham Lincoln the formal right not only to take the slaves of disloyal owners but also to seize their other property as well. But implementing that law depended on a cumbersome judicial process, and at Lincoln's insistence Congress had stipulated that when expropriated rebels died, all their confiscated property (other than slaves) must be returned to their heirs.[31] As a result, that law affected very little land at all.[32]

Another set of laws, however, bared sharper teeth. In August 1861, Congress levied a tax upon all states to help fund the war effort, and the following June it passed a second law to enforce that tax in "insurrectionary districts within the United States." That second law empowered the federal government to seize and sell the property of individuals who failed to pay the tax bills levied upon them. A third law, enacted in July 1864, directed that lands abandoned by owners "engaged, either in arms or otherwise, in aiding or encouraging the rebellion" be used in one way or another "for the employment and general welfare" of former slaves.

As chairman of the Ways and Means Committee, Stevens shepherded such measures through the House. Along with ad hoc military actions, they had placed more than 850,000 acres of confiscated or abandoned southern farmland into the Freedmen's Bureau's hands by 1865. That included all the soil that General William T. Sherman had set aside for provisionally settling liberated slaves, except the small fraction to which freedpeople had managed to obtain legal title by then.[33]

Lincoln initially leaned toward helping emancipated slaves to obtain farms on such lands, but his administration soon changed course. It did accept General Sherman's field order granting "possessory title" of coastal acreage to freedpeople. But instead of assisting freedpeople to obtain full legal title to that or other confiscated lands, the government prioritized selling such properties to northern investors (to help defray the costs of war) or returning them to former owners (hoping thereby to smooth the way to national reconciliation).[34]

Andrew Johnson sharply accelerated the return of landed property to former owners. And when Freedman's Bureau chief O. O. Howard tried to exempt from restoration those parcels that freedpeople were already working, the president overruled him. As a result, within a year of the war's conclusion, more than half of the acreage once in the Bureau's hands had been handed back to former owners; most of the rest would be returned during the next two years.[35]

During the war Stevens had called repeatedly for seizing and re-selling plantation lands in the form of small farms. But he did not at first press for getting those farms into the hands of freedpeople. In May 1864, in fact, he explicitly looked forward to former slaves work-ing the land for others. He and other congressional Republicans, he said then, "are for leaving them on the soil to cultivate it for wages."[36]

Once the war ended, however, Stevens began to urge transfer-ring confiscated lands into the hands of the black population. He had always assumed that only those with at least a minimum of wealth could make good use of the franchise. Thirty years earlier, when Stevens served as a delegate to Pennsylvania's constitutional convention, that assumption had inclined him against fully universal manhood suffrage. In the very different conditions of the Civil War's aftermath, Stevens turned that principle on its head. If, as he had concluded, giving impoverished freedmen the vote was the only way to protect them politically, then they must also own some property. They would need farms of their own if they were to vote freely, without succumbing to economic pressure by white employers.[37] And a more equal distribution of landed property would sustain a more egalitarian form of society. "It is impossible that any practical equality of rights can exist," Stevens told a Lancaster audience in the fall of 1865, "where a few thousand men monopolize the whole landed property." For "how can republican institutions, free schools, free churches, free social intercourse exist in a mingled community of nabobs and serfs"? Creating and safeguarding such institutions re-quired seizing and redistributing the land of the elite. Without that, "such men [freedmen] can not become useful citizens."[38]

This argument for using the law to create greater economic

equality seemed to depart strikingly from some views that he had expressed in earlier years. The younger Stevens accepted considerable differences in wealth among the population as inevitable byproducts of civilization's advance. As the need to destroy slavery in the United States had pushed him to reverse his youthful condemnation of revolutions, so now the revolutionary transformation that he sought compelled Stevens to recognize extreme economic inequality as a threat to democracy. No doubt aiding that recognition was a belief that in the South such inequality in landed wealth was born of and sustained by the illegitimate system of slavery.

In September 1865, Stevens called for confiscating the plantations of those southerners who owned at least two hundred acres of land. He had no designs, he said, on the property of "the poor, the ignorant, and the coerced" among the white population. They "should be forgiven" because they had only "followed the example and teachings of their wealthy and intelligent neighbors." The latter deserved no such consideration, and taking their land would provide the government with far more acreage than the Freedmen's Bureau had ever controlled. It would mean, he calculated, seizing nearly four hundred million acres of land. "Divide this land into convenient farms. Give, if you please, forty acres to each adult male freedman." Then sell the rest of the confiscated land "to the highest bidders." The proceeds of those sales should fund pensions for Union soldiers, indemnify loyal citizens who had suffered property losses to Confederate raiders during the war, and pay off the national debt.[39]

Stevens advanced a specific plan along these lines in 1866 when Congress discussed extending the Freedmen's Bureau's lease on life. The law that had created the Bureau in March 1865 authorized its director to rent confiscated southern land to freedpeople and white unionist refugees in the form of forty-acre plots on three-year leases. Thereafter those renters might purchase at a price equal to the land's market value "such title thereto as the United States can convey."

This ambiguous language about land title reflected Congress's lack of confidence that the federal government truly owned that land and its consequent uncertainty about whether it could transfer full title to freedpeople.[40]

Lyman Trumbull's January 1866 bill to extend the life of the Freedmen's Bureau did address the subject of confiscated and abandoned land. It proposed to "confirm and make valid the possessory titles" that General Sherman's Special Field Order No. 15 had granted to freedpeople along the Atlantic coast. And it suggested that President Johnson set aside up to three million acres of *publicly owned* land in Florida, Mississippi, and Arkansas for leasing to white refugees and freedpeople, charging an annual rent that was, once again, "based upon a valuation of the land." Finally, Trumbull proposed to allow freedpeople eventually to purchase those farms by paying a price equal to the land's market value.[41]

Stevens considered Trumbull's proposal wholly inadequate. In the states that Trumbull named, the public land was poor in quality, and the sale prices that Trumbull proposed were too high for people who only yesterday had been enslaved. Perhaps most important to Stevens, Trumbull's bill left plantations owned by what Stevens called "reeking rebels" untouched in most of the former Confederacy.[42]

In early February 1866, therefore, Stevens put forward a substitute for Trumbull's plan. It sought to assure to freedpeople free and clear legal title to the Sherman lands. And it proposed to take the additional three million acres of fertile soil that Trumbull talked about not only from publicly owned lands but also from "unoccupied" land and "from forfeited estates of the enemy." It would do that, moreover, not just in three states but in five, adding Alabama and Louisiana. Stevens's bill also aimed to keep both rental and sale prices for freedpeople low.[43]

As a party floor leader whose proposals had often proved essential throughout the war era, Stevens enjoyed great authority among

Republicans. But on this subject, very few of his colleagues were willing to follow him. Just one day after Stevens introduced his bill, the House overwhelmingly rejected it. More than two-thirds of the Republicans who voted (including even some radicals, such as James M. Ashley) joined the Democrats in opposition and another ten abstained. The House then passed Trumbull's bill by a comparable margin.[44]

Although Stevens ultimately voted for Trumbull's bill, he warned his colleagues that denying to "every adult freedman a homestead on the land where he was born and toiled and suffered" would earn them "the censure of mankind and the curse of Heaven." So he tried again in March 1867, this time seeking to modify the judicial land-seizure procedures that hobbled the Second Confiscation Act. Stevens urged bypassing the courts entirely in favor of "a more convenient and speedy" executive department mechanism for seizing and redistributing the landed property. He also proposed transferring all publicly owned land throughout the former Confederacy to the federal government. From that combined trove of confiscated and transferred land, Stevens would then provide to every adult male and any widowed household head among the freedpeople a forty-acre homestead and the sum of fifty dollars with which to erect buildings on that land.[45]

As before, Stevens aimed to confiscate holdings only of the ex-Confederate elite. No one's land would be seized whose total wealth equaled less than five thousand dollars, a substantial sum at the time. Those affected by that bill, he estimated, made up fewer than 2 percent of the South's white population. The people who would benefit, in contrast, were the "four millions of injured, oppressed, and helpless men, whose ancestors for two centuries have been held in bondage" and forced to perform the labor that paid for the land in question. If left propertyless, those four million "must necessarily . . . be the servants and victims of others." Instead, let us "make them independent of their old masters . . . by giving them a small tract of land to cultivate for themselves." Only then will they "not be compelled to work" for others on "unfair terms." In the process, we will also "elevate the character of the freedman," making him more independent politically as well as economically, since "nothing is so likely to make a man a good citizen as to make him a freeholder."[46]

Printed copies of Stevens's speech circulated through the South, and literate freedpeople read it aloud to others at their meetings, encouraging popular agitation for land confiscation. In Congress, however, his bill horrified many. Stevens dismissed their objections. The steps proposed "can be condemned only by the [secessionist] criminals and their immediate friends, and by that unmanly kind of men whose intellectual and moral vigor has melted into a fluid weakness which they mistake for mercy, and which is untempered with a single grain of justice, and to those religionists who mistake meanness for Christianity, and who forget that the essence of religion is to 'do unto others what others have a right to expect from you.'" The House, this time unmoved by his words, postponed and then forgot about Stevens's bill, and the Senate rejected Charles Sumner's similar efforts.[47]

Why did congressional Republicans reject these land reform proposals? They did not object, it soon developed, to allotting lands previously in the public domain to freedpeople or other settlers. Both houses passed, with little trouble, bills confined to such lands. Just two days after rejecting Stevens's substitute Freedmen's Bureau bill, Republican congressmen approved almost unanimously George Julian's Southern Homestead Act, which opened all *publicly owned* land in the South to settlement and gave blacks and loyal whites preferential access to it through 1867.[48]

The principal obstacle confronting Stevens's proposals was his party's aversion to abolishing the private-property rights of plantation owners in peacetime. The challenge of treason and armed rebellion had reconciled those northern politicians to the abolition of a form of property that they already considered sinful and illegitimate—human property. But most balked at infringing upon claims to another form of property, property in land, that remained as close to their hearts as ever. And many feared that black landowners would refuse to grow cotton (a crop they associated with slavery), thereby harming New England's textile industry.

Republicans also wondered nervously where—if they began redistributing landed property to exploited and impoverished people—that road would lead. "If Congress is to take cognizance of the claims of labor against capital," Henry Raymond's *New York Times* warned, "there can be no decent pretence [*sic*] for confining the task to the slave-labor of the South. It is a question . . . of the fundamental relation of industry to capital; and sooner or later, if begun at the South, it will find its way into the cities of the North." Boston's *Daily Advertiser* worried similarly that opposing the existence of landed aristocracies "is two-edged," since "there are socialists who hold that *any* aristocracy" is anathema, including the North's own economic elite. Stoking such fears was a rising tide of labor organizing and strikes in the North that was driving a wedge between many Republicans and workers.[49]

If Stevens could not provide freedpeople with the farms he believed they needed and deserved, he would still fight to secure their civil and political rights and personal safety. And it soon became apparent that not even the Reconstruction Act of 1867 would guarantee either. The enactment of that law did not put an end to Andrew Johnson's campaign to obstruct congressional action in the ex-Confederacy. The new Reconstruction law did place the army in temporary control of ten southern states. But the president, as the army's commander in chief, retained his power to hamper that law's enforcement.

Johnson proved determined to do just that. In June 1867 he issued directives aimed at limiting the discretion of military commanders in dealing with state and local officials.[50] He then moved directly against Secretary of War Edwin M. Stanton, whom he regarded by then as too close to the radical Republicans. Johnson suspended Stanton from office on August 12, 1867, replacing him on an interim basis with Ulysses S. Grant, with whom he had a better relationship. He then removed generals in command of one after another of the Reconstruction Act's military districts. General Philip Sheridan commanded the Louisiana-Texas district; General Dan Sickles commanded the Carolinas district. Both men clashed with the president when they sought to exercise power over recalcitrant white politicians and courts. Despite Grant's objections, Johnson replaced both men. He also replaced General John Pope as commander in the Florida-Georgia-Alabama district when that officer drew the fire of southern notables. And he removed General Edward O. C. Ord, commander of the Mississippi-Arkansas district, as well as General Wager Swayne, the head of the Alabama branch of the Freedmen's Bureau. Bureau chief O. O. Howard saw these and related acts as "doubtless intended to utterly defeat reconstruction." No wonder that Stevens's sometime ally, Representative James M. Ashley, called Andrew Johnson "the recognized leader" of the "counter-revolution."[51]

Mustering out the wartime army magnified the impact of Johnson's attack on the military's power in the South. About a million men wore Union blue in the spring of 1865. By year's end, demobilization reduced that number to about 150,000. By the autumn of 1866, the administration had cut it down to 38,000, of whom only 25,000 remained in the states of the former Confederacy.[52]

The meaning of all this for freedpeople and white unionists in the South was impossible to miss. Ulysses Grant, who initially favored demobilization, turned against it during the fall of 1866 because "the

right[s] and safety of all class of citizens in the states lately in rebellion" were palpably imperiled. Thaddeus Stevens shared with the
House reports that "the most horrible murders and outrages that it is
possible for man to imagine are daily being committed in these States
without there being . . . any effort made, to punish the perpetrators."[53]

For Reconstruction to succeed, Stevens concluded, Andrew Johnson had to go. That meant impeachment, which Stevens supported
from an early date.

Johnson's supporters would attribute efforts to impeach him to
personal animus toward the president. Stevens had certainly come to
despise Johnson. When another congressman tried to excuse him on
the grounds that Johnson was, after all, "a self-made man," Stevens
replied acidly that he was "glad to hear it, for it relieves God Al-
mighty of a heavy responsibility." But Stevens was far less concerned
with punishing a hated individual or penalizing past crimes than
with clearing the path for positive congressional action in the South.
When a Democratic opponent denounced impeachment's motives
as political, Stevens readily agreed. The fight to remove Johnson, he
acknowledged, was "wholly political" in purpose—it was, he meant,
indissolubly bound up with a struggle over government policy. He
told his party's congressional caucus in early January 1867, in a reporter's account, that "it was impossible to reconstruct the South"
with Andrew Johnson in the White House. For "so long as he remained there the laws of Congress would be inoperative, and the
power of the army, which might be required to enforce the laws of
Congress, would be subject to the control of Andrew Johnson"—the
man who was in fact "the head and front of all opposition" to Reconstruction.[54]

The U.S. Constitution authorizes impeachment of a president on the
grounds of "treason, bribery, or other high crimes and misdemean-

ors." Jurists and politicians differed about what that should mean in practice. According to a narrow interpretation, a president could be removed only for breaking some specific law. Upholders of a broader interpretation believed a president could be discharged for abusing or failing conscientiously to carry out the duties of office.[55]

Stevens consistently rejected the narrow understanding of what were impeachable acts. "In order to sustain impeachment under our Constitution," he said, "I do not hold that it is necessary to prove a crime as an indictable offense. . . ." Impeachment was "a purely political proceeding. It is intended as a remedy for malfeasance [that is, improper conduct] in office and to prevent the continuance thereof." It was "not intended as a personal punishment for past offenses." "We are to treat this question . . . as wholly political, in which, if an officer of the Government abuse his trust or attempt to pervert it to improper purposes, . . . he becomes subject to impeachment and removal from office."[56]

Stevens had begun urging Johnson's removal in 1866 and supported a failed attempt to create a special impeachment committee in the House in December of that year. Early the next month James Ashley asked the House to instruct its Judiciary Committee to investigate whether Johnson should be impeached. The House agreed to do so (by a vote of 108 to 39). Although the committee's majority voted that summer not to proceed with impeachment, Johnson's aggressive conduct subsequently reversed that decision; in late November, the Judiciary Committee issued a report that called upon the House to impeach. That report based itself on a broad interpretation of impeachment's legitimate grounds, and radical committee member George Boutwell defended the report on that basis. But the House rejected the report the following month in a vote of 57 to 108. The opposition included a majority (66) of all Republicans voting, who claimed that a president could be removed from office only for breaking a specific law.[57]

That House vote further emboldened Johnson. He now openly defied Congress by dismissing his troublesome secretary of war, Edwin M. Stanton, an apparent violation of the recently passed Tenure of Office Act, which forbade a president to dismiss certain appointed officials without the consent of the Senate.[58]

That step broke the dam. On February 22, 1868, Stevens's Reconstruction Committee recommended that the president be impeached, and this time the House assented, by a margin of 126 to 47, with the support of every Republican who cast a vote. Enthusiastic messages of encouragement poured into Washington from Republican voters and state conventions. Few doubted that the party's rank and file supported putting the president in the dock. In Congress, even many Republican moderates who had been unwilling previously to proceed were now ready to remove Johnson. The Speaker of the House appointed a committee to draw up a list of formal articles of impeachment to bring before the Senate. Stevens was a member of that committee, but swiftly declining health prevented him from participating actively in its deliberations, and he failed to persuade its members to follow his lead. Conscious, moreover, that the House had earlier refused to proceed with an indictment framed broadly, the committee framed this case narrowly, emphasizing violation of law. The ten articles that they drafted focused on the Tenure of Office law and collateral matters.[59]

Stevens was unhappy with that result. Johnson had consistently sought "to defeat instead of to execute the laws of Congress," and that amounted to a "monstrous usurpation" of power. Unfortunately, Stevens said, the ten articles of impeachment were silent about acts of obstruction and usurpation that constituted "much more fundamental offenses" than those they cited. The acts upon which they instead concentrated, while serious enough to justify impeachment and removal from office, were "trivial by comparison." Stevens regained some ground on March 3 when the House adopted an eleventh impeachment article. This one accused Johnson not only of violating the Tenure of Office Act but also of striving "to prevent the execution" of the Reconstruction Act, denying "that the legislation of said Congress was valid or obligatory upon him," and denying "the power of the said thirty-ninth Congress to propose amendments to the Constitution."[60]

To manage and present the case against the president, the House appointed seven men, including both radicals and moderates—Thaddeus Stevens as well as his frequent intraparty adversary, John A. Bingham, who had earlier opposed impeachment. The Senate trial began on March 30, with Supreme Court chief justice Salmon P. Chase presiding. It lasted six weeks. When the eleventh impeachment article seemed to enjoy the most support in the Senate, the House managers arranged for it to come up for a vote first.[61]

A conviction would require the assent of two-thirds of the Senate. On May 16 came the verdict. William P. Fessenden and six other Republicans joined with the Democrats to acquit Johnson by a one-vote margin. Fessenden had opposed impeachment from the start, fearing that removing Johnson would undermine the power of and public respect for the presidency and help the radicals, whose influence he abhorred, to gain control of the government. Stevens had taken Fessenden's measure years earlier. "He has too much of the vile ingredient called conservatism," he told a confidant in 1862. The intervening years did nothing to change his mind. Fessenden and his circle, Stevens advised Edward McPherson in the summer of 1867, were "a base set" who "will ruin us."[62]

Aghast at the acquittal, Stevens tried unsuccessfully to bring forth additional charges against Johnson. But the trial was effectively over and would come to a formal close before the month was out.[63]

CHAPTER ELEVEN

"Equality of Man Before His Creator"

D uring Thaddeus Stevens's years in Congress, fellow Republicans would often draw close when he rose to speak. Before the war they did that to protect him from physical assault by slavery's infuriated southern champions. During the war and postwar years, however, would-be attackers were gone from the House of Representatives; they had walked out when their states left the Union, and they were later kept out by Stevens and his party. When Republicans crowded around him during the Reconstruction era, they did so not to shield the old man from violence but because his voice had grown too weak to hear from any distance, so weak that stenographers had trouble recording his words.[1]

With growing frequency, therefore, Stevens now had to ask others to read his words aloud in the House of Representatives. When it came time to deliver a key impeachment speech, that task fell to longtime ally Edward McPherson. Another old associate, Alexander Hood, nonetheless congratulated the old man on the result. It was a "great" speech, Hood judged, adding that "as your body wears out, the spiritual essence, the reasoning power becomes clearer than ever." An appreciative Philadelphian urged Stevens in a letter to continue fighting anything "that debars any class of human beings from enjoying *Free & Equal Rights*" and to "raise from the dust the down trodden [*sic*] of our day." That man hoped "that you may be spared to see your triumph over the enemies of Freedom."[2] Many others harbored the same hope.

But more than Stevens's voice had by now grown weak. Rheumatism had for years been torturing his body, and many of his organs were giving out. During the Senate trial, he was carried into the Capitol in a chair and swathed in blankets. That is how he entered the Senate chamber on the day in May when Andrew Johnson eked out his acquittal. By then Stevens seemed to be surviving only by the sheer force of will. "His illness [is] progressing rapidly," the French observer Georges Clemenceau noted, "but his energies [are] mounting still faster. Once in a while a sardonic smile, like a grimace, flickers over his livid face. If it were not for the fire smoldering in the depths of his piercing eyes, one might imagine life had already fled from that inert body, but it still nurses all the wrath of a Robespierre." Late in the House's 1868 summer session, Stevens seemed to rally. "For a few days the old vivacity returned," a colleague later remembered, along with "the brilliant repartee and unexpected sallies that all enjoyed so much." But that was only the guttering flame's final flicker. On August 11, at age seventy-six, Thaddeus Stevens died.[3]

And so passed away one of the central leaders of the Second American Revolution. He had dedicated much of his life to creating a more egalitarian and democratic form of capitalist society than the one he found, one that "freed them from every vestige of human oppression, of inequality of rights, of the recognized degradation of the poor, and the superior caste of the rich," one in which "no distinction would be tolerated . . . but what arose from merit and conduct." That vision drew on the legacy of Vermont's early struggles against landlordism and for democratic government as well as his mother's evangelical Protestantism, all tempered by his own study of republican classics and works inspired by the Enlightenment.[4]

Stevens's devotion to creating a better society had animated his successful fight in the 1830s to protect Pennsylvania public schools from their narrow-minded opponents and especially his decades-long fight against slavery and racial oppression. The passing of time and his accumulation of years only increased the determination and consistency with which he pursued that goal. In that respect, as in so many others, he was unusual. As a fellow Pennsylvania congressman observed, "too frequently in men of all stations the generous impulses and noble sentiments of youth give place, with advancing years and prosperity, to the fossil petrifaction of humanity called conservatism. . . . But this dry rot of the soul never tainted Thaddeus Stevens."[5] To a radical Republican contemporary, indeed, he came to seem the very "embodied spirit of revolution," adding that had he lived in France during its Great Revolution, Stevens would cheerfully have plunged into "the glorious work of tearing to shreds monarchy and aristocracy, and lifting to their feet the poor, degraded, oppressed peasants of France." A European observer described him as "the Robespierre, Danton, and Marat of America all rolled into one."[6]

Stevens was of course no plaster saint. He had his flaws, and in pursuit of political effectiveness he took a number of missteps. His sojourn among nativists, which violated his democratic principles, was one of those. So was his sometime support for colonization. Recurring doubts about universal manhood suffrage, still another.

On key issues of the day, however, Stevens regularly staked out a position well in advance of public opinion. He did that when he fought for public education for all and when he rejected a discriminatory Pennsylvania state constitution, when he supported abolitionism, when he participated in the Underground Railroad, and when he opposed concessions to the slave states in 1850. Most important, he did that during the 1850s and 1860s when he pushed the young Republican Party to face down threats of secession, to confiscate and emancipate slaves, and to welcome black men into the ranks of Union armies. He continued to do that after the war as he strove to secure civil rights for the South's freedpeople and when he came to champion their right to participate equally in politics and government. Time after time, Stevens forged ahead when others, including members of his own party, hung back. As many of his contemporaries noted, he preferred to shape public opinion rather than bow before it. "It was in thus educating people and party up to his views," wrote an insightful journalist, "that Mr. Stevens did his greatest work in national politics."[7] That he sometimes failed in that goal, as when he proved unable to provide land for the freedpeople, testified in its own way to his determined staking out of advanced positions.

Stevens was famously savage in verbal combat with the paladins of inequality and oppression. But he could also be unsparing about allies who seemed to him backward, cowardly, or simply laggard. Many writers have since faulted him for so sternly criticizing Abraham Lincoln's refusal to move more swiftly and decisively than he did in support of emancipation and black rights generally. After all, those writers held, as a shrewd tactician Lincoln knew that politics is the art of the possible, and practicing that art requires not getting too far ahead of public opinion. In response, one of Stevens's early biographers reasonably asked "how public opinion was ever to be brought to a higher plane . . . if the surgent and radical anti-slavery men had all kept still, or had uttered nothing but pleasant and honeyed words for Lincoln and his Cabinet."[8]

The course of Stevens's career as an antislavery fighter paralleled that of the Second American Revolution. The trajectories of revolutions commonly exhibit both ascending and descending halves of a curve. The same is often true of their leaders' careers. For Stevens, the curve's ascending half included his efforts among the small but growing cadre of abolitionists in the 1830s, his adherence to the fledgling Republican Party in the 1850s, his successful congressional fight for a revolutionary war policy, and his postwar struggles to unseat Johnson's racist southern state governments and their black codes, to enfranchise southern black men, and to impose military rule long enough for southern units of the Republican Party to form and attempt to govern.

The Second American Revolution, like many others, eventually reached the limits of its resources and capacity. Here began the curve's descending half. The northern public, never firmly devoted to racial equality, tired of the seemingly endless struggle in the South. For many commercial and manufacturing interests, moreover, the stakes of the sectional conflict had always been limited. They had not liked the prospect of slavery expanding into the West in the 1850s, and a few years later they emphatically refused to permit secessionists to tear the country and its market in half. If resisting those perils had once compelled them to accept radical measures, however, that time had passed by the end of the 1860s. Continuing sectional strife now seemed simply bad for business. In Congress, Republican moderates whom Stevens and his allies had earlier pushed or hauled into supporting strong measures now began applying the brakes. They fretted that bold action in support of equal rights had alienated the white South and would continue to do so if sustained. They placed a far higher premium on reconciling with those southern whites than on making good on the promise of freedom and democracy to black Americans.

Outright slavery was dead and buried, and northern moderates would not surrender that achievement. But neither would they remove from office a reactionary president in league with the southern elite. Nor would they maintain federal control over the rebel states for the purpose of transforming them. Nor employ federal troops long and thoroughly enough to stamp out white-supremacist terrorism. And they certainly would not turn plantation lands over to the freedpeople.

That conservative mindset informed the obituary for Stevens that appeared in Henry J. Raymond's *New York Times*. When the war ended, it argued, the time had come for "hastening reconciliation" with the South and thereby "restoring friendly relations between the sections." But Stevens, said the *Times*, "had so fostered hatred of the nation's enemies, that he refused, even in their helplessness, to extend the fraternal hand." "His spirit was unchristian," that paper therefore judged, "and his measures were unjust and impolitic."[9]

In the midst of ebbing support, radicals faltered, backed down, or—as in Stevens's case—simply died off, helping thereby to clear the way for the North's retreat. Edward McPherson judged that it was in Stevens's role as a firm opponent of retreat that "his loss will be most seriously felt. We have many men in our ranks who otherwise are of remarkable ability but who are sadly deficient in this respect." As if in corroboration, moderate Republican congressman James G. Blaine sighed in relief that "the death of Stevens is an emancipation for the Republican Party."[10]

Reconstruction did not end in 1868 when Stevens died. Southern Republicans governed some states well into the 1870s. They managed to do so despite Congress's refusal to give freedpeople the land that Stevens thought they needed in order to act politically in their own interests. As it turned out, Stevens had underestimated their determination and ability to resist economic intimidation. Cases abounded in which black men voted despite employer threats to discharge them. In Montgomery, Alabama, one such landowner spotted an employee standing in a voting line and fired him then and there. The freedman just smiled, looked down, said nothing, and cast his ballot. Contrary to Stevens's lifelong assumptions, propertyless and even illiterate laborers proved perfectly capable of grasping and boldly acting in their own political interests.

When Reconstruction did die later in the 1870s, therefore, it was not because impoverished black citizens had succumbed to economic extortion but because white supremacist bands terrorized them and killed their leaders while erstwhile northern allies turned their backs. Meanwhile, judges took advantage of weaknesses and holes in the postwar constitutional amendments to undermine them. As a result, the fight to further democratize U.S. society was thrown back, and the Second American Revolution was left unfinished.[11]

In his last year of life, Stevens already thought he saw such an outcome on the horizon. In that dark mood, he told a writer that his principal "regret is that I have lived so long and so uselessly." But others held his achievements in higher regard. Some who did so could not yet foresee the defeats that lay ahead. Others, because they understood that those defeats would not be complete, that key achievements of the Second American Revolution—especially the abolition of slavery—would endure. And still others, because they believed that the achievements that survived and the example that Stevens and others set would help future generations to reconquer lost ground.

Two black ministers came to Stevens's sickbed at the end to pray for him and to report that the rest of the country's black population was doing the same. A postwar freedpeople's convention called him a "beacon light of our race." Black people in the nation's capital district named a school in his honor. Frederick Douglass hung Stevens's portrait on his wall. The great twentieth-century scholar W. E. B. DuBois praised his "grim and awful courage" as a "seer of democracy."[12]

On August 13, 1868, a racially integrated corps of pallbearers carried Thaddeus Stevens's body into the Capitol's Rotunda. There it lay in state with an honor guard of black Union soldiers, the Butler Zouaves from the District of Columbia. Five or six thousand people, white and black, came to view him. His body was then removed for burial to Lancaster, Pennsylvania, where between fifteen and twenty thousand mourners—again, black and white—reportedly attended his funeral.[13]

In his later years, as his health declined, Stevens had more than once contemplated his own epitaph. He did so in January 1865 while responding to an Ohio Democrat's criticism of the proposed Thirteenth Amendment. That critic, Stevens said, "may have his epitaph written . . . , 'Here rests the ablest and most pertinacious defender of slavery and opponent of liberty.'" As for himself, Stevens continued, "I will be satisfied if my epitaph shall be written thus: 'Here lies one who never rose to any eminence'" and who harbored only "'the low ambition to have it said that he had striven to ameliorate the condition of the poor, the lowly, the downtrodden of every race and language and color.'"[14]

The inscription upon which Thaddeus Stevens finally settled was chiseled onto the face of his monument in the only racially integrated cemetery in Lancaster, and there it remains to this day. "I repose in this quiet and secluded spot," it reads, "not from any natural preference for solitude. But, finding other cemeteries limited as to race, by charter rules, I have chosen this that I might illustrate in my death the principles which I advocated through a long life: EQUALITY OF MAN BEFORE HIS CREATOR."

Acknowledgments

Like most historians, I owe much of whatever value this book has to offer to the generous and invaluable assistance of many people. Before receiving her own doctorate, Sally Heinzel served as a fine research assistant, and the Campus Research Board of the University of Illinois at Urbana-Champaign (UIUC) supported her assistance. Roy Ritchie, then research director at the Huntington Library, offered me a yearlong residential fellowship, during which full-time work on this manuscript began. Steve Hindle, Roy's successor, warmly hosted me at that wonderful institution. Tom Bedwell of the UIUC History Department skillfully and energetically pushed my application for the supplementary funds that made my stay at the Huntington possible. Dan Green, literary agent par excellence, brought me to Simon & Schuster, where Tom LeBien signed me up. When Tom went off to other pastures, Alice Mayhew, assisted by Amar Deol and Maria Mendez, worked hard and ably to improve this manuscript, and Jonathan Evans copyedited it with great skill. After Alice died in early 2020, Megan Hogan ably piloted the book through to publication. My deepest gratitude to the Simon & Schuster production team of Paul Dippolito, Lisa Erwin, Lisa Healy, Kimberly Goldstein, and Gabby Robles for their work in designing this beautiful book.

In addition to Dan Green and Alice Mayhew, the following hardy folks read the entire manuscript and shared their reactions with me: Stephen V. Ash, John Ashworth, Joshua Brown, Fred Chase, Paul Escott, Eric Foner, Steve Hahn, Ross Hetrick, Ruth Hoffman, Kate Masur, Geoff Mirelowitz, Beverly Palmer, Bruce Thompson, and Scott Ware. Jonathan Beecher, Les Benedict, Tim Breen, Richard Carwardine, Chris Clark, and Edward Countryman read and provided discerning feedback on selected chapters, which improved them all. My gratitude to all of these folks is boundless. The book is no doubt weaker for my inability to follow *all* of their suggestions.

Among those who helped me to track down various puzzle pieces of Stevens's story are Kate Rousmaniere, Alex Keyssar, Randall Miller, John Joseph Wallis, Louise Stevenson, Van Gosse, Alan Taylor, Tim Breen, Randolph Harris, and Emma Lapsansky-Werner—as well as Sharon Lakey, the Director of the Danville Vermont Historical Society; Wendy Somers, the town clerk and treasurer of Danville, Vermont; Thomas Galinat, the town clerk and treasurer of Peacham, Vermont; Patrick Kerwin of the Library of Congress; Ross Hetrick of the Thaddeus Stevens Society; Karen Lewis of the Peacham, Vermont, Historical Association; Morgan Swan, the Special Collections Education & Outreach Librarian at the Rauner Special Collections Library of Dartmouth College; Prudence Doherty, Public Services Librarian of Special Collections at the University of Vermont; David Haugaard, Director of Research Services of the Historical Society of Pennsylvania; Mary Haegert of Harvard's Houghton Library; and attorney Ernest Tobias Balivet. And, as anyone can tell from scanning my endnotes, this project would have been immeasurably more difficult without the prior prodigious and meticulous labors of Beverly Wilson Palmer and Holly Byers Ochoa in compiling and preparing Stevens's papers for microfilming and then selecting and editing two volumes of them for publication in book form.

A few opportunities to test some of the book's arguments in public were very useful. Thanks to Manisha Sinha for inviting me to participate in an excellent conference on Reconstruction at the University of Connecticut. Patrick Clarke, Michael Birkner, Randall Miller, and John Quist graciously brought me to the campus of LancasterHistory.org as keynote cospeaker (with Jim Oakes) of the 2015 President James Buchanan National Symposium. Thanks, too, to Tom Ryan and Robin Sarratt of Lancasterhistory.org, who subsequently returned me to that city to participate in a richly informative conference about restoring the Thaddeus Stevens–Lydia Hamilton Smith House in Lancaster.

Throughout my work on this book and the various personal travails that occurred along the way, Mike, Dennis, and Emma kept me smiling and laughing. And, as always, Ruth Hoffman continued and continues to make life worth living.

Notes

Introduction

1 *Cleveland Daily Leader*, Sept. 10, 1863; Jubal Anderson Early, *Narrative of the War between the States* (1912; reprint, New York: Da Capo, 1991), pp. 255–56; Stevens to Simon Stevens, July 11, 1863, in *The Selected Papers of Thaddeus Stevens*, ed. Beverly Wilson Palmer and Holly Byers Ochoa, 2 vols. (Pittsburgh: University of Pittsburgh Press, 1997), vol. 1, p. 402 [henceforth abbreviated as *SPTS*]; Philip S. Foner, ed., *The Life and Writings of Frederick Douglass*, 5 vols. (New York: International, 1955), vol. 4, pp. 217–18.

2 James K. Moorhead (R-PA) in *Memorial Addresses on the Life and Character of Thaddeus Stevens* (Washington, DC: Government Printing Office, 1869), pp. 14–15.

3 Ignatius L. Donnelly (R-MN) in *Memorial Addresses*, p. 64.

4 Alexander K. McClure, *Abraham Lincoln and the Men of War-Times* (Philadelphia: Times, 1892), p. 279; *New York Times*, Aug. 13, 1868.

5 *Memphis Argus*, quoted in Eugene D. Genovese, *Roll, Jordan, Roll: The World the Slaves Made* (New York: Pantheon Books, 1974), p. 110; George E. B. Clemenceau, *American Reconstruction*, ed. Fernand Balensperger (New York and Toronto: Dial Press and Longmans, Green, 1926), p. 294; Karl Marx and Frederick Engels, *Collected Works*, 50 vols. (Moscow: Progress, 1975–2005), vol. 42, p. 48; Richard Taylor to Samuel L. M. Barlow, Dec. 13, 1865, in the Samuel Latham Mitchell Barlow Papers, Huntington Library.

6 *SPTS*, vol. 1, p. 323; Edward McPherson, untitled biographical sketch

of Stevens, p. 5, in the Edward McPherson Papers, Library of Congress (hereafter cited as McPherson, *Sketch*); *New York Herald*, March 9, 1868.

7 Henry L. Cake (R-PA) and Moorhead in *Memorial Addresses*, pp. 14–15.

8 Fawn M. Brodie, *Thaddeus Stevens: Scourge of the South* (1959; reprint, New York: Norton, 1966), p. 145; *Congressional Globe* (hereafter CG), 38th Congress, 1st session, p. 1223, 37th Congress, 2nd session, p. 2054; Hans L. Trefousse, *Thaddeus Stevens: Nineteenth-Century Egalitarian* (Chapel Hill: University of North Carolina Press, 1997), p. 127; William M. Hall, *Reminiscences and Sketches, Historical and Biographical* (Harrisburg, PA: Meyers Printing House, 1890), p. 14.

9 *New York Times*, Aug. 13, 1868.

10 William A. Dunning, *Reconstruction, Political and Economic, 1865–1877* (1907; reprint, New York: Harper & Row, 1962), pp. 86–87; J. G. Randall, *Lincoln the President: Midstream* (New York: Dodd, Mead, 1953), p. 104.

11 Lloyd Paul Stryker, *Andrew Johnson: A Study in Courage* (New York: Macmillan, 1929), pp. 248, 440, 691; James T. Adams, *The Epic of America* (Boston: Little, Brown, 1931), p. 275; John F. Kennedy, *Profiles in Courage* (New York: Harper & Row, 1955), p. 131.

12 Brodie, *Stevens*, p. 22.

13 Richard N. Current, *Old Thad Stevens: A Story of Ambition* (1942; reprint, Westport, CT: Greenwood Press, 1980), pp. iii–iv.

14 Alexander H. Hood, "Thaddeus Stevens," in Alexander Harris, A *Biographical History of Lancaster County* (Lancaster, PA: Elias Barr, 1872), pp. 568–69.

Chapter 1: A Son of Vermont

1 CG, 40:3, pp. 129, 132; Luke P. Poland in *Memorial Addresses*, p. 13.

2 Email message to author from Danville town clerk Wendy Somers, Aug. 26, 2016; Hans Trefousse, *Thaddeus Stevens: Nineteenth-Century Egalitarian* (Chapel Hill: University of North Carolina Press, 1997), p. 1; email message to author from Sharon Lakey, director, Danville Historical Society, Oct. 26, 2016, conveying information supplied by attorney Ernest Tobias Balivet.

3 *Harper's Weekly*, vol. 12 (Aug. 29, 1868), p. 548.

4 *Harper's Weekly*, vol. 12 (Aug. 29, 1868), p. 548; Hall, *Reminiscences and Sketches*, p. 6; *SPTS*, vol. 1, p. 34.

5 Samuel W. McCall, *Thaddeus Stevens* (Boston: Houghton, Mifflin, 1899), pp. 4–7; Fawn M. Brodie, *Thaddeus Stevens: Scourge of the South* (1959; reprint, New York: Norton, 1966), p. 23; *Memorial Addresses*, p. 13.

6 Chilton Williamson, *Vermont in Quandary* (Montpelier: Vermont Historical Society, 1949), pp. 10–12; David Bennett, *A Few Lawless Vagabonds: Ethan Allen, The Republic of Vermont, and the American Revolution* (Philadelphia: Casemate, 2014), p. 30; Edward Countryman, *A People in Revolution: The American Revolution and Political Society in New York, 1760–1790* (Baltimore: Johns Hopkins, 1981), p. 48.

7 The structure and functioning of government in colonial New York abetted landlord power. Legislative districts were unequally represented in the colonial assembly, and long terms of office for legislators made it difficult for voters to replace those who displeased them. Meanwhile, the government's most powerful offices, those of the governor and the council, were not elected at all but appointed by the British king. The governor, furthermore, had the power to call, adjourn, or dissolve the legislature at will. Countryman, *People in Revolution*, pp. 74–77; Williamson, *Vermont in Quandary*, pp. 16–18, 62.

8 Williamson, *Vermont in Quandary*, pp. 20, 45; Bennett, *A Few Lawless Vagabonds*, pp. 34–40; Mary Greene Nye, ed., *Sequestration, Confiscation and Sale of Estates* (1941), vol. 6 of *Vermont State Papers*, pp. 38, 56; Randolph A. Roth, *The Democratic Dilemma: Religion, Reform, and the Social Order in the Connecticut River Valley of Vermont, 1791–1850* (Cambridge: Cambridge University Press, 1987), p. 23.

9 Countryman, *People in Revolution*, pp. 42–45, 48, 50; Williamson, *Vermont in Quandary*, pp. 10–12; Bennett, *A Few Lawless Vagabonds*, p. 30; Ira Allen, *The Natural and Political History of the State of Vermont* (London: J. W. Meyers, 1798), pp. 19–21.

10 Nye, *Sequestration*, p. 7; Williamson, *Vermont in Quandary*, pp. 69, 73–75; 84; E. P. Walton, ed., *Records of the Council of Safety and Governor and Council of the State of Vermont*, 8 vols. (Montpelier, VT: J. & J. M.

Poland, 1873–80), vol. 1, pp. 134–35; Bogart, *Peacham*, p. 57; Paul S. Gillies, "Ruminations. The Question of Sequestration: Condemnation without Compensation in a Time of War," *Vermont Bar Journal*, no. 14 (December 2004); Edward Countryman, The American Revolution (New York: Hill and Wang, 1985), p. 132.

11 Countryman, *People in Revolution*, p. 52; Bogart, *Peacham*, p. 3; Roth, *Democratic Dilemma*, p. 21. The meeting of town representatives that founded the Vermont republic opened with an invocation by Rev. Aaron Hutchinson that reminded the gathering of those values. The minister elaborated upon an injunction in the book of Zachariah: All must "shew mercy and compassion every man to his brother. And oppress not the widow, nor the fatherless, the stranger, nor the poor: and let none of you imagine evil against his brother in your heart." So a farmer, Hutchinson explained, must not set "an exorbitant price for the necessaries of life," should not "use extortion, and make a neighbour's necessity my opportunity to exact more than is meet." Nor should a lawyer charge a high fee to a "poor client, at the head of a needy family." A merchant, too, must avoid asking excessive prices for wares. And a harsh employer should think, "if I was the poor servant, should I not think such severity hard and unjust, and quite unbecoming one that has a master in heaven, with whom there is no respect of persons?" Aaron Hutchinson, "A well tempered self-love a rule of conduct towards others: A sermon preached at Windsor, July 2, 1777, before the representatives of the towns in the counties of Charlotte, Cumberland, and Gloucester, for forming the state of Vermont," pp. 6–9, accessed at https://quod.lib .umich.edu/e/evans/N12546.0001.001/1:3?rgn=div1;view=fulltext.

12 Countryman, *People in Revolution*, p. 168; Jon L. Wakelyn, ed., *America's Founding Charters: Primary Documents of Colonial and Revolutionary Era Governance*, 3 vols. (Westport, CT: Greenwood, 2006), vol. 2, pp. 793–94.

13 Williamson, *Vermont in Quandary*, pp. 63–64; Chilton Williamson, *American Suffrage from Property to Democracy, 1760–1860* (Princeton, NJ: Princeton University Press, 1960), p. 98.

14 Harvey Amani Whitfield, *The Problem of Slavery in Early Vermont, 1777–1810: Essays and Primary Sources* (Barre: Vermont Historical Society, 2014). Whitfield notes that the lack of serious enforcement of this

constitutional provision in fact allowed the enslavement of people in the state to continue for decades.

15 Paul Chouinard, "Thaddeus Stevens in the Limelight—Early Life in Danville," website of the Danville Vermont Historical Society, accessed at http://www.danvillevthistorical.org; CG, 38th Cong., 2d sess., p. 265.

16 *SPTS*, vol. 1, p. 6; Henry Crocker, *History of the Baptists in Vermont* (Bellows Falls, VT: P. H. Gobie Press, 1913), pp. 313–14, 318; email message from Karen Lewis of the Peacham Historical Association to the author, August 21, 2016.

17 Perry Miller, *The New England Mind: From Colony to Province* (1953; reprint, Cambridge, MA: Harvard University Press, 1983), p. 83; Christopher Hill, *Puritanism and Revolution: The English Revolution of the 17th Century* (New York: Schocken, 1964), pp. 244–46, 267; Christopher Hill, *The World Turned Upside Down: Radical Ideas during the English Revolution* (New York: Viking, 1972), pp. 80, 84–85.

18 "Once give up christening the whole parish [in] infancy," an English Baptist minister foresaw, "and then farewell [to] that parish posture which the Pope set up in all Christendom some six hundred years ago," and then down too would fall all other aspects of "Popish" religion. "Amen," he added: "so be it." Hill, *The World Turned Upside Down*, pp. 80, 84–85.

19 Christopher Hill, *Society and Puritanism in Pre-Revolutionary England* (London: Panther Books, 1969), p. 287.

20 Roth, *Democratic Dilemma*, p. 28; Alexander Hood, "Thaddeus Stevens," in Alexander Harris, *A Biographical History of Lancaster County* (Lancaster, PA: Elias Barr, 1872), pp. 570–71.

21 David M. Ludlum, *Social Ferment in Vermont, 1791–1850* (Montpelier: Vermont Historical Society, 1948), pp. 92–93; William H. Brackney, *Baptists in North America: A Historical Perspective* (Hoboken, NJ: John Wiley, 2006), p. 50; John E. Goodrich, *Immigration to Vermont: A Paper . . . Read before the Vermont Historical Society on November 10th, 1908* (Montpelier, Vt.: n.p., 1909), pp. 73–75.

22 Alexander Harris, *A Review of the Political Conflict in America, from the Commencement of the Anti-Slavery Agitation to the Close of Southern*

Reconstruction (New York: T. H. Pollock, 1876), pp. 9–10, 12–13; Paul Chouinard, "Thaddeus Stevens in the Limelight—The School Years," accessed at http://danvillevthistorical.org/?p=1837; Hood, "Stevens," pp. 570–71; Thomas Frederick Woodley, *Thaddeus Stevens* (Harrisburg, Pa.: Telegraph Press, 1934), p. 14. Few sources refer to his attending elementary school, but Pennsylvania congressman Oliver J. Dickey, who began his career in Stevens's law office, who knew him for many years, and who eventually took Stevens's House seat after the older man died, attested to that. CG, 40:3, p. 130. See also Current, *Old Thad Stevens*, p. 5.

23 Herbert Darling Foster, "Webster and Choate in College," *Dartmouth Alumni Magazine*, vol. 19 (April 1927), pp. 511–13.

24 Samuel W. McCall, *Thaddeus Stevens* (Boston: Houghton Mifflin, 1899), p. 14. On Stevens's exacting attitude toward university study, see his advice to his nephew in Stevens to Thaddeus Stevens Jr., Oct. 23, 1854, in *SPTS*, vol 1, p. 147.

25 Henry F. May, *The Enlightenment in America* (New York: Oxford University Press, 1976), p. 348.

26 William Paley, *The Principles of Moral and Political Philosophy* (1785; reprint, Indianapolis: Liberty Fund, 2002), p. 66.

27 We have more detailed information about Dartmouth's curriculum than about the University of Vermont's, but we do know that the latter's junior year studies included classics and what was called "natural philosophy." Julian Ira Lindsay, *Tradition Looking Forward: The University of Vermont: A History, 1791–1904* (Burlington, VT: [University of Vermont and State Agricultural College,] 1954), p. 87; Foster, "Webster and Choate in College," pp. 511–13. A journal called the *Anti-Jacobin Review* complained in 1802, thus, that in Paley's work "the most determined Jacobin might find a justification of his principles, and a sanction for his conduct." D. L. Le Mahieu, "Foreword" to Paley, *The Principles of Moral and Political Philosophy*, p. xii.

28 CG, 38th Cong., 2d. sess., p. 265; Betty Bandel, "Student Debates . . . and Thaddeus Stevens," in *The University of Vermont: The First Two Hundred Years*, ed. Robert V. Daniels (Hanover, NH: University Press of New England, 1991), pp. 51–52; Paley, *The Principles of Moral and Political Philosophy*, pp. 136–38.

29 Paley, *The Principles of Moral and Political Philosophy*, pp. 136–38.
30 *SPTS*, vol. 1, p. 4.
31 Notice in the *Adams Centinel*, Dec. 18, 1816, in the *Thaddeus Stevens Papers* (microfilm), henceforth *TSP(M)*; Frederick Watts, letter dated January 16, 1868, reprinted in Hall, *Reminiscences and Sketches*, pp. 29–31; Harris, *Review of the Political Conflict*, p. 90; Hood, "Thaddeus Stevens," p. 596.
32 *SPTS*, vol. 2, p. 243; letter from Edward McPherson, dated January 1887, in Hall, *Reminiscences and Sketches*, p. 20.
33 Hood, "Thaddeus Stevens," p. 573; McPherson, Sketch of Stevens.
34 McPherson *Sketch*; Hood, "Thaddeus Stevens," p. 573.
35 Abraham Lincoln apparently embraced just such an understanding. Noting that Thomas and Nancy Hanks Lincoln were also, like Stevens's family, Calvinist-minded Baptists, religion scholar Peter J. Thuesen suggests that even though "Lincoln never joined a church himself, his early exposure" to the doctrine of predestination "contributed to his lifelong belief in fate or necessity." Lincoln expressed that belief in the midst of the Civil War, writing that "I claim not to have controlled events, but confess plainly that events have controlled me." Peter Johannes Thuesen, *Predestination: The American Career of a Contentious Doctrine* (New York: Oxford University Press, 2009), p. 197; *The Collected Works of Abraham Lincoln*, ed. Roy P. Basler et al., 8 vols. (New Brunswick, NJ: Rutgers University Press, 1953), vol. 7, p. 282 (henceforth *ALCW*); CG, 37:1, p. 439; *SPTS*, vol. 1, pp. 242, 395.
36 Hood, "Thaddeus Stevens," p. 593.
37 McPherson, *Sketch*.
38 CG, 40:2, p. 3791.
39 Hood, "Thaddeus Stevens," pp. 593–94; Blanchard, "Thaddeus Stevens," *Christian Cynosure*, December 29, 1868; CG, 39:1, p. 4304; Hall, *Reminiscences and Sketches*, p. 21; *Memorial Addresses*, p. 7.
40 *Memorial Addresses*, p. 63; *SPTS*, vol. 1, p. 24.
41 Hood, "Thaddeus Stevens," p. 570. The Tennessee unionist and Republican congressman Horace Maynard, for example, recorded that Stevens "evinced little respect for mere taste and refinement and delicacy and

luxury. . . ." William M. Hall agreed that Stevens "set no store by money, and was generous and liberal with it." *Memorial Addresses*, p. 21; Hall, *Reminiscences and Sketches*, p. 11.

42 *SPTS*, vol. 1, p. 3.

Chapter 2: A Young Man's Outlook

1 Olivier Fraysse, *Lincoln, Land, and Labor, 1809–60* (Urbana: University of Illinois Press, 1994), esp. pp. 30–32. Lincoln's words appeared in a short autobiographical memo he wrote in 1859. See *ALCW*, vol. 3, p. 511. On Greeley, see his *Recollections of a Busy Life* (New York: J. B. Ford, 1868), pp. 34–38, 60.

2 These same words also illuminate the early evolution of Stevens's religious views. His argument here significantly departed from the one he had encountered in William Paley, who attributed these same achievements to the spread of the Christian faith. Stevens's commencement speech, labeled as "Conference by Sen. Stevens for next Commencement—July 9th 1814," is in the Thaddeus Stevens Papers, Rauner Special Collections Library, Dartmouth College.

3 CG, 32:1, Appendix, pp. 742, 745. Historian Daniel Walker Howe has summarized this outlook's core tenet: "Industrial capitalism was the high point of civilization." This same opinion was then becoming widespread across the transatlantic world. Such harsh critics of industrial capitalism as Karl Marx and Friedrich Engels would readily acknowledge at mid-century that this economic system had "accomplished wonders far surpassing Egyptian pyramids, Roman aqueducts, and Gothic cathedrals" and had thereby "been the first to show what man's activity can bring about." Daniel Walker Howe, *The Political Culture of the American Whigs* (Chicago: University of Chicago Press, 1979), pp. 101–2; Karl Marx and Friedrich Engels, *Collected Works*, 47 vols. (New York: International, 1975–2001), vol. 6, p. 487.

4 "Conference by Sen. Stevens."

5 *Proceedings and Debates of the Convention of the Commonwealth of Pennsylvania, to Propose Amendments to the Constitution: Commenced and*

Held at Harrisburg, on the Second Day of May, 1837, 14 vols. (Harrisburg, PA: n.p., 1837–39), vol. 7, pp. 157–58.

6 *SPTS*, vol. 1, pp. 12–14; *Proceedings and Debates*, vol. 1, pp. 545–47.

7 *SPTS*, vol. 1, p. 22.

8 *SPTS*, vol. 1, p. 23.

9 *Memorial Addresses*, p. 15; Alexander K. McClure, *Old Time Notes of Pennsylvania*, 2 vols. (Philadelphia: John C. Winston, 1905), vol. 1, p. 20; Charles McCarthy, *The Antimasonic Party: A Study of Political Antimasonry in the United States, 1827–1840* (Washington, DC: U.S. Government Printing Office, 1903), pp. 427–28.

10 Emphasis added.

11 *SPTS*, vol. 1, pp. 19–30. Emphasis added.

12 *Report of the Commissioner of Education for the Year 1898–99* (Washington, DC: U.S. Government Printing Office, 1900), p. 518; *SPTS*, vol. 1, p. 30n8; McClure, *Old Time Notes*, I, 21; *Proceedings and Debates*, vol. 5, pp. 288, 300; Rosalind L. Branning, *Pennsylvania Constitutional Development* (Pittsburgh: University of Pittsburgh Press, 1960), p. 29.

13 This stance served the interests of wealthy southern Democrats, too. As landowners rather than merchants or manufacturers, they resented tariffs that raised the prices they paid for imported manufactured goods, and they opposed federal support for roads, canals, and other improvements that were constructed principally in the North.

14 *Proceedings and Debates*, vol. 7, pp. 133, 156–57.

15 *SPTS*, vol. 1, p. 14; Christopher Hill, *Puritanism and Revolution: The English Revolution of the 17th Century* (New York: Schocken, 1958), pp. 305–8; C. B. McPherson, *The Political Theory of Possessive Individualism: Hobbes to Locke* (Oxford: Oxford University Press, 1962), pp. 248–49, 252, 263–64, and passim; Howe, *Political Culture*, pp. 51, 76–77; J. G. A. Pocock, *The Machiavellian Moment: Florentine Political Thought and the Atlantic Republican Tradition* (Princeton, NJ: Princeton University Press, 1975), pp. 386–87; Donald K. Pickens, "The Republican Synthesis and Thaddeus Stevens," *Civil War History* 31 (1985): 57–73.

16 *Proceedings and Debates of the Convention*, vol. 1, p. 169; vol. 2, pp. 473–74; vol. 3, pp. 33, 167–78; Branning, *Pennsylvania Constitutional Development*, p. 22.

17 The vote was 71 to 42. *Proceedings and Debates*, vol. 2, p. 476; vol. 3, pp. 167, 170. An opponent held that Stevens's ardent championing of the poor during the public schools discussion was inconsistent with his stance on voting rights. Stevens's support for universal public education, this critic said, should make him welcome universal manhood suffrage. Stevens did not respond to the jibe. Like others, however, he looked upon public education as at least a partial safeguard against misuse of the suffrage. John Ashworth, *"Agrarians" and "Aristocrats": Party Political Ideology in the United States, 1837–1846* (Cambridge: Cambridge University Press, 1983), pp. 161–63.

18 Howe, *Political Culture*, p. 51; "Conference by Sen. Stevens."

19 "To Our Constituents," an open letter published in the *Adams Centinel*, Jan. 20, 1830, from Stevens and others concerning the editorship of an anti-Masonic newspaper, in *TSP(M)*, reel 1, frame 0030.

20 *The Autobiography of William H. Seward*, ed. Frederick W. Seward (New York: Appleton, 1877), vol. 1, p. 79; Ashworth, *"Agrarians" and "Aristocrats,"* p. 170; McCarthy, *The Antimasonic Party*, pp. 483, 487–88, 544; Kathleen Smith Kutolowski, "Antimasonry Reexamined: Social Bases of the Grass-Roots Party," *Journal of American History* 71 (September 1984): 274, 280. Anti-Masons (who were numerous in rural districts) generally despised Jackson's National Republican critics (who were strong in Philadelphia) as high-handed aristocrats and neo-Federalists, and the contempt was mutual. Michael F. Holt, *The Rise and Fall of the Whig Party* (New York: Oxford University Press, 1999), pp. 13–14.

21 Original emphasis. Paul Goodman, *Towards a Christian Republic: Antimasonry and the Great Transition in New England, 1826–1836* (New York: Oxford University Press, 1988), pp. 12, 25; Howe, *Political Culture*, p. 56; Ronald P. Formisano and Kathleen Smith Kutolowski, "Antimasonry and Masonry: The Genesis of Protest, 1826–1827," *American Quarterly* 29 (Summer 1977): 139–65; Roth, *Democratic Dilemma*, pp. 98–99, 101, 152–53; Ludlum, *Social Ferment*, pp. 92–93; *The Proceedings of the Second United States Anti-Masonic Convention Held at Baltimore, September, 1831* (Boston: Boston Type & Stereotype Foundry, 1832), p. 61.

22 *SPTS*, vol. 1, p. 10; James Albert Woodburn, *The Life of Thaddeus Ste-*

vens: A Study in American Political History (Indianapolis: Bobbs-Merrill, 1913), p. 318; McCarthy, *Anti-Masonic Party*, pp. 557–58. Former president John Quincy Adams similarly argued in 1833 that "Masonic oaths and mysteries give a tenfold power to the knot of association [among its members], and, by the secrecy vital to the institution, it becomes a conspiracy of exclusive privilege to the members at the expense of all the rest of the community." *Memoirs of John Quincy Adams*, ed. Charles Francis Adams, 12 vols. (Philadelphia: J. B. Lippincott, 1874–77), vol. 9, pp. 16–17.

23 In 1832, the voters of Peacham cast almost three-quarters of their ballots for Anti-Mason candidates. By the following year, Anti-Masons predominated in Vermont's Connecticut River valley as a whole.

24 *SPTS*, vol. 1, p. 6; McCarthy, *The Antimasonic Party*, pp. 504–14; Goodman, *Towards a Christian Republic*, pp. 4, 17, 122–23, 132, 136; Roth, *Democratic Dilemma*, p. 157.

25 Of those who voted Anti-Mason in 1832, most who remained politically active four years later seem to have cast ballots for Whigs. McCarthy, *The Antimasonic Party*, pp. 506, 509; Goodman, *Towards a Christian Republic*, pp. 139, 145.

26 CG, 38:2, p. 265.

27 Hall, *Reminiscences and Sketches*, pp. 21–22; Thomas P. Slaughter, *Bloody Dawn: The Christiana Riot and Racial Violence in the Antebellum North* (New York: Oxford University Press, 1991), p. 50; Harris, *Review of the Political Conflict*, p. 90; Bradley R. Hoch, *Thaddeus Stevens in Gettysburg: The Making of an Abolitionist* (Gettysburg, PA: Adams County Historical Society, 2005), pp. 230–31; Paul Finkelman, *An Imperfect Union: Slavery, Federalism, and Comity* (Union, NJ: Lawbook Exchange, 2000), pp. 54–56. In this respect, too, Stevens's record mirrored that of Illinois's Abraham Lincoln. See Eric Foner, *The Fiery Trial: Abraham Lincoln and American Slavery* (New York: Norton, 2010), pp. 47–48.

28 James Brewer Stewart, *Holy Warriors: The Abolitionists and American Slavery*, rev. ed. (New York: Hill & Wang, 1996), pp. 51–53; Manisha Sinha, *The Slave's Cause: A History of Abolition* (New Haven, CT: Yale University Press, 2016), p. 226.

29 William H. Brackney, *Baptists in North America* (Malden, MA: Blackwell,

2006), p. 232; Ludlum, *Social Ferment*, pp. 163–64; Bogart, *Peacham*, p. 219; Hoch, *Stevens in Gettysburg*, p. 235.

30 William W. Freehling, *Prelude to Civil War: The Nullification Controversy in South Carolina, 1816–1836* (New York: Harper & Row, 1966), p. 263.

31 Freehling, *Prelude*, p. 257.

32 *SPTS*, vol. 1, p. 14; CG, 31:1, Appendix, p. 1108.

33 Russel B. Nye, *Fettered Freedom: Civil Liberties and the Slavery Controversy, 1830–1860* (East Lansing: Michigan State College Press, 1949), p. 37; Leonard L. Richards, *The Slave Power: The Free North and Southern Dominion, 1780–1860* (Baton Rouge: Louisiana State University Press, 2000), pp. 128–29.

34 Nye, *Fettered Freedom*, 34; William J. Cooper Jr., *Liberty and Slavery: Southern Politics to 1860* (Columbia: University of South Carolina Press, 2000), p. 64.

35 Many of the resolutions adopted at those meetings were collected in "Proceedings of the Various Counties of Virginia, and Several of the Non-Slaveholding States, on the Subject of Abolition," in the *Journal of the House of Delegates of the Commonwealth of Virginia . . . on Monday, the Seventh Day of December, One Thousand Eight Hundred and Thirty-Five* (Richmond, VA: Samuel Shepherd, 1835); *Niles Weekly Register*, vol. 13 (Sept. 5, 1835), pp. 9–10.

36 *Autobiography of Seward*, p. 79.

37 Gettysburg *Star and Republican Banner*, Oct. 19, 1835. The precise substance of his remarks does not appear in this account, but the anti-abolitionist resolutions quoted above reportedly passed "unanimously." *Niles' Weekly Register*, vol. 13 (Sept. 5, 1835), pp. 9–10; Eric Ledell Smith, "The Pittsburgh Memorial: A Forgotten Document of Pittsburgh History," *Pittsburgh History* (Fall 1997): 107.

38 James B. Stewart, "Abolitionists, Insurgents, and Third Parties: Sectionalism and Partisan Politics in Northern Whiggery, 1836–1844," in Alan M. Kraut, ed., *Crusaders and Compromisers: Essays on the Relationship of the Antislavery Struggle to the Antebellum Party System* (Westport, CT: Greenwood, 1983), p. 25; Nye, *Fettered Freedom*, pp. 40–41; Freehling, *Prelude*, 346–58.

39 *SPTS*, vol. 1, p. 37.

40 *SPTS*, vol. 1, p. 50.

41 *SPTS*, vol. 1, pp. 36–38, emphasis added; "Fourth Annual Report of the American Anti-Slavery Society," *Quarterly Antislavery Magazine*, vol. 2, no. 4 (July 1837), p. 360. Richard N. Current erroneously claimed that Stevens's report "agreed with the Virginians that Congress had no constitutional power to abolish slavery . . . in the District of Columbia." See Current, *Old Thad Stevens*, pp. 33–34.

42 *ALCW*, vol. 1, pp. 74–75.

43 The bill Lincoln had in mind would have compelled children born to enslaved mothers to labor as "apprentices" for their mothers' owners until adulthood, at which point they would become free. Slaves who were already adults in 1850 would remain enslaved for the rest of their lives unless their owners voluntarily liberated them. The federal government would compensate any owner who chose to do that for the "full cash value" of the people they manumitted. Lincoln decided not to introduce the bill when he found himself "abandoned by my former backers" in the House. ALCW, vol. 2, pp. 20–22; Foner, *The Fiery Trial*, pp. 56–57.

44 Blanchard to Stevens, May 12, 1847, in *TSP(M)*, reel 1, frame 0497; Hoch, *Stevens in Gettysburg*, p. 238.

45 Jonathan Blanchard, "Thaddeus Stevens," *Christian Cynosure*, December 29, 1868. Emphasis added.

46 "Proceedings of the Convention, of the Integrity of the Union," May 1837, at Duke University Libraries Digital Collection, accessed at http://library.duke.edu/digitalcollections/broadsides_bdspa012367/.

47 *SPTS*, vol. 1, pp. 50–51.

48 Eric Foner, *Free Soil, Free Labor, Free Men: The Ideology of the Republican Party before the Civil War* (New York: Oxford University Press, 1970), pp. 76–77, 117.

49 *Proceedings and Debates*, vol. 3, p. 694.

50 Stevens to Samuel Webb and others, May 4, 1838, reprinted in the *Pennsylvania Freeman*, May 17, 1838, in *TSP(M)*, reel 1, frame 0200; *SPTS*, vol. 1, pp. 65–66; Leonard L. Richards, *Gentlemen of Property and Standing: Anti-Abolition Mobs in Jacksonian America* (New York: Oxford

University Press, 1970), p. 156; Hans L. Trefousse, *The Radical Republicans: Lincoln's Vanguard for Racial Justice* (New York: Knopf, 1969), pp. 29–30; David G. Smith, *On the Edge of Freedom: The Fugitive Slave Issue in South Central Pennsylvania, 1820–1870* (New York: Fordham University Press, 2013), p. 54; *Proceedings and Debates*, vol. 1, p. 191.

51 Smith, *On the Edge of Freedom*, p. 54.

52 *Proceedings and Debates*, vol. 1, p. 191; vol. 2, p. 200. Although New York State did not absolutely bar blacks from the polls, it did impose a discriminatory property requirement upon their franchise.

53 *Proceedings and Debates*, vol. 2, p. 472.

54 Eric Ledell Smith, "The Pittsburgh Memorial: A Forgotten Document of Pittsburgh History," *Pittsburgh History* (Fall 1997): 106–11. The memorial misdated the gradual-emancipation law to 1790.

55 *Proceedings and Debates*, vol. 3, pp. 684–85.

56 *Proceedings and Debates*, vol. 3, p. 693; emphasis added.

57 Agnew's party colleague Ebenezer W. Sturdevant went further, complaining that to "yield a right to the negro" in "an attempt to elevate him" would "degrade us." And black suffrage, Sturdevant also claimed, would represent a gain for "the anti-American doctrines of the abolitionists" and therefore so offend the South that it "may result finally in the overthrow of the Union." *Proceedings and Debates*, vol. 9, pp. 328, 365; Nicholas Wood, "'A Sacrifice on the Altar of Slavery': Doughface Politics and Black Disenfranchisement in Pennsylvania, 1837–1838," *Journal of the Early Republic* 31 (Spring 2011): 96.

58 Wood, "Sacrifice," pp. 80, 96–97; *Proceedings and Debates*, vol. 3, pp. 69, 82–88; *SPTS*, vol. 1, pp. 55–56.

59 *Proceedings and Debates*, vol. 10, p. 106; McClure, *Old Time Notes*, vol. 2, p. 279.

60 Foner, *Free Soil*, chapter 3; Patrick Cudmore, *The Civil Government of the States* (New York: P. Cudmore, 1875), p. 206.

61 Chase to Stevens, April 1, 1842, in *TSP(M)*, reel 1, frames 0352–55; *SPTS*, vol. 1, pp. 82–83.

62 Aileen S. Kraditor, *Means and Ends in American Abolitionism: Garrison and His Critics in Strategy and Tactics, 1834–1850* (New York: Pantheon, 1967), pp. 144–45.

63 Stevens to Blanchard, May 24, 1842, in *TSP(M)*, reel 1, frames 0386–87.

64 Stevens to Jeremiah Brown, sometime in 1847, in Charles D. Spotts, "The Pilgrim's Pathway: The Underground Railroad in Lancaster," *Community History* 5 (December 1966): 42-43 (also in *TSP(M)*, reel 1, frame 0520).

Chapter 3: Resisting Slavery's Expansion

1 Holt, *Whig Party*, p. 55.

2 CG, 28 Cong., 2 Sess., p. 132; Current, *Old Thad Stevens*, p. 43; Chaplain W. Morrison, *Democratic Politics and Sectionalism: The Wilmot Proviso Controversy* (Chapel Hill: University of North Carolina Press, 1967), p. 6.

3 Morrison, *Democratic Politics and Sectionalism*, pp. 7, 14; Eric Foner, *The Fiery Trial: Abraham Lincoln and American Slavery* (New York: Norton, 2010), pp. 52–53.

4 Holman Hamilton, *Prologue to Conflict: The Crisis and Compromise of 1850* ([Lexington:] University of Kentucky Press, 1964), p. 114; CG, 30:1, Appendix, p. 680; *Niles National Register* 71 (Feb. 6, 1847): 353; Richards, *The Slave Power*, p. 153; Morrison, *Democratic Politics and Sectionalism*, p. 37.

5 Trefousse, *The Radical Republicans*, p. 45; Richard H. Sewell, *Ballots for Freedom: Antislavery Politics in the United States, 1837–1860* (New York: Norton, 1976), p. 159.

6 Frederick J. Blue, *The Free Soilers: Third Party Politics, 1848–1854* (Urbana: University of Illinois Press, 1973), pp. 137, 166–67, 207; David Herbert Donald, *Charles Sumner and the Coming of the Civil War* (1960; reprint, Chicago: University of Chicago Press, 1980), pp. 189–201. Prominent among the Free Soil congressmen were Preston King of New York, David Wilmot of Pennsylvania, Joshua Giddings of Ohio, George Julian of Indiana, and Horace Mann of Massachusetts.

7 *SPTS*, vol. 1, p. 103n.

8 Mueller, *Whig Party in Pennsylvania*, p. 151; Holt, *Whig Party*, p. 344; *SPTS*, vol. 1, pp. 102–3.

9 *Examiner and Herald,* Aug. 23, 30, 1848; *Huntingdon Journal,* Sept. 12, 1848. The pro-Democratic *Intelligencer and Journal* (Aug. 22 and 29, 1848) said that Smith was preferred by "the *ultra* whigs," favored by "the 'Old Hunkers' of the Whig party."

10 *Lancaster Intelligencer and Journal,* Aug. 29, 1848. When Stevens publicly denied any intent to interfere directly with slavery in the states, the *Intelligencer and Journal* withdrew the charge in its edition of Sept. 5, 1848.

11 Letter reprinted in the *Intelligencer and Journal,* Sep. 26, 1848; *Intelligencer and Journal,* Oct. 17, 1848.

12 *Examiner and Herald,* Aug. 16, Sep. 27, 1848; Gettysburg *Star and Banner,* Sep. 29, 1848; letter to the *Intelligencer and Journal,* Sep. 26, 1848.

13 CG, *31:1,* p. 195.

14 CG, 31:1, pp. 18–28, 201–4; Hamilton, *Prologue,* p. 44.

15 Mark J. Stegmaier, *Texas, New Mexico, and the Compromise of 1850: Boundary Dispute & Sectional Crisis* (Kent, OH: Kent State University Press, 1996), pp. 27, 32; Holt, *Whig Party,* p. 519.

16 Robert V. Remini, *Henry Clay: Statesman for the Union* (New York: Norton, 1991), pp. 731–32; J. J. Bowden, "The Texas–New Mexico Boundary Dispute along the Rio Grande," *Southwestern Historical Quarterly* 63 (October 1959): 228. In the event, the federal government agreed to pay Texas $10 million.

17 *United States Statutes at Large,* chap. 7, p. 302.

18 Application to the National Parks Service to make Stevens's home and office in Lancaster a site in the NPS's Network to Freedom project, Jan. 27, 2011, p. 4; James A. Delle and Marry Ann Levine, "Excavations at the Thaddeus Stevens and Lydia Hamilton Smith Site, Lancaster, Pennsylvania: Archaeological Evidence for the Underground Railroad?" *Northeast Historical Archaeology* 33 (2004): 131–52; William J. Switala, *Underground Railroad in Pennsylvania,* second ed. (Mechanicsburg, Pa.: Stackpole Books, 2008), pp. 116–17.

19 *U.S. Statutes at Large,* chap. 9, pp. 446–58, 462–65.

20 CG, 31:1, p. 246.

21 CG, 31:1, pp. 150, 175.

22 CG, 31:1, Appendix, p. 141.

23 CG, 31:1, Appendix, p. 142.

24 CG, 31:1, Appendix, p. 142.

25 CG, 31:1, Appendix, pp. 142–43.

26 CG, 31:1, Appendix, p. 143.

27 CG, 31:1, Appendix, pp. 141–42.

28 CG, 31:1, Appendix, p. 142; Woodley, *Stevens*, p. 220.

29 *Memorial Addresses*, p. 16.

30 CG, 31:1, Appendix, p. 143.

31 CG, 31:1, Appendix, pp. 462, 768–69.

32 CG, 31:1, Appendix, p. 769.

33 Blanchard to Stevens, March 13, 1850, *TSP(M)*, reel 1, frames 728–30; Giddings to Sumner, Oct. 28, 1850, Charles Sumner Papers, MS Am 1 (2545), Houghton Library, Harvard University; McClure, *Recollections*, p. 418.

34 CG, 31:1, Appendix, p. 768.

35 Alexander Hood to Stevens, July 10, 1850, in *TSP(M)*), reel 1, frame 0759; Hamilton, *Prologue*, p. 163; David M. Potter, *The Impending Crisis, 1848–1861*, ed. Don E. Fehrenbacher (New York: Harper & Row, 1976), p. 113.

36 *The Pennsylvania Freeman*, Nov. 20, 1851, in *TSP(M)*, reel 1, frame 0827; *SPTS*, vol. 1, p. 134.

37 CG, 31:1, Appendix, p. 122; Robert V. Remini, *Daniel Webster: The Man and His Time* (New York: Norton, 1997), p. 693; *The American Whig Review* (June 1852), p. 479; *ALCW*, vol. 2, p. 130.

38 CG, 31:1, Appendix, p. 1109.

39 *Jefferson Davis, Constitutionalist: His Letters, Papers, and Speeches*, ed. Dunbar F. Rowland (Jackson: Mississippi Department of Archives and History, 1923), vol. 1, pp. 484–85.

Chapter 4: From Whig to Republican

1 John Miller to Stevens, June 3, 1850; George Ford to Stevens, August 6, 1850; James Aiken et al. to Stevens, Oct. 8, 1850, all in *TSP(M)*, reel 1, frames 0749, 0769, 0782; Holt, *Whig Party*, pp. 575, 578; Henry Wilson, *History of the Rise and Fall of the Slave Power in America*, 3 vols. (Boston:

James B. Osgood, 1874), vol. 2, p. 362; Harris, *Biographical History*, p. 156n; *Examiner and Herald*, August 5, 1850.

2   Harris, *Biographical History*, p. 156n.

3   Holt, *Whig Party*, p. 576; *SPTS*, vol. 1, pp. 131, 142–43.

4   Eric Foner, *Gateway to Freedom: The Hidden History of the Underground Railroad* (New York: Norton, 2015), pp. 145–49.

5   Thomas P. Slaughter, *Bloody Dawn: The Christiana Riot and Racial Violence in the Antebellum North* (New York: Oxford University Press, 1991), p. 52.

6   Slaughter, *Bloody Dawn*, chapters 3 and 4.

7   Slaughter, *Bloody Dawn*, p. 115; W. U. Hensel, *The Christiana Riot and the Treason Trials of 1851: An Historical Sketch* (Lancaster, PA: New Era, 1911), p. 62.

8   Slaughter, *Bloody Dawn*, pp. 107–8; *SPTS*, vol. 1, pp. 136–37. On the abduction of free blacks in southern Pennsylvania for sale into slavery, see R. J. M. Blackett, *The Captive's Quest for Freedom: Fugitive Slaves, the 1850 Fugitive Slave Law, and the Politics of Slavery* (Cambridge: Cambridge University Press, 2018), pp. 293–94.

9   Hensel, *Christiana Riots*, pp. 87–90, 98–100; Slaughter, *Bloody Dawn*, p. 133.

10   Slaughter, *Bloody Dawn*, pp. 134–7; *Examiner and Herald*, May 26, 1852, Dec. 10, 1851; Hensel, *Christiana Riots*, p. 49.

11   George Ford to Stevens, Aug. 6, 10, 1850, in *TSP(M)*, reel 1, frames 0769 and 0776; letter in the *Examiner and Herald*, Dec. 24, 1851; Mueller, *Whig Party in Pennsylvania*, p. 184n.

12   Franklin Ellis and Samuel Evans, *History of Lancaster County, Pennsylvania* (Philadelphia: Everts & Peck, 1883), pp. 503–4; *Examiner and Herald*, Dec. 10, 17, 24, 1851.

13   Holt, *Whig Party*, p. 679; *New York Times*, Dec. 3, 1851; *Weekly Raleigh Register*, Dec. 10, 1851; CG, 32:1, pp. 6, 9, 132; *Examiner and Herald*, Dec. 24, 1851.

14   Horace Greeley and John F. Cleveland, eds., *A Political Textbook for 1860* (1886; reprint, New York: Greenwood, 1969), p. 19.

15   *Examiner and Herald*, June 30, 1852.

16   *Examiner and Herald*, Dec. 24, 31, 1851, Sep. 15, 1852.

17 *Examiner and Herald*, Dec. 31, 1851.

18 *Examiner and Herald*, Feb. 11, 1852.

19 Andrew Robertson, "The Idealist as Opportunist: An Electoral Analysis of Thaddeus Stevens' Support in Lancaster County Pennsylvania, 1843–1866," *Journal of the Lancaster County Historical Society* 84 (1980): 64; Ellis and Evans, *History of Lancaster County*, pp. 239, 510; *Examiner and Herald*, July 21, 28, Oct. 20, 1852.

20 As noted, it was Reigart for whom Stevens tried to obtain the Whig nomination for Lancaster's seat in the U.S. House in 1852.

21 Mueller, *Whig Party in Pennsylvania*, p. 154; Harris, *Biographical History*, p. 478; David R. Keller, "Nativism or Sectionalism: A History of the Know-Nothing Party in Lancaster County, Pennsylvania," *Journal of the Lancaster County Historical Society* 75 (1971), p. 82; Tyler Anbinder, *Nativism and Slavery: The Northern Know Nothings & the Politics of the 1850s* (New York: Oxford University Press, 1992), pp. 151–52; letter from Stevens and four others to J. Lefever, published in the *Adams Centinel*, Jan. 20, 1830, in *TSP(M)*, reel 1, frame 0029, original emphasis.

22 *SPTS*, vol. 1, p. 154; Foner, *Free Soil*, p. 227. Stevens clung to such beliefs for the rest of his life. "What would be the condition of the State of New York," he demanded in September 1865, "if it were not for her independent yeomanry? She would be overwhelmed and demoralized by the Jews, Milesians [Irish] and vagabonds of licentious cities." *SPTS*, vol. 2, p. 23.

23 The name reflected the party's secretive origins, when members allegedly were to answer any questions about it by saying, "I know nothing."

24 James L. Huston, "The Demise of the Pennsylvania American Party, 1854–1858," *Pennsylvania Magazine of History and Biography* 109 (1985): 477.

25 Anbinder, *Nativism and Slavery*, pp. 166–67.

26 *SPTS*, vol. 1, p. 86; *History of the Rise, Progress and Downfall of Know Nothingism in Lancaster County by Two Expelled Members* (Lancaster, PA: n.p., 1856), pp. 18–19; CG, 39:1, p. 255; Keller, "Nativism or Sectionalism," pp. 60–62; Huston, "Demise," pp. 480–81. For my understanding of the Whigs' collapse and of the relationship between Know Nothingism and slavery, see Levine, "Conservatism, Nativism, and Slav-

ery: Thomas R. Whitney and the Origins of the Know Nothing Party,"
Journal of American History 88 (September 2001): 455–88; and Levine,
"'The Vital Element in the Republican Party': Antislavery, Nativism,
and Abraham Lincoln," in the *Journal of the Civil War Era* (December 2011): 481–505, also reprinted in Nicholas Buccola, ed., *Abraham
Lincoln and Liberal Democracy* (Lawrence: University Press of Kansas,
2016), pp. 139–63.

27 Huston, "Demise," pp. 483, 486–88; Keller, "Nativism or Sectionalism,"
pp. 61, 65, 82–84; *The Inland Weekly* (Lancaster), November 11, 1854.
The Inland Weekly was the nativist party's local newspaper. Its front page
prominently displayed the national Know Nothing platform, including
a call for an "extension of the term of residence for the naturalization
of foreigners to twenty-one years." But in the edition of November 11,
1854, the editor printed a statement alongside that platform that considerably narrowed the scope of the paper's avowed nativism. It insisted
that Know Nothings "make no war upon foreigners simply because they
are foreigners. . . . They know that there are hundreds of thousands of
natives of Germany, Scotland, England, Ireland and France at heart as
truly *American* as any born on our own soil. These they respect, and
will fight to protect them in all their legitimate rights. Neither do they
oppose Roman Catholicism as a religion. . . ." Their "only object" was
to defeat "*Jesuit conspirators*" who sought "to establish the supremacy of
the Pope in this country."

28 Robert W. Johannsen, *Stephen A. Douglas* (Urbana: University of Illinois
Press, 1997), pp. 402–3.

29 William W. Freehling, *The Road to Disunion: Secessionists at Bay, 1776–
1854* (New York: Oxford University Press, 1990), pp. 536–42, 560.

30 Enoch Lewis to Stevens, Feb.[?] 9, 1854, in *TSP(M)* reel 1, frame 0892.

31 *SPTS*, vol. 1, pp. 86, 148–49.

32 Greeley and Cleveland, *Political Textbook*, pp. 22–23.

33 Allan Nevins, *Ordeal of the Union*, vol. 1, *Fruits of Manifest Destiny,
1847–1852* (New York: Charles Scribner's Sons, 1947), p. 12. The
Know Nothing platform that year tried to have it both ways on the subject of territorial slavery. One clause seemed to endorse the principle of
popular sovereignty while another criticized the same Kansas-Nebraska

Act that imposed popular sovereignty. Greeley and Cleveland, *Political Textbook*, p. 23.

34 *SPTS*, vol. 1, p. 154.

35 *SPTS*, vol. 1, p. 151; William E. Gienapp, *The Origins of the Republican Party, 1852–1856* (New York: Oxford University Press, 1987), p. 336.

36 Gienapp, *Origins of the Republican Party*, pp. 414–15; Stevens to E. D. Gazzam, Dec. 4, 1856, in *TSP(M)*, reel 1, frame 1005.

37 Anbinder, *Nativism and Slavery*, p. 261; Gienapp, *Origins of the Republican Party*, pp. 407, 415–16, 420; Thomas O. Allen to Stevens, June 4, 1856, in *TSP(M)*, reel 1, frames 0992–94; Stevens to E. D. Gazzam, Aug. 24, 1856, in *TSP(M)* reel 1, frame 0998; *SPTS*, vol. 1, p. 152n.

Chapter 5: "If This Union Should Be Dissolved"

1 Don E. Fehrenbacher, *The Dred Scott Case: Its Significance in American Law and Politics* (Oxford: Oxford University Press, 1978), chaps. 14 and 15.

2 Fehrenbacher, *The Dred Scott Case*, pp. 348–49.

3 Kenneth M. Stampp, *America in 1857: A Nation on the Brink* (New York: Oxford University Press, 1990), pp. 266–75, 281–82.

4 Stampp, *America in 1857*, pp. 158, 278–79, 291, 306.

5 Stampp, *America in 1857*, pp. 278, 302; Johannsen, *Douglas*, p. 656.

6 Holt, *Political Crisis*, pp. 204–5; Johannsen, *Douglas*, p. 698.

7 Foner, *Free Soil*, pp. 254–55; McClure, *Old Time Notes*, I, 300–301; Anbinder, *Nativism and Slavery*, p. 261.

8 Foner, *Free Soil*, p. 255; Anbinder, *Nativism and Slavery*, pp. 262–63.

9 Stevens to Salmon P. Chase, Sept. 25, 1858, in *TSP(M)*, I/1059-59; McClure, *Old Time Notes*, I, 336.

10 *SPTS*, vol. 1, p. 156.

11 Bruce Collins, "The Democrats' Loss of Pennsylvania in 1858," *Pennsylvania Magazine of History and Biography* 109 (October 1985): 499–536; John F. Coleman, *The Disruption of the Pennsylvania Democracy, 1848–1860* (Harrisburg: Pennsylvania Historical and Museum Commission, 1975), pp. 116–17.

12 *The Daily Evening Express*, Dec. 22, 1858; *Lancaster Intelligencer*, Dec. 28, 1858.

13 Noah Brooks, *Washington in Lincoln's Time* (New York: Century, 1895), p. 17; A. G. Riddle, *Recollections of War Times: Reminiscences of Men and Events in Washington, 1860–1865* (New York: G. P. Putnam's Sons, 1895), p. 31.

14 Stephen B. Oates, *To Purge This Land with Blood: A Biography of John Brown* (Amherst: University of Massachusetts Press, 1984); F. B. Sanborn, ed., *The Life and Letters of John Brown* (1885; reprint, New York: New American Library, 1969), pp. 562–69; *New York Herald*, October 21, 1859.

15 Sanborn, *Life and Letters of John Brown*, pp. 584–85.

16 Oates, *To Purge This Land*, pp. 310, 353; CG, 36:1, pp. 24–25; McClure, *Old-Time Notes*, p. 371.

17 CG, 36:1, pp. 24–25; Alfred R. Conkling, *The Life and Letters of Roscoe Conkling: Orator, Statesman, Advocate* (New York: Charles L. Webster, 1889), pp. 96–97; Brodie, *Thaddeus Stevens*, p. 135; *Memorial Addresses*, p. 16; *SPTS*, vol. 1, p. 159–60.

18 On this point, see the able discussion in James Oakes, *Freedom National: The Destruction of Slavery in the United States, 1861–1865* (New York: Norton, 2013), passim.

19 Greeley and Cleveland, *Political Textbook*, pp. 26–27.

20 *New York Times*, Sep. 28, 1860.

21 ALCW, 2:453.

22 Foner, *Fiery Trial*, pp. 64–65, 95, 106-107; *ALCW*, vol. 2, pp. 461, 491, 501, 514–15, vol. 3, pp. 146–47, 522–50; ALCW, vol. 3, pp. 145-146.

23 *SPTS*, vol. 1, p. 164.

24 CG, 36:1, 584–86; McClure, *Recollections*, p. 419.

25 *New York Times*, Sep. 28, 1860.

26 Foner, *Free Soil*, p. 107.

27 Foner, *Free Soil*, pp. 107, 258; William E. Gienapp, "Who Voted for Lincoln?" in *Abraham Lincoln and the American Political Tradition*, ed. John L. Thomas (Amherst: University of Massachusetts Press, 1986), p. 65; James F. Babcock to Mark Howard, Aug. 4, 1860, Mark Howard Papers, Connecticut Historical Society.

28 Richmond *Examiner*, November 9, 1860, in Lowell Dumond, *Southern Editorials on Secession* (1931; reprint, Gloucester, MA: Peter Smith, 1964), pp. 223 (emphasis added), 231, 278; William Kaufmann Scarborough,

Masters of the Big House: Elite Slaveholders of the Mid-Nineteenth Century (Baton Rouge: Louisiana State University Press, 2003), p. 416; "American Slavery in 1857," *Southern Literary Messenger* 25 (August 1857): 81.

29 Steven A. Channing, *Crisis of Fear: Secession in South Carolina* (New York: Norton, 1974), pp. 284–85.

30 Kenneth M. Stampp, *And the War Came: The North and the Secession Crisis, 1860–1861* (Baton Rouge: Louisiana State University Press, 1950), pp. 86, 133–35. Delegates from Texas, arriving later, declared their state's adherence to the new government as well.

31 Stampp, *War Came*, pp. 47, 86; CG, 36:2, pp. 1–4.

32 Stampp, *War Came*, pp. 80, 94; CG, 36:2, p. 623; Stevens to Edward McPherson, Dec. 19, 1860, and S. Austin Allibone to Stevens, Dec. 29, 1860, in *TSP(M)*, reel 1, frames 1112 and 1115.

33 CG, 36:2, pp. 621–24; the recollection of Massachusetts congressman Henry L. Dawes was quoted in *Biographical Annals of Lancaster County, Pennsylvania; Containing Biographical and Genealogical Sketches of Prominent and Representative Citizens and Many of the Early Settlers* ([Chicago]: J. H. Beers, 1903), p. 40.

34 *ALCW*, vol. 4, p. 270; James G. Blaine, *Twenty Years of Congress: From Lincoln to Garfield*, 2 vols. (Norwich, CT: Henry Hill, 1884), I, 266. The history of this failed amendment is told in Daniel W. Crofts, *Lincoln and the Politics of Slavery: The Other Thirteenth Amendment and the Struggle to Save the Union* (Chapel Hill: University of North Carolina Press, 2016).

35 Stampp, *War Came*, pp. 129–30; Martin Duberman, *Charles Francis Adams, 1807–1886* (Stanford, CA: Stanford University Press, 1960), pp. 239–40.

36 *ALCW*, vol. 4, pp. 172n, 183; SPTS, vol. 1, p. 180n.; CG, 36:2, pp. 341, 343; John A. Campbell, "Memoranda Relative to the Secession Movement in 1860–61," *Southern Historical Society Papers* 42 (October 1917): 43; Russell McClintock, *Lincoln and the Decision for War: The Northern Response to Secession* (Chapel Hill: University of North Carolina Press, 2008), p. 73; Duberman, *Charles Francis Adams*, pp. 240–41.

37 CG, 36:2, pp. 621–22.

38 Stevens to Salmon P. Chase, Jan. 4, 1861, in *TSP(M)*, reel 1, frame 1117;

SPTS, vol. 1, p. 200; Stampp, *War Came*, pp. 129, 143; *SPTS*, vol. 1, pp. 182–83, 194–95.

39 Stampp, *War Came*, pp. 143–44, 146, 167; *SPTS*, vol. 1, pp. 197–98; McClintock, *Lincoln and the Decision for War*, p. 8.

40 CG, 36:2, pp. 621–24.

41 CG, 36:2, p. 624.

Chapter 6: Stevens's Civil War, Part I

1 *Memorial Addresses*, pp. 22, 25–26.

2 CG, 37:1, p. 152.

3 *ALCW*, vol. 4, p. 147.

4 Stevens had believed this, he repeatedly reminded the Congress, from the start of the conflict. CG, 37:1, p. 251; 38:1, p. 338.

5 *SPTS*, vol. 1, p. 391.

6 Trefousse, *Stevens*, p. 113; McClure, *Recollections*, pp. 421–22. After the war, the House divided the responsibilities of the Committee on Ways and Means among three committees. In December 1865 Stevens became head of one of them, the Appropriations Committee.

7 William D. Kelley, in *Memorial Addresses*, pp. 25–26; William Horatio Barnes, *History of the Thirty-Ninth Congress of the United States* (New York: Harper, 1868), p. 29.

8 Donald K. Pickens, "The Republican Synthesis and Thaddeus Stevens," *Civil War History* 31 (1985): 63; John W. Howe to Stevens, Feb. 2, 1861, in *TSP(M)*, reel 2, frame 0006; R. Weiser to Stevens, April 12, 1862, in *TSP(M)*, reel 2, frame 3066; D. E. Conery to Stevens, June 5, 1862, in *TSP(M)*, reel 2, frame 0423; M. R. Hall to Stevens, April 18, 1862, in *TSP(M)*, reel 2, frame 0388; David Montgomery, *Beyond Equality: Labor and the Radical Republicans, 1862–1872* (New York: Knopf, 1967), pp. 84–85.

9 Leonard P. Curry, *Blueprint for Modern America: Nonmilitary Legislation of the First Civil War Congress* (Nashville, TN: Vanderbilt University Press, 1968); Philip Shaw Paludan, *"A People's Contest": The Union and the Civil War, 1861–1865* (New York: Harper & Row, 1988), esp. chaps. 5 and 6.

10 *Speeches, Correspondence, and Political Papers of Carl Schurz*, ed. Frederic Bancroft, 6 vols. (1913; reprint, New York: Greenwood Press, 1969), vol. 1, p. 156.

11 Henry Wilson, *The Rise and Fall of the Slave Power in America*, 3 vols. (Boston: James R. Osgood, 1874), vol. 2, p. 698; Isaac N. Arnold, *The History of Abraham Lincoln and the Overthrow of Slavery* (Chicago: Clark, 1866), p. 226.

12 *ALCW*, vol. 6, p. 48.

13 *ALCW*, vol. 4, p. 506.

14 *New York Times*, April 24, 1862. And see the remarks of Wisconsin Republican senator Timothy Howe in CG, 37:1, p. 191.

15 Riddle, *Recollections of War Times*, p. 41.

16 Schurz, *Speeches, Correspondence, and Political Papers*, I, 230.

17 Benjamin F. Butler, *Butler's Book: Autobiography and Personal Reminiscences* . . . (Boston, 1892), vol. 1, pp. 256–58; Edward McPherson, *Political History of the United States during the Great Rebellion* (Washington, DC: Philp & Solomons, 1865), p. 244; *The War of the Rebellion: A Compilation of the Official Records of the Union and Confederate Armies*, 128 vols. (Washington, DC: U.S. Government Printing Office, 1880–1901), ser. 1, vol. 2, pp. 648–52; ser. 3, vol. 1, p. 243. Henceforth referred to as OR.

18 McPherson, *Political History during the Rebellion*, pp. 247–51.

19 CG, 37:1, p. 32; McPherson, *Political History during the Rebellion*, p. 286.

20 The best treatment of this subject can be found in Oakes, *Freedom National*, pp. 128–31.

21 George W. Julian, *Political Recollections, 1840–1872* (1884; reprint, Westport, CT: Greenwood Press, 1970), p. 198; CG, 37:1, pp. 223, 265; Blaine, *Twenty Years*, p. 341; Riddle, *Recollections of War Times*, pp. 42–43. The House divided the resolution into two parts. The first part blamed the war on southern disunionists. The second defined Union war aims. Stevens abstained on both parts. Julian endorsed the first and abstained on the second.

22 CG, 37:1, p. 217. The amendment referred to "persons" whose labor was claimed by others rather than to "slaves" because Republicans generally denied that human beings could be held as property.

23 The final text of Trumbull's amendment omitted the provision that confiscated slaves would be "discharged from such service," but Trumbull denied that anything substantive had changed thereby. CG, 37:1, pp. 219, 427, 431.

24 John G. Nicolay, *The Outbreak of the Rebellion* (New York: Charles Scribner's Sons, 1881–83), pp. 208–9; Arnold, *The History of Abraham Lincoln*, p. 226. Arnold, an Illinois Republican, served in the House of Representatives throughout the war. CG, 37:1, p. 219.

25 Wilson, *Rise and Fall*, vol. 2, p. 11; Henry Wilson, *History of the Antislavery Measures of the Thirty-seventh and Thirty-eighth United States Congresses, 1861–1864* (Boston: Walker, Wise, 1864), p. 10.

26 Wilson, *Rise and Fall*, vol. 3, pp. 8–10; Wilson, *Antislavery Measures*, pp. 12–13.

27 Wilson, *Antislavery Measures*, p. 14; SPTS, vol. 1, p. 223; CG, 37:1, pp. 410–15.

28 CG, *37:1, p. 414, 37:2, pp. 439–41.*

29 CG, 37:2, p. 440.

30 Emer de Vattel, *The Law of Nations*, ed. Bela Kapossy and Richard Whatmore (1797; reprint, Indianapolis: Liberty Fund, 2008), p. 87.

31 SPTS, vol. 1, p. 247.

32 In fact, Lincoln embraced a kindred logic regarding the constitutionality of some of his actions as wartime commander in chief. "I felt that measures, otherwise unconstitutional," he wrote in the spring of 1864, "might become lawful, by becoming indispensable to the preservation of the constitution, through the preservation of the nation. Right or wrong, I assumed this ground, and now avow it." ALCW, vol. 7, p. 281.

33 SPTS, p. 248.

34 CG, 37:3, p. 50.

35 Curry, *Blueprint for Modern America*, p. 77n.

36 CG, 37:1, p. 43, 37:2, p. 197.

37 Julian, *Political Recollections*, p. 198; CG, 37:1, p. 415.

38 CG, 37:1, p. 415.

39 ALCW, vol. 5, p. 506.

40 SPTS, vol. 1, p. 226; CG, 37:2, p. 6.

41 Smith to Stevens, Dec. 6, 1861, published in the *National Anti-Slavery Standard* of Dec. 21, 1861, *TSP(M)*, reel 2, frame 0139; Timothy Davis to Stevens, Feb. 11, 1862, *TSP(M)*, reel 2, frame 0228–30; Stewart to Stevens, Feb. 14, 1862, *TSP(M)*, reel 2, frame 0266; Keith to Stevens, Aug. 2, 1862, *TSP(M)*, reel 2, frame 0229; Bruner to Stevens, Aug. 1, 1862, *TSP(M)*, reel 2, frame 0223–24; Philip Columbus Croll et al., eds., *The Pennsylvania-German: A Popular Magazine of Biography, History, Genealogy, Folklore, Literature, Etc.* (Lebanon, PA: P. C. Croll, 1900–11), vol. 8, p. 55.

42 *ALCW*, vol. 5, p. 49. According to Massachusetts radical Henry Wilson, this last phrase of Lincoln's "very clearly indicat[ed] the drift of his thought and purposes on the subject" at that point. Wilson, *Rise and Fall*, vol. 3, p. 247.

43 *New York Times*, Dec. 10, 1861.

44 McPherson, *Political History during the Rebellion*, p. 287; CG, 37:2, p. 15; Blaine, *Twenty Years of Congress*, I, 354.

45 CG, 37:2, pp. 439–41.

46 John Beatty, *The Citizen-soldier: Or, Memoirs of a Volunteer* (Cincinnati: Wilstach, Baldwin, 1879), p. 119; George L. Wood, *The Seventh Regiment: A Record* (New York: James Miller, 1865), p. 77; Stephen V. Ash, *When the Yankees Came: Conflict & Chaos in the Occupied South, 1861–1865* (Chapel Hill: University of North Carolina Press, 1995), pp. 31–32, 153–54; United States Congress, *Report of the Joint Committee of the Conduct of the War. In Three Parts. Part 3: Department of the West* (Washington, DC: U.S. Government Printing Office, 1863), p. 642; OR, ser. 1, vol. 10, p. 162.

47 CG, 37:2, pp. 440, 2054.

48 *SPTS*, vol. 1, p. 397; CG, 37:2, p. 441.

49 CG, 37:2, p. 441.

50 CG, 37:2, p. 440.

51 OR, ser. 1, vol. 14, p. 341.

52 *ALCW*, vol. 7, p. 282, vol. 5, pp. 222–24; Foner, *Fiery Trial*, p. 206.

53 CG, 37:2, p. 3125.

54 CG, 37:2, pp. 958–59, 1142.

55 CG, 37:2, pp. 1643, 1649. As already noted, in 1850 Congress had out-
    lawed only the interstate slave trade in the capital district, not slavery
    itself.

56 *ALCW*, vol. 5, p. 192; *New York Times*, April 15, 1862.

57 CG, 37:2, pp. 2042, 2047, 2054.

58 CG, 37:2, pp. 2053–54, 2068; Wilson, *Antislavery Measures*, p. 108.

59 *New York Times*, April 24, 1862; CG, 37:2, pp. 3331–32. Stevens would
    later tell the Treasury secretary that he intended the colonization funds
    to be used to transport slaves liberated in the District of Columbia.
    Stevens to Salmon P. Chase, Aug. 25, 1862, *TSP(M)*, reel 2, frame
    0478.

60 *SPTS*, vol. 1, p. 322; Wilson, *Antislavery Measures*, p. 174; CG, 37:2, pp.
    3267–68.

61 *Diary of Gideon Welles, Secretary of the Navy under Lincoln and
    Johnson*, 2 vols. (Boston: Houghton Mifflin, 1911), vol. 1, pp. 70–71.
    The president said much the same thing a few months later to his
    portraitist in explaining the genesis "of the emancipation policy." By
    "midsummer, 1862," Lincoln told Francis Carpenter, "things had gone
    on from bad to worse, until I felt that we had reached the end of our
    rope on the plan of operations we had been pursuing; that we had
    about played our last card." He had therefore decided that the Union
    "must change our tactics, or lose the game!" F. B. Carpenter, *Six Months
    at the White House with Abraham Lincoln: The Story of a Picture* (New
    York, 1866), pp. 20–22. And Lincoln explained himself in similar
    terms to the northern businessman and writer John R. Gilmore: He
    had steadfastly resisted "military emancipation" until he finally judged
    it an "indispensable military necessity." Only at that point, he said, did
    he feel "driven to the alternative of either surrendering the Union, and
    with it, the Constitution, or of laying strong hands upon the colored
    element. I chose the latter." John R. Gilmore, *Personal Recollections of
    Abraham Lincoln and the Civil War* (Boston: L. C. Page, 1898), p. 76;
    ALCW, vol. 7, pp. 282–82.

62 *ALCW*, vol. 5, pp. 343–45.

63 *ALCW*, vol. 5, p. 434.

64 Stevens to Simon Stevens, Sep. 5, 1862, in *SPTS*, vol. 1, p. 323; Noah

Brooks, *Lincoln Observed: Civil War Dispatches of Noah Brooks*, ed. Michael Burlingame (Baltimore: Johns Hopkins University Press, 1998), pp. 151, 155; CG, 37:3, Appendix, p. 81.

65 Office of the Historian, Office of Art & Archives, House of Representatives at https://history.house.gov/Institution/Party-Divisions/Party-Divisions; Adam J. P. Smith, *No Party Now: Politics in the Civil War North* (New York, 2006), p. 57.

66 Stevens to Edward McPherson, October 30, 1862, in *TSP(M)*, reel 2, frame 0495; Edward McPherson to Stevens, Oct. 31, 1862, in *SPTS*, vol. 1, p. 327; Blaine, *Twenty Years of Congress*, I, 444; *Lancaster Intelligencer*, Oct. 21, 1862. Stevens helped McPherson to become the clerk of the House of Representatives in December 1863; *SPTS*, vol. 1, p. 416.

67 CG, 37:1, p. 307.

68 Richard F. Miller, ed., *States at War*, vol. 3, *A Reference Guide for Pennsylvania in the Civil War* (Lebanon, NH: University Press of New England, 2014), p. 261.

69 CG, 38:1, p. 19, and Appendix, p. 201.

70 Wilson, *Antislavery Measures*, pp. 283–92.

71 *SPTS*, vol. 1, pp. 393–94.

72 Jubal Anderson Early, *Narrative of the War between the States* (1912; reprint, New York: Da Capo, 1991), pp. 255–56; *Baltimore American*, quoted in Carl Sandburg, *Abraham Lincoln, The War Years*, 4 vols. (New York: Harcourt, Brace, 1939), vol. 3, p. 150.

73 James T. Currie, *Enclave: Vicksburg and Her Plantations, 1863–1870* (Jackson: University Press of Mississippi, 2007), p. 73; William J. Minor, Plantation Diary 35, entry for January 3, 1863, William J. Minor and Family Papers, Mss. 519, Louisiana and Lower Mississippi Valley Collection, Special Collections, Louisiana State University Libraries; Ira Berlin, et al., *The Destruction of Slavery* (Cambridge: Cambridge University Press, 1985), p. 676.

74 CG, 36:1, pp. 1805–6.

75 Najia Aarim-Heriot, *Chinese Immigrants, African Americans, and Racial Anxiety in the United States, 1848–1882* (Urbana: University of Illinois Press, 2003), pp. 71–72; CG, 37:2, p. 2939.

76 CG, 37:2, pp. 2938–39.

Chapter 7: Stevens's Civil War, Part II

1 OR, ser. 3, vol. 1, p. 133; William O. Stoddard, *Inside the White House in War Times: Memoirs and Reports of Lincoln's Secretary*, ed. Michael Burlingame (Lincoln: University of Nebraska Press, 2000), p. 173; *The Diary of Orville Hickman Browning*, ed. Theodore Calvin Pease, 2 vols. (Springfield: Illinois State Historical Library, 1925), vol. 1, p. 555.

2 McPherson, *Political History during the Rebellion*, p. 249.

3 Foner, *Fiery Trial*, p. 188; *SPTS*, vol. 1, p. 230n2; James M. McPherson, *The Struggle for Equality: Abolitionists and the Negro in the Civil War and Reconstruction* (Princeton, NJ: Princeton University Press, 1964), p. 194; *New York Semi-Weekly Tribune*, Dec. 10, 1861.

4 OR, ser. 3, vol. 2, p. 198; *New York Times*, May 22, 1862; Dudley Taylor Cornish, *The Sable Arm: Black Troops in the Union Army, 1861–1865* (Lawrence: University Press of Kansas, 1987), pp. 33–53.

5 CG, 37:2, pp. 3125–27.

6 CG, 37:2, pp. 3126.

7 Wilson, *Antislavery Measures*, pp. 216–17.

8 *ALCW*, vol. 5, pp. 356–57; *Chase Diary*, pp. 96–100, 105; Bruce Levine, *The Fall of the House of Dixie: The Civil War and the Social Revolution That Transformed the South* (New York: Random House, 2013), pp. 134–36.

9 CG, 37:3, pp. 282, 598–99.

10 *ALCW*, vol. 8, p. 1, vol. 7, p. 500.

11 CG, 38:1, p. 1996; Cornish, *Sable Arm*, pp. 265, 288; Joseph T. Glatthaar, *Forged in Battle: The Civil War Alliance of Black Soldiers and White Officers* (New York: Penguin, 1990), p. 167.

12 Glatthaar, *Forged in Battle*, p. 170; CG, 38:1, pp. 133, 1991, 1995.

13 *SPTS*, vol. 1, pp. 228–29, 416–17, 436; *TSP(M)*, reel 2, frames 0136, 0854; Martha S. Jones, *Birthright Citizens: A History of Race and Rights in Antebellum America* (Cambridge: Cambridge University Press, 2018), pp. 151–52.

14 CG, 37:3, Appendix, p. 79.

15 *ALCW*, vol. 6, p. 410.

16 *ALCW*, vol. 7, p. 514.

17 *SPTS*, vol. 1, p. 413–14, 500; Allan Nevins, *The War for the Union: The Organized War to Victory, 1864–1865* (New York: Charles Scribner's Sons, 1971), pp. 105–7; Donald Bruce Johnson, comp., *National Party Platforms*, rev. ed., 2 vols. (Urbana: University of Illinois Press, 1978), vol. 1, pp. 34–35.

18 Johnson, *Party Platforms*, vol. 1, pp. 35–36; *ALCW*, vol. 7, pp. 380, 435, 440–42, 451; James M. McPherson, *Tried by War: Abraham Lincoln as Commander in Chief* (New York: Penguin, 2008), pp. 234–35; CG, 38:1, p. 2105; *SPTS* vol. 1, p. 409.

19 McClure, *Old Time Notes*, vol. 2, p. 141.

20 *SPTS*, vol. 1, p. 500; *OR*, ser. 1, vol. 47, pt. 2, pp. 39–40; James M. McPherson, *Battle Cry of Freedom: The Civil War Era* (New York: Oxford University Press, 1988), pp. 841–42.

21 Miller, *States at War*, vol. 3, p. 261.

22 CG, 38:1, pp. 1490, 2995.

23 *SPTS*, vol. 1, p. 503.

24 Arnold, *The History of Abraham Lincoln*, pp. 585–87; CG, 38:2, p. 531; Michael Vorenberg, *Final Freedom: The Civil War, the Abolition of Slavery, and the Thirteenth Amendment* (Cambridge: Cambridge University Press, 2001), pp. 198–207; *ALCW*, vol. 8, p. 149.

25 CG, 38:1, pp. 2043, 2105; *SPTS*, vol. 1, p. 409n., vol. 2, p. 196.

26 Herman Belz, *Reconstituting the Union: Theory and Policy during the Civil War* (Ithaca, NY: Cornell University Press, 1969), p. 56; Foner, *Fiery Trial*, p. 270.

Chapter 8: Steven's Civil War, Part III

1 CG, 39:1, p. 3148; *SPTS*, vol. 2, p. 23.

2 *ALCW*, vol. 5, p. 318; Ira Berlin et al., eds., *The Wartime Genesis of Free Labor: The Upper South* (Cambridge: Cambridge University Press, 1993), pp. 367, 374.

3 Berlin, *Wartime Genesis: Lower South*, pp. 426–27, 455; Steven Hahn, *A Nation under Our Feet: Black Political Struggles in the Rural South from Slavery to the Great Migration* (Cambridge, MA: Harvard University Press, 2003), p. 97; Willie Lee Rose, *Rehearsal for Reconstruction: The*

Port Royal Experiment (Oxford: Oxford University Press, 1964), p. 22; *OR*, ser. 3, vol. 3, pp. 430–54.

4 Berlin, *Wartime Genesis: Lower South*, pp. 69, 356–58, 367, 455; Hahn, *Nation under Our Feet*, pp. 171, 174, 214; Berlin, *The Wartime Genesis: Upper South*, p. 68.

5 *Proceedings of the National Convention of Colored Men, Held in the City of Syracuse, N.Y. . .* (Boston: Rand & Avery, 1864).

6 Philip S. Foner and George E. Walker, eds., *Proceedings of the Black State Conventions, 1840–1865*, 2 vols. (Philadelphia: Temple University Press, 1980), vol. 2, pp. 242–53; James G. Hollandsworth Jr., *The Louisiana Native Guards: The Black Military Experience during the Civil War* (Baton Rouge: Louisiana State University Press, 1995), pp. 33, 78; Hahn, *Nation under Our Feet*, pp. 107–9.

7 *Proceedings of the Convention in Syracuse*, pp. 55–56; Foner and Walker, *Proceedings of the Black Conventions*, vol. 1, p. 349.

8 James McKaye, *The Emancipated Slave Face to Face with His Old Master: A Report to Edwin M. Stanton, Secretary of War* (New York: William C. Bryant, 1864), pp. 3, 21; Louis S. Gerteis, *From Contraband to Freedman: Federal Policy toward Southern Blacks, 1861–1865* (Wesport, CT: Greenwood, 1973), p. 92; Joseph Carlyle Sitterson, *Sugar Country: The Cane Sugar Industry in the South, 1753–1950.* ([Lexington]: University of Kentucky Press, 1953), p. 221; Berlin, *Wartime Genesis: Lower South*, p. 761; *New York Times*, March 24, 1864; *OR*, ser. 4, vol. 3, pp. 393–98; James L. Roark, *Masters without Slaves: Southern Planters in the Civil War and Reconstruction* (New York: Norton, 1977), pp. 117, 134, 119–20.

9 In a July 1863 letter to Union general Stephen A. Hurlbut, Lincoln specified that upon Arkansas's return to the Union slaves already freed should remain free while the condition of those not yet actually liberated might be shaped by "some plan, substantially being gradual emancipation, [that] would be better for both white and black" than immediate freedom. He evidently repeated the offer verbally in November to a unionist judge from Texas. Lincoln told Thomas H. Duval (as paraphrased in the latter's diary) that he "saw nothing inconsistent" between "the gradual emancipation of slavery and his own declaration."

ALCW, vol. 6, p. 358; Don E. Fehrenbacher and Virginia Fehrenbacher, eds., *Recollected Words of Abraham Lincoln* (Stanford, CA: Stanford University Press, 1996), p. 146.

10 *ALCW*, vol. 6, pp. 1, 365, vol. 7, pp. 53–56; emphasis added.

11 *ALCW*, vol. 7, p. 56.

12 He had done the same thing earlier. Back in January, just a week after issuing his Emancipation Proclamation, Lincoln suggested to General John McClernand that if states returned to the Union they might avoid being too severely "hurt by" that proclamation by simply "adopt[ing] systems of apprenticeship for the colored people" of the kind that had often followed emancipation in other states and other lands. Lincoln repeated that suggestion, this time to General Nathaniel Banks in Louisiana, in early November. *ALCW*, vol 6, p. 49, vol. 7, p. 1.

13 *ALCW*, vol. 7, pp. 54–55. Despite the vague language, Lincoln was certainly here referring again to apprenticeship, acknowledging subsequently that this had been a "suggestion about apprenticeship for freed-people." Lincoln made this suggestion over the objections of his Treasury secretary, as he later acknowledged. *ALCW*, vol. 7, pp. 51, 145, and vol. 8, p. 402. See also John Niven et al., eds., *The Salmon P. Chase Papers*, 5 vols. (Kent, OH: Kent State University Press, 1997), vol. 4, pp. 203–4; Roark, *Masters without Slaves*, pp. 114–15; Berlin, *Wartime Genesis: Lower South*, pp. 414–15.

14 *ALCW*, vol. 7, p. 54.

15 *Diary of Gideon Welles, Secretary of the Navy under Lincoln and Johnson*, 3 vols. (Boston: Houghton Mifflin, 1911), vol. 2, p. 237; *ALCW*, vol. 7, p. 243, vol. 8, pp. 389, 403–7. Lincoln's correspondent ignored the president's recommendation.

16 Niven, *Chase Papers*, vol. 4, p. 6.

17 *SPTS*, vol. 2, p. 13; Stevens to Simon Stevens, Sep. 5, 1862, *TSP(M)*, reel 2, frame 0481.

18 *SPTS*, vol. 2, pp. 13–19.

19 CG, 37:2, pp. 736–37, 986.

20 *SPTS*, vol. 1, p. 386.

21 *SPTS*, vol. 2, p. 16. Emphasis in original.

22 Robert J. Cook, *Civil War Senator: William Pitt Fessenden and the Fight to Save the American Republic* (Baton Rouge: Louisiana State University Press, 2011), pp. 214–35 (quote on p. 235).

23 CG, 38:1, p. 1465.

24 CG, 38:1, p. 2989.

25 CG, 38:1, p. 2042.

26 Peyton McCrary, *Abraham Lincoln and Reconstruction: The Louisiana Experiment* (Princeton, NJ: Princeton University Press, 1978), p. 354; CG, 38:2, p. 125. The Hollywood film *Lincoln* (2012) depicted Stevens's words as a prudent public retreat from radicalism toward moderation, a retreat executed under duress for the sake of passing the Thirteenth Amendment. But, as noted above, championing equality before the law at that moment was not a cautious but an ambitious stand.

27 Edward McPherson, *Political History of the United States of America during the Great Rebellion*, 2nd ed. (Washington, DC: Philp & Solomons, 1865), pp. 317–18; John David Smith, ed., *A Just and Lasting Peace: A Documentary History of Reconstruction* (New York: Penguin, 2013), pp. 18–23.

28 CG, 38:1, pp. 2041–42; SPTS, vol. 1, p. 386; interview in the *New York Herald*, July 8, 1867, clipping in the Edward McPherson Papers, Library of Congress.

29 CG, 38:1, pp. 2107–8, 3491; Herman Belz, *Reconstructing the Union: Theory and Policy during the Civil War* (Ithaca, NY: Cornell University Press, 1969), pp. 211–13.

30 ALCW, vol. 7, pp. 433–34; SPTS, vol. 1, pp. 391, 500.

31 CG, 37:2, p. 1950, 38:1, p. 2042; SPTS, vol. 1, pp. 392, 473n; Belz, *Reconstructing the Union*, p. 212.

Chapter 9: "In the Midst of a Revolution"

1 CG, 38:2, p. 734.

2 Paul H. Bergeron, *Andrew Johnson's Civil War and Reconstruction* (Knoxville: University of Tennessee Press, 2011), pp. 74–87.

3 CG, 40:1, p. 207, 40:2, appendix, pp. 2–3; *Journal of the House of Rep-*

resentatives of the United States, vol. 40, no. 2 (Washington, DC: U.S. Government Printing Office, 1868), p. 18; Edward McPherson, ed., *The Political History of the United States from April 15, 1865 to July 15, 1870* (Washington, DC: Philp & Solomons, 1871), p. 19. The Republican moderate James G. Blaine later noted that this "imprudent language" demonstrated that Johnson had suggested enfranchising some black men merely out of political expediency and "not from any proper conception of its inherent justice." Blaine, *Twenty Years of Congress*, vol. 2, pp. 81–82.

4 *SPTS*, vol. 2, pp. 4, 6, 9–10; George Julian, *Political Recollections, 1840 to 1872* (1884; reprint, Westport, CT: Greenwood, 1970), p. 243; Frederick Douglass, *Life and Times of Frederick Douglass* (1892; reprint, London: Collier Books, 1962), p. 364; Tyler Dennett, ed., *Lincoln and the Civil War in the Diaries and Letters of John Hay* (1939; reprint, Cambridge, MA: Da Capo, 1988), p. 108.

5 Blaine, *Twenty Years of Congress*, vol. 2, p. 68.

6 Roark, *Masters without Slaves*, p. 134.

7 Bergeron, *Johnson's Civil War and Reconstruction*, p. 75; Foner, *Reconstruction*, p. 191.

8 Foner, *Reconstruction*, p. 189; James M. McPherson and James K. Hogue, *Ordeal by Fire: The Civil War and Reconstruction*, 4th ed. (Boston: McGraw-Hill, 2009), pp. 534–35; Blaine, *Twenty Years of Congress*, vol. 2, pp. 84–85; CG, 40:1, p. 206; Hans L. Trefousse, *Andrew Johnson: A Biography* (New York: Norton, 1989), pp. 232–33.

9 *Report of the Joint Committee on Reconstruction* (1866; reprint, New York: Greenwood Press, 1969), pp. 120–21. In November 1865 Stevens heard from a professedly unionist former slaveowner in Mississippi that "whatever genuine union sentiment was forming and would in time have grown up, has been checked by the Johnson course." Ex-rebels saw Johnson as their ally "and hence the south is encouraged in the course she is now pursuing." Robert W. Fluornoy to Stevens, Nov. 20, 1865, *TSP(M)*, reel 4, frames 0380–85. A group of North Carolina unionists told Stevens much the same thing, that "the Cecesionist [*sic*] have Taken Fresh Courage by the pres[ident's] Course towards them." *SPTS*, vol. 2, p. 267; *TSP(M)*, reel 5, frame 0082. See also Michael Les

Benedict, *The Impeachment and Trial of Andrew Johnson* (New York: Norton, 1973), p. 49n.

10 *SPTS*, vol. 2, p. 5.

11 *SPTS*, vol. 2, pp. 6–10.

12 Edward McPherson, ed., *The Political History of the United States of America, During the Period of Reconstruction* (Washington, DC: Solomons & Chapman, 1875), pp. 66–67.

13 Bergeron, *Johnson's Civil War and Reconstruction*, pp. 82–84; Trefousse, *Andrew Johnson*, pp. 229–30; John Hope Franklin, *Reconstruction after the Civil War*, 2nd ed. (Chicago: University of Chicago Press, 1994), p. 43.

14 Roark, *Masters without Slaves*, p. 138.

15 Samuel Thomas to Carl Schurz, n.d., in United States Congressional Serial Set, vol. 1237 (Washington, DC: U.S. Government Printing Office, 1866), p. 81; Schurz, *Speeches, Correspondence, and Political Papers*, vol. 1, p. 320; Eric Foner, *Nothing but Freedom: Emancipation and Its Legacy* (Baton Rouge: Louisiana State University Press, 1983), p. 49.

16 Claude F. Oubre, *Forty Acres and a Mule: The Freedmen's Bureau and Black Land Ownership* (Baton Rouge: Louisiana State University Press, 1978), p. 26.

17 Laura F. Edwards, *Gendered Strife and Confusion: The Political Culture of Reconstruction* (Urbana: University of Illinois Press, 1997), pp. 39–48; Foner, *Reconstruction*, p. 201.

18 CG, 39:1, p. 2459; Bergeron, *Johnson's Civil War and Reconstruction*, p. 88.

19 *TSP(M)*, reel 4, frames 0727–28; George C. Rable, *But There Was No Peace: The Role of Violence in the Politics of Reconstruction* (Athens: University of Georgia Press, 1984), pp. 27–29.

20 Blaine, *Twenty Years of Congress*, vol. 2, p. 93; Foner, *Reconstruction*, pp. 224–25, 272–73.

21 *SPTS*, vol. 2, p. 25; CG, 39:1, p. 74.

22 Horace Edgar Flack, *The Adoption of the Fourteenth Amendment* (Baltimore: Johns Hopkins University Press, 1908), pp. 11–12; CG, 39:1, pp. 3–5.

23 CG, 39:1, p. 3984, 39:2, p. 251.

24 Michael Les Benedict, *A Compromise of Principle: Congressional Republicans and Reconstruction, 1863–1869* (New York: Norton, 1974), pp. 352–53.

25 CG, 39:1, pp. 943–50; McPherson, *Political History during Reconstruction*, p. 72n.

26 McPherson, *Political History during Reconstruction*, pp. 68–74, 147–151.

27 McPherson, *Political History during Reconstruction*, pp. 78–81; Foner, *Reconstruction*, p. 244; Eric Foner, *The Second Founding: How the Civil War and Reconstruction Remade the Constitution* New York: Norton, 2019), p. 63; Smith, *Just and Lasting Peace*, pp. 186–92.

28 McPherson, *Political History during Reconstruction*, pp. 74–78.

29 Bingham, who sympathized with the bill's purpose, nonetheless considered it an unconstitutional infringement on states' rights. He therefore voted against its passage and then apparently abstained in the vote to override Johnson's veto. McPherson, *Political History during Reconstruction*, p. 81; Gerard N. Magliocca, *American Founding Son: John Bingham and the Invention of the Fourteenth Amendment* (New York: New York University Press, 2013), p. 120.

30 McPherson, *Political History during Reconstruction*, p. 92; Foner, *Reconstruction*, p. 272; CG, 39:1, pp. 421, 688.

31 CG, 39:1, pp. 10, 2286.

32 McPherson, *Political History during Reconstruction*, p. 102.

33 Foner, *Second Founding*, p. 61.

34 CG, 39:1, pp. 2545, 2459. Senators voting "no" included Democrats, conservative Republicans, and a small handful of radicals, including Sumner, who objected to the amendment's failure to guarantee black suffrage outright.

35 Benjamin B. Kendrick, *The Journal of the Joint Committee of Fifteen on Reconstruction* (1914; reprint, New York: Greenwood Press, 1969), p. 101.

36 CG, 39:1, pp. 2459–60.

37 CG, 39:1, p. 2545.

38 CG, 39:1, p. 3148; Foner, *Reconstruction*, p. 259.

39 CG, 39:1, pp. 3041–42, 39:2, pp. 290–92; McPherson, *Political History during Reconstruction*, pp. 151–52, 194; William Horatio Barnes, *History of the Thirty-ninth Congress of the United States* (New York: Harper, 1868), pp. 473–74; Benedict, *Compromise of Principle*, pp. 186, 198; Eric L. McKitrick, *Andrew Johnson and Reconstruction* (1960; reprint, New York: Oxford University Press, 1988), p. 469.

40 *SPTS*, vol. 2, p. 192.

41 Bergeron, *Andrew Johnson's Civil War and Reconstruction*, p. 127.

Chapter 10: "Perfecting a Revolution"

1 Benedict, *Compromise of Principle*, pp. 29, 359; McKitrick, *Johnson and Reconstruction*, p. 447; CG, 39:2, p. 715; David O. Stewart, *Impeached: The Trial of President Andrew Johnson and the Fight for Lincoln's Legacy* (New York: Simon & Schuster, 2009), pp. 53, 69.

2 *Saint Paul Daily Press*, Dec. 1, 1866; CG, 39:2, p. 251; Foner, *Reconstruction*, p. 259.

3 CG, 39:2, p. 251; *TSP(M)*, reel 4, frames 0727–29, reel 5, frames 0220–21, 0257–58.

4 CG, 39:2, pp. 251–52; Foner, *Reconstruction*, p. 272.

5 CG, 39:2, pp. 250, 594; *Barnes, History of the Thirty-ninth Congress*, pp. 506–8.

6 CG, 39:2, p. 251.

7 Magliocca, *American Founding Son*, pp. 132–39; Foner, *Second Founding*, p. 12; CG, 39:2, pp. 816–17, 1213; *SPTS*, vol. 2, p. 222n; Benedict, *Compromise of Principle*, p. 227; McKitrick, *Johnson and Reconstruction*, p. 477.

8 Hahn, *Nation under Our Feet*, pp. 151–52; Steven V. Ash, *A Massacre in Memphis: The Race Riot That Shook the Nation One Year after the Civil War* (New York: Hill & Wang, 2013), p. 180; CG, 39:1, p. 2544; James G. Hollandsworth Jr., *An Absolute Massacre: The New Orleans Race Riot of July 30, 1866* (Baton Rouge: Louisiana State University Press, 2001), p. 3; Benedict, *Compromise of Principle*, pp. 205–6.

9 Foner, *Reconstruction*, pp. 270–71, 277; McKitrick, *Johnson and Reconstruction*, pp. 475–76; Kendrick, *Journal of the Joint Committee*, pp. 379–80.

10 CG, 39:2, p. 1036.

11 CG, 39:2, pp. 1213–14.

12 CG, 39:2, p. 1215. The vote was 109 in favor, 55 against, with 26 abstaining.

13 CG, 39:2, pp. 1400, 1645; McPherson, *Political History during Recon-*

struction, pp. 102, 191–92; interview with Stevens in the *New York Herald*, July 8, 1867, clipping in the McPherson Papers, Library of Congress.

14 McPherson, *Political History during Reconstruction*, pp. 166–173; CG, 39:2, p. 815. Congress passed three supplementary bills by the summer clarifying and only slightly modifying the first one.

15 Foner, *Reconstruction*, pp. 281–84; *SPTS*, vol. 2, p. 266–71.

16 CG, 39:1, pp. 75, 536, 4304; *SPTS*, vol. 2, pp. 11, 16.

17 CG, 39:1, p. 311; McPherson *Political History during Reconstruction*, pp. 116–17, 160, 184; Kate Masur, *An Example for All the Land: Emancipation and the Struggle over Equality in Washington, D.C.* (Chapel Hill: University of North Carolina Press, 2010), pp. 139–45.

18 Kelley in *Memorial Addresses*, pp. 26–27.

19 As Republican attorney Richard H. Dana Jr. argued, "The conquering party may hold the other in the grasp of war until it has secured whatever it has a right to require." *New York Times*, June 24, 1865.

20 Brooks D. Simpson, "Land and the Ballot: Securing the Fruits of Emancipation," *Pennsylvania History* 60 (April 1993): 178; *Memorial Addresses*, pp. 26–27; CG, 39:1, p. 74; Foner, *Reconstruction*, pp. 270–71.

21 CG, 39:2, pp. 251–52.

22 CG, 39:2, pp. 253, 291–92.

23 McPherson and Hogue, *Ordeal by Fire*, p. 580; Foner, *Reconstruction*, pp. 314–20, 331–33.

24 Leon Litwack, *Been in the Storm So Long: The Aftermath of Slavery* (New York: Knopf, 1979), p. 600; Arnold H. Taylor, *Travail & Triumph: Black Life and Culture in the South Since the Civil War* (Westport, CT: Greenwood Press, 1976), p. 18; *TSP(M)*, reel 5, frame 0221; A South Carolinian, "The Political Condition of South Carolina," *Atlantic* 39 (February 1877): 193–94.

25 Benedict, *Compromise of Principle*, pp. 271–74; Magliocca, *Founding Son*, p. 141; Foner, *Reconstruction*, p. 315.

26 CG, 40:2, pp. 1790, 1822, 2138, 2211, 2216; Benedict, *Compromise of Principle*, pp. 316–19.

27 CG, 40:2, pp. 2214, 2216–17, 2399, 3090, 3097; Benedict, *Compromise of Principle*, pp. 320–22.

28 *SPTS*, vol. 2, pp. 323–24; CG, 40:2, pp. 1966–67; Foner, *Second Found-*

ing, p. 97. Stevens excoriated the Republicans' 1868 national convention when it refused to endorse nationwide universal manhood suffrage in its platform. "I regret I cannot speak favorably of the Chicago Platform," he wrote to a fellow Pennsylvanian. "It is like most of the Republican platforms for the past six years,—tame and cowardly . . . They are just as timid now as they were before the war." But "universal suffrage" is "an *inalienable* right," and "this question must be met; the sooner it is done the more successful it will be." *SPTS*, vol. 2, pp. 440–41.

29 Berlin, *Wartime Genesis: Lower South*, pp. 195, 438–39, 460; James S. Allen, *Reconstruction: The Battle for Democracy* (New York: International, 1937), p. 44; Sidney Andrews, *The South since the War* (1866; reprint, Boston: Houghton Mifflin, 1971), p. 233; Joseph Carlyle Sitterson, *Sugar Country: The Cane Sugar Industry in the South* ([Lexington]: University of Kentucky Press, 1953), p. 210; Hahn, *Nation under Our Feet*, pp. 81–82; Litwack, *Been in the Storm So Long*, p. 438.

30 OR, ser. 3, vol. 3, p. 437; William S. McFeeley, *Grant: A Biography* (New York: Norton, 1981), p. 20; James M. McPherson, *The Negro's Civil War: How American Negroes Felt and Acted during the War for the Union* (1965; reprint, Urbana: University of Illinois Press, 1982), p. 298; *Proceedings of the National Convention of Colored Men in Syracuse*, p. 42; Julie Saville, *The Work of Reconstruction: From Slave to Wage Laborer in South Carolina, 1860-1870* (Cambridge: Cambridge University Press, 1996), p. 95; Foner, *Reconstruction*, p. 291.

31 OR, ser. 3, vol. 2, pp. 276–77.

32 *ALCW*, vol. 5, pp. 329–31.

33 Berlin, *Wartime Genesis: Lower South*, pp. 36, 222n; *Official Opinions of the Attorney General of the United States Advising the President and Heads of Departments*, ed. J. Hubley Ashton, 12 vols. (Washington, DC: W. H. & O. H. Morrison, 1869), vol. 11, p. 357; Steven Hahn et al., eds., *Land and Labor, 1865* (Chapel Hill: University of North Carolina Press, 2008), p. 425n.

34 *ALCW*, vol. 7, p. 55; John Niven, *Salmon P. Chase: A Biography* (New York: Oxford University Press, 1995), p. 329. By the beginning of 1865, Lincoln had evidently decided that the freedpeople would simply have to make the best of the difficult economic situation in which they found themselves. Carpenter, *Six Months at the White House*, p. 211.

35 *Autobiography of Oliver Otis Howard,* 2 vols. (New York: Baker & Taylor, 1907), vol. 2, pp. 234–35; McPherson, *Political History . . . to 1870,* p. 12; Trefousse, *Andrew Johnson,* p. 226; George R. Bentley, *A History of the Freedmen's Bureau* (Philadelphia: University of Pennsylvania Press, 1955), p. 102; Oubre, *Forty Acres and a Mule,* p. 37; Foner, *Reconstruction,* pp. 158–59. By April 1866, O. O. Howard reported, his Bureau had returned some 430,000 acres of land to prewar owners, including more than 14,000 acres that Union forces had previously assigned to freedpeople. By 1868, fewer than 140,000 acres remained in the Bureau's hands. *The Reports of Committees of the House of Representatives for the First Session of the Fortieth Congress, 1867* (Washington, DC: U.S. Government Printing Office, 1868), pp. 1086–89.

36 CG, 38:1, p. 2042.

37 *SPTS,* vol. 2, p. 18.

38 CG, 40:2, p. 4136.

39 *SPTS,* vol. 2, pp. 18–19.

40 CG, 38:2, p. 1182; Smith, *Just and Lasting Peace,* p. 45.

41 CG, 39:1, p. 209.

42 CG, 39:1, p. 658; Eric Foner, *Politics and Ideology in the Age of the Civil War* (New York: Oxford University Press, 1980), p. 139.

43 CG, 39:1, p. 655.

44 CG, 39:1, p. 688; Foner, *Politics and Ideology,* p. 139. The vote for Trumbull's bill was 133 to 36, with 13 abstentions.

45 CG, 39:1, p. 2459, 40:1, pp. 203–4.

46 CG, 40:1, pp. 204–5.

47 Foner, *Reconstruction,* p. 309; CG, 40:1, p. 204.

48 Foner, *Politics and Ideology,* p. 142.

49 *New York Times,* July 9, 1867 (emphasis added); Benedict, *Compromise of Principle,* p. 258; Montgomery, *Beyond Equality;* Heather Cox Richardson, *The Death of Reconstruction: Race, Labor, and Politics in the Post–Civil War North, 1865–1901* (Cambridge, MA.: Harvard University Press, 2001). The moderate Republican leader William Pitt Fessenden, thus, had gone along only reluctantly even with the Second Confiscation Act (1862). Charles A. Jellison, *Fessenden of Maine: Civil War Senator* (Syracuse, NY: Syracuse University Press, 1962), pp. 145–46.

50 As Eric McKitrick noted, "The effect of this order would have been to give the existing state governments the most extensive control over the pending elections and to guarantee the largest possible white vote." McKitrick, *Johnson and Reconstruction*, p. 493.

51 Benedict, *Compromise of Principle*, pp. 288–89; Bergeron, *Johnson's Civil War and Reconstruction*, pp. 160–66; McKitrick, *Johnson and Reconstruction*, pp. 494–95; Trefousse, *Andrew Johnson*, pp. 293–304; CG, 39:2, p. 784.

52 Gregory P. Downs, *After Appomattox: Military Occupation and the End of War* (Cambridge, MA: Harvard University Press, 2015), pp. 89–111; Foner, *Reconstruction*, p. 148.

53 Downs, *After Appomattox*, p. 106; CG, 40:2, pp. 265–266.

54 Michael Les Benedict, *The Impeachment and Trial of Andrew Johnson* (New York: Norton, 1973), p. 74; James M. Scovel, "Thaddeus Stevens," *Lippincott's Monthly Magazine* 61 (January–June 1898): 545; *New York Times*, January 7, 1867. Fawn M. Brodie also ascribed to Stevens "a compulsion to punish" that "result[ed] in the sordid impeachment proceedings." Brodie, *Stevens*, p. 22.

55 Benedict, *Impeachment and Trial*, chapter 2.

56 CG, 40:2, p. 1399.

57 Although a majority of House members voting in January 1867 supported the creation of a special impeachment committee, that initiative failed because passage required a two-thirds affirmative vote. McPherson, *Political History during Reconstruction*, pp. 187–88, 264–65; Stewart, *Impeached*, pp. 83, 101; Benedict, *Impeachment and Trial*, pp. 74–75, 85, 254; CG, 40:1, pp. 791–92, 40:2, p. 68, and Appendix, pp. 54–62. In championing a broad interpretation of the impeachment grounds, Representative George Boutwell pointed out that there was "no law which declares that it shall be a high crime or misdemeanor for the President to decline to recognize the Congress of the United States." But did that mean that if a president refused to administer its laws, Congress must be denied the power to remove him? That, Boutwell warned, would spell "virtually the end of Government."; CG, 40:2, Appendix, p. 57.

58 Benedict, *Impeachment and Trial*, pp. 102–3. In 1926, a Supreme Court majority ruled that a president has no need to gain congressional ap-

proval in order to remove a cabinet member. Justices Louis Brandeis and Oliver Wendell Holmes dissented from that opinion.

59 Stewart, *Impeached*, pp. 156, 168; CG, 40:2, p. 1400.

60 CG, 40:2, pp. 1612, 1642; McPherson, *Political History during Recon-struction*, pp. 266–69.

61 CG, 40:2, pp. 71, 230; *SPTS*, vol. 2, p. 320; Stewart, *Impeached*, p. 256.

62 Benedict, *Impeachment and Trial*, pp. 132–33, 173, 178–79; *SPTS*, vol. 1, p. 328, vol. 2, pp. 324, 334–35.

63 CG, 40:2, p. 2530, Supplement, pp. 411–15; *SPTS*, vol. 2, p. p. 431n; Robert J. Cook, *Civil War Senator: William Pitt Fessenden and the Fight to Save the American Republic* (Baton Rouge: Louisiana State University Press, 2011), pp. 214–35; McKitrick, *Johnson and Reconstruction*, p. 506; Stewart, *Impeached*, p. 280.

Chapter 11: "Equality of Man Before His Creator"

1 Clemenceau, *American Reconstruction*, pp. 226–27; *SPTS*, vol. 2, p. 358n.

2 *SPTS*, vol. 2, pp. 358n, 360, 365.

3 Clemenceau, *American Reconstruction*, pp. 165, 226–27; *Memorial Ad-dresses*, p. 20.

4 *SPTS*, vol. 2, p. 156.

5 *Memorial Addresses*, p. 32.

6 *Memorial Addresses*, p. 64; "The American Constitution and the Im-peachment of the President," *Blackwood's Edinburgh Magazine* 103 (June 1868): 717.

7 *Harper's Weekly* 12 (Aug. 29, 1868): 548.

8 James Albert Woodburn, *The Life of Thaddeus Stevens* (Indianapolis: Bobbs-Merrill, 1913), p. 190.

9 *New York Times*, Aug. 13, 1868.

10 George F. Hoar, *Autobiography of Seventy Years*, 2 vols. (New York: Charles Scribner's Sons, 1903), vol. 1, p. 239; McPherson, *Sketch*.

11 Taylor, *Travail & Triumph*, p, 14; Litwack, *Been in the Storm So Long*, p. 556.

12 *Harper's Weekly* 12 (Aug. 29, 1868): 548; Samuel W. McCall, *Thaddeus Stevens* (Boston: Houghton Mifflin, 1899), p. 352; Eric Foner, "Thaddeus Stevens and the Imperfect Republic," *Pennsylvania History* 60 (April 1993): 150; newspaper article originally published in the *Cincinnati Enquirer*, reprinted in the *Freeborn County Standard* (Albert Lee, Minn.), May 26, 1886, and *Worthington Advance* (Worthington, Minn.), May 27, 1886; *The Elevator* (San Francisco), Jan. 1, 1869; W. E. B. Du Bois, *Black Reconstruction in America, 1860–1880* (1935; reprint, New York: Atheneum, 1983), p. 197.

13 *Harper's Weekly*, vol. 12 (Aug. 29, 1868), p. 549; *New York Times*, Aug. 18, 1868; Ralph Korngold, *Thaddeus Stevens: A Being Darkly Wise and Rudely Great* (New York: Harcourt, Brace, 1955), p. 440. A militia unit called the Butler Guard had earlier formed in Baltimore; it is not clear whether that was the same unit referred to here. See Jones, *Birthright Citizens*, pp. 149–50.

14 CG, 38:2, p. 266.

Index

Page numbers beginning with 247 refer to notes.

Index

Index

emancipation:
    arguments for gradual, 20–21
    differing interpretations of, 182
    Lincoln's overruling of Frémont's
      ordering of, 139
    Lincoln's overruling of Hunter's
      ordering of, 146
    universal, TS's call for, 144–45
emancipation, immediate:
    Lincoln's reluctance to push for,
      122–23, 128, 140, 278
    Lincoln's turnaround on support
      for, 150–51
    northern opposition to, 43–44
    Republicans' wartime embrace of,
      127–28
    TS's advocacy of, 123, 134, 143,
      144–45, 153–54, 167–68
    TS's House resolution for, 139–45
Emancipation Proclamation, 162, 172,
    181
    backlash against, 152
    TS on, 151–52
Emerson, John, 95–96
ends and means, TS on morality of,
    136
Enlightenment, 11
    TS's exposure to ideas of, 9, 18–20
Epic of America, The (Adams), 7
equal rights, *see* African Americans,
    civil rights of; egalitarianism
Examiner and Herald (Lancaster, Pa.),
    77, 81–82, 100
Ex parte Milligan, 210

farmers, small:
    freedpeople as, 224
    Republican support for, 105, 127
    TS's praise of, 67–68, 265
    in Vermont, 13–14
Fessenden, William Pitt, 181, 197, 221,
    236

Fillmore, Millard, 60, 73, 75, 83, 84,
    92, 93, 110
films, TS as portrayed in, 7–8, 9, 280
Florida, readmitted to statehood, 222
Fort Monroe, fugitive slaves in,
    129–30, 158, 173
Fort Sumter, 111, 113, 122
Fourteenth Amendment, 202, 213,
    215, 223
    black voting rights and, 203–5
    Johnson's denunciation of, 207
    ratification of, 206
    TS and, 204–7
free blacks, prewar, 51, 78
Freedmen's Bureau, 227, 232
    extension of, 199–200, 228
    land redistribution and, 225–28, 287
freedpeople (former slaves):
    campaign to deny personal rights
      to, 194–97; *see also* black codes
    civil rights of, *see* African
      Americans, civil rights of
    education desired by, 173
    enfranchisement of, *see* African
      Americans, voting rights of
    forced "apprenticeship" of children
      of, 195, 259
    hopes and goals of, 172–74
    land redistribution and, 223–31
    Lincoln on treatment and rights of,
      177–79, 196, 259, 279, 286
    Reconstruction-era voting by, 220
    Sherman's allotment of land to,
      179, 225, 228
    TS's call for extending political
      rights of, 211–12
    violence against, 196, 210, 211, 212–13
free labor, as Republican Party
    principle, 196
Freemasons, 37–38, 257
Free Soil Party, 59–60, 62, 75
    TS declines to join, 60–61, 85

Index

Index

Index

Index

North Carolina, readmitted to statehood, 222
Northwest Ordinance (1787 and
1789), 96
nullification crisis, 41–42
nullification doctrine, 48

Ord, Edward O. C., 232

Paley, William, 18, 19, 20–21, 252, 254
Parker, William, 79
Peacham, Vt., 12, 41
Peacham Academy, 18
Pendleton, George H., 168–69
Pennsylvania, 3
    black enfranchisement in, 217
    Christiana "riot" in, 78–81, 96
    concessions to South widely
        opposed by, 118
    defeat of Lee's raid in, 154
    nativism in, 99, 266
    pro-slavery sentiment in, 39
    public education fight in, 30–32,
        239, 256
    TS's burial in, 244
    TS's move to, 21
    Whigs in, 57
Pennsylvania Antislavery Society,
    50–51
Pennsylvania constitutional convention
    (1837–38), 51
    black Pittsburghers' petition to, 52–53
    blacks disenfranchised by, 54
    taxpayer qualification for voting
        preserved by, 36
    TS as delegate at, 3, 22, 32, 33,
        34–35
    TS's antislavery speech at, 49–50
    TS's opposition to black
        disenfranchisement by, 3, 53–54,
        239
    voting law revision at, 35

Pennsylvania House of Representatives,
    TS in, 21–22, 29, 30–32, 36, 46,
    256
Pennsylvania People's Party, 99, 100–101
Pierce, Franklin, 90
Pittsburgh, Pa., early black voting in,
    52–53
Poland, Luke, 13
political parties and partisan spirit:
    TS's evolving view of, 36
    see also specific parties
Polk, James K., 58
Pope, John, 149, 232
popular sovereignty, 62
    1850 Compromise and, 64, 74, 76
    Kansas-Nebraska Act and, 89–90
    Supreme Court's nullification of,
        97
Port Hudson, Grant's capture of, 154
poverty:
    Greeley's experience of, 27
    Lincoln's experience of, 27
    TS's childhood experience of, 12,
        24–25
predestination, 16, 23, 253
presidency, constitutional powers of,
    114, 134–35
Principles of Moral and Political
    Philosophy (Paley), 19, 20
private-property rights, Republican
    support for, 230–31
Profiles in Courage (Kennedy), 7
public opinion, TS as shaper of, 126
public schools, TS as advocate for,
    30–32, 37, 239, 256
Pugh, W. W., 176
Puritans, Puritanism, 16–17

racism, racial discrimination, 174
    and issue of blacks in Union armies,
        157, 159–60
    of Johnson, 189–90, 201

Index

Index

Index

Vallandigham, Clement, 102
Van Buren, Martin, 58–60, 62
Vattel, Emer de, 135
Vermont, University of, 18, 20, 252
Vermont, Vermonters:
  as Anti-Masonry bastion, 38
  Baptists in, 16–17
  conflict between large landowners
    and small farmers in, 13–14
  democratic and egalitarian
    traditions of, 13, 14–16, 17, 238
  initial unicameral legislature of, 15
  as self-governing republic, 14, 250
  separation of church and state
    favored by, 17
  slavery condemned in constitution
    of, 15–16
  Stevens family in move to, 12
  transparency of government
    demanded by, 17
  TS's character as shaped by
    childhood in, 11, 238
Vicksburg, Grant's capture of, 154,
  156, 169
voting rights:
  of blacks, see African Americans,
    voting rights of
  TS's support for taxpayer
    requirements in, 35–36
  of women, 101

Wade, Benjamin, 183
Wade-Davis bill:
  Lincoln's pocket veto of, 184–85
  TS's criticism of, 183–84, 185–86
War Department, U.S., employment of
  fugitive slaves authorized by, 130

Washington, D.C., see District of
  Columbia
Webster, Daniel, 64, 74, 75, 80
Weld, Theodore Dwight, 49
West Virginia, 137
Whig national convention (1852),
  Scott nominated by, 83
Whigs, Whig Party:
  Anti-Masons' joining of, 38
  antislavery faction of, in
    Pennsylvania, 59, 61
  black disenfranchisement and, 54
  conservative wing of, 104
  declining national support for, 87,
    100
  Mexican War opposed by, 58
  slavery as divisive issue among, 57
  TS in, 56
  TS attacked by, 84–85
white supremacy, 182–83, 243
  Johnson's espousal of, 189–90
  Lincoln's equivocation on, 106–7
  TS's opposition to, 153
Wickliffe, Charles A., 160
Williams, George H., 213
Wilmot, David, 59, 99
Wilmot Proviso, 59, 60, 61, 62, 87,
  106
Wilson, Henry, 59, 77, 88, 128
Wise, Henry A., 112
women's suffrage, TS's endorsement
  of, 101
Worth, Jonathan, 193

York Academy, 21
Young Men's Colonization Society
  (Gettysburg), 51

Illustration Credits